AN ELEMENTARY TREATISE

ON

AMERICAN GRAPE CULTURE

AND

WINE MAKING.

BY

PETER B. MEAD.

Illustrated with nearly 200 Engravings drawn from Nature.

NEW-YORK:
Harper & Brothers, Publishers, Franklin Square.

1867.

JOHN A. GRAY & GREEN,
PRINTERS,
16 & 18 Jacob Street, New-York.

PREFACE.

THE present volume has been prepared in compliance with the urgent request of friends in various parts of the country.

We conceive that an elementary work on the vine, to possess the highest practical value for the amateur, as well as the gardener and vineyardist, should treat of all the facts and principles involved in the subject, laying them clearly in order before the student, and linking them together with just so much of the theory as is necessary to explain lucidly their relation to each other, and unite them in the mind of the student in one harmonious and systematic whole. This is what we have aimed to accomplish in the present work, indulging in no theorizing speculations, and introducing nothing of doubtful verification. We have given a simple record of our own practice and experience, stating no fact that we have not repeatedly verified, and which may not be repeated by others, with like results. We have striven to make it a safe guide to all.

Although Grape Culture, and especially Wine-Making, are yet in their infancy in this country, the principles and conditions upon which success depends are so well established that, if we walk in the full light of the knowledge we have, we need tread no doubtful path. Though the work is strictly elementary, we have by no means intended to make it in any degree superficial, and have therefore labored to leave no important practical question unsolved; indeed, some points, that have heretofore been entirely neglected, or very briefly noticed, are here treated with a degree of minuteness somewhat commensurate with their importance, as will be seen, among others, in the chapters on "Varieties," "Ripening," and "Taste."

The engravings are so true to life, and so admirably executed, that they may be said, in some sense, to present a treatise in themselves, from which may be obtained a good knowledge of the operations to be performed, as well as the manner of doing them. Our acknowledgments are made elsewhere.

February 5, 1867. PETER B. MEAD.

CONTENTS.

AMERICAN GRAPE CULTURE.

CHAPTER I.

INTRODUCTION.

THERE are few material interests that at present claim a larger share of public attention than the culture of the grape. This is true, whether we regard the grape as something that ministers to our enjoyments, or fills our pockets with gold. We have thought, therefore, that an elementary work on the grape, plain and practical, would now possess a certain degree of interest, and be of some value to the public. It would not be possible, of course, to exhaust such a subject in an elementary work; we must necessarily treat it with much brevity, but we shall endeavor to present such a *resumé* of the details and principles of grape culture as will enable any intelligent person to grow good grapes, and even make good wine. The subject, indeed, is worthy of profound study for the sake of its own pure and simple pleasures. It may at first seem a little dry in its details to the uninformed; but in its fruition it possesses a degree of fascination which can be claimed for no other culture. Besides what may be termed its intellectual pleasures, it has an interest of a more material kind, which will address itself not only to those who wish to grow their own grapes and drink their own wine, but more especially to that large class who look at the subject from the stand-point of profit.

We do not propose to indulge in figures, whether of arithmetic or the imagination; but we may say that grape culture is fast working itself up to the first position among the productive interests of the country. The capital invested in it may already be counted by millions; and a time will come when the products of grape culture will be found among the exports of the country. It is not claimed that we shall make better wines than those of Europe; but we can and shall make them purer than most of those sent to us; and *pure* wines will always find a good market and high prices wherever wines are used. Besides, our best wines will possess a fruity bouquet natural to but few of the wines of Europe; a bouquet that grows upon the taste, and which will make our wines sought after by all connoisseurs. It is safe, then, to say that the products of grape culture will at no distant day have an important commercial value, as respects our foreign trade. They already have a very considerable value in our internal trade; for, not to speak of the vast quantities of grapes that are consumed for the table, it is an indisputable fact that American wines, some of them confessedly impure and of inferior quality, are to-day selling in New-York for higher prices than imported wines of better quality. This is an anomaly, however, which must soon necessarily disappear. The purchasers of these inferior wines are not found among those who know what a really pure and good wine is; and there are unmistakable indications that the public taste is happily being educated up to that point where pure and excellent wines will be the rule, and impure and faulty ones the exception. There we may safely leave the subject.

Fears are sometimes expressed that grape culture will soon be carried to excess; that the market will be overstocked, and prices, consequently, cease to be remunerative. More than fifteen years ago we heard the same fears expressed in very much the same terms; and to-day we have a sufficient answer in the fact, that grapes are now selling for three and four times as much as they did fifteen years ago. This is readily accounted for in the simple fact, that the demand has kept steadily in advance of the supply, notwithstanding the largely increased area of cultivation. A little reflection will convince the most obdurate of doubters that this must continue to be the case for many years to come. Let us for a moment look at some plain facts, within the reach and comprehension of any common-sense man. Taking the last census tables as a basis, we may safely assume that our population will increase for the next hundred years at the rate of forty per cent per decade. Let us then take into consideration the fact, that the taste for grapes and other good fruits is rapidly spreading among all classes of the people, so that fruit consumers hereafter will form a relatively larger proportion of the community than heretofore. If we put these two facts together, we may even take as a standard the rapid increase in grape culture which has been witnessed during the past five years, and the conclusion will still be unavoidable, that the demand will be far in advance of the supply: the mouths will multiply faster than they can be filled. This must be the case, however large the number of propagators may be, or however vast their facilities for multiplying the vine. The man has yet to be born who will be able to purchase our best native grapes for less than fifteen cents a pound. We know that grapes can be profitably grown for much less than ten.

From what has been said, we are justified in concluding that grape culture is rich in the elements of pleasure and profit. There is one other point that may be glanced at before proceeding to the more immediate object of this work. A good deal has been said, at times, about the morality of the subject; the wickedness of growing grapes for the purpose of making wine. We do not propose to discuss this point. The limits prescribed to this book will not permit it; besides, it is really not necessary in this connection. We may remark, however, that our efforts to benefit mankind will be successful just in proportion as we deal with them as they are, and not as we would have them. We usually fail because we begin by supposing men to be what we only propose to make them: an inversion which defeats our purpose.

Men will drink wine of some kind, reason as we may. Accept the fact, and strive to teach them to drink only that which is pure, and thus prepare them for the next higher step in moral progress, the drinking of no wine at all, if that be necessary, which some will doubt. Wine is not the only blessing that is abused; but it can hardly be said that pure wine makes drunkards. The wine countries of Europe prove quite the contrary. We have no hesitation in recording our conviction, that grape culture may be made the handmaiden of the temperance cause.

CHAPTER II.

CLIMATE—LOCATION—EXPOSURE—SHELTER.

Is our Climate adapted to the Vine?—We do not propose in this little volume to give a botanical description of the grape vine. Those who are in present need of that knowledge may consult Gray's Botany, or some other within their reach. The question, however, naturally arises at the start, whether our climate is adapted to the successful growth of the vine. This question, often asked, may be answered by pointing to the many successful vineyards scattered over the country. The vine, in fact, is indigenous to almost every part of the American continent. As it is the improved forms of our native kinds that we depend upon, there ought to be no doubt of the compatibility of our climate with success. Foreign varieties have been tried, and failed. Seedlings of the native vines have been grown with eminent success.

Their relative merits will be discussed hereafter.

Location.—Having determined upon planting a vineyard, the first point to engage our attention will be the selection of a proper location. We attach more importance to this than some others do. It is said that we need not be particular on this point, since the vine is found growing wild almost every where, even in swamps. This is true; but the fruit produced upon vines growing in wet places is very ill-flavored; redolent, indeed, of that peculiar odor popularly called "foxy;" the skin is thick, tough, and acrid, and the flesh hard and indigestible. If the same vine be removed to dry soil, and cultivated, these offensive characteristics become in a small degree mitigated; showing conclusively the ameliorating influence of culture and position. The fruit even of the cultivated vine is more or less affected by what is called a "wet season:" it is found to lose a portion of its tenderness, and to deteriorate in flavor. These, and other facts, must necessarily lead us to attach much importance to the selection of a location that is naturally dry; and the experience of the great mass of cultivators will be found to agree with this. An opposite opinion will be found to prevail only among those whose experience in the vineyard is of a limited nature. If circumstances should compel the selection of a location not naturally dry, then recourse must be had to artificial drainage, and this should be of the most thorough kind. We should give a decided preference to tile drain. If tile can not be readily procured, then we must use stone; and these should be so well laid in the bottom as to prevent the possibility of their being disturbed or clogged up by the adjacent soil. The location must not only be dry, but *the grade must be such that no surface water can remain on it at any season of the year.* Surface water, especially in the winter, is a prevalent cause of the winter-killing of vines, both old and young, but particularly the latter.

In selecting a site for a vineyard, low grounds should, if possible, be avoided. There are many objections to them, chief among which are these: they are subject to heavy cold fogs and vapors, and strong currents of cold air; they are more or less damp in spring and fall, and liable to early and late frosts; all of which are great impediments to the successful culture of the grape. Hillsides have always been favorite spots for the grape; cultivators concede their peculiar fitness with great unanimity. Declivities, gentle slopes, in short, almost any elevated spot free from dampness, may be selected as a suitable place for a vineyard. But the best of all places is, undoubtedly, some elevated spot bordered by a large body of water. Hence the fewer casualties, the greater certainty of the crop, and the superior quality of the fruit grown in such localities as the Hudson River and the Lakes. There are several reasons for this, the chief being the ameliorating influence exercised by the water. The temperature of the surrounding air is very even; sudden changes being comparatively rare, or at least shorn of most of their ill effects. Early and late frosts are not of such frequent occurrence, and the growing season is thus prolonged These facts will account for individual cases of failure or success, which seem at first to set at naught all our efforts to refer them to any particular cause; though it can not be denied that hidden causes are often at work, the results of which may be seen, but can not well be overcome. The cause of disease being unknown, the application of remedies becomes altogether a matter of chance: we are just as apt to kill as cure.

In selecting a site for a vineyard, wherein no inconsiderable capital must necessarily be employed, prudence would suggest that we seek the advice of some experienced friend, whose practiced eye would quickly detect most of the conditions which are favorable or unfavorable to the successful growth of the vine. We have received many letters, asking whether some particular spot is adapted to the grape, to which we have but one reply: the conditions can only be safely determined on the spot; and it should not be concealed, that in some cases, even where the best judgment has been exercised, hidden local causes will operate to defeat in a measure our purpose.

Exposure.—Having thus briefly treated of the location, we pass next to the subject of *exposure*, by which is meant the aspect which the vineyard should have in reference to the points of the compass. On this point some diversity of opinion exists among practical men, owing, no doubt, to the fact that good grapes have been grown in various exposures. There is a pretty general agreement, however, that a southern exposure is best, some claiming a preëminence for one facing southeast, and others again, but fewer in number, one looking to the southwest. Our own preference, all things considered, is for one facing the southeast. But, after all, the exposure must, in some degree, be determined by the local surroundings. A vineyard may be safely planted with an exposure ranging any where from east to south and west; but we should hesitate to plant one looking due north, if we proposed to make wine. We might, under certain circumstances, plant one thus situated, and expect to get some good grapes for the table, but ripening a few days later than those having a southern exposure.

The objects to be attained by exposure consist chiefly in the admission to the soil and vines of a due proportion of the sun's vivifying rays, and shelter from prevailing cold winds; and here, again, we must bring to our aid the exercise of a discerning judgment.

Shelter.—This is so intimately connected with location and exposure, that we shall treat of it here. It is a subject of very great importance in its bearings on the well-being of the vineyard, and one to which, strangely enough, vineyardists have hitherto given very little attention. We know of vineyards that only require appropriate shelter to make them yield highly remunerative returns. There are probably many such all over the country, the owners of which are mourning over their small success, while their vines are a prey to early and late frosts, mildew, tempests, and other casualties, which could be measurably controlled by proper shelter. The object of shelter is to protect the vineyard from high and cold winds, and incidentally to secure freedom from unseasonable frosts, mildew, and analogous casualties. The atmosphere that surrounds the vineyard should be warm, and not liable to sudden changes. The heat and moisture that exhale from the earth should not be liable to be blown suddenly away. The leaves should not be torn and twisted by strong winds. With all these, we should avoid destroying the life of the air: there should be gentle breezes passing around and between the plants, the leaves, and the fruit. Shut out rude Boreas, but let the Zephyrs wanton as they will.

These leading objects can be measurably attained by affording proper shelter. A board fence will often answer a good purpose, and is always better than no shelter at all; for simple as it may seem, the influence of such a fence is felt for several hundred feet. In some cases sufficient shelter may be found in the natural wood surrounding the selected site; but in others, and the great majority of cases, it will be necessary to make the shelter by planting trees. Of deciduous trees, we should select the birch or the maple. If the ground could be spared, we should plant two rows of trees, though one row will answer the purpose very well. The birch we should plant three feet apart each way; the maple, four feet apart. Of evergreen trees, we should select the Norway spruce, and plant four feet apart. The evergreens will make much the best shelter. The sheltering belt should be so arranged as to afford protection against prevalent winds, and these, in most cases, proceed from the northeast, north, and northwest; sometimes from some point south. Wherever they come from, let them be shut off by belts or clumps of trees.

A caution may be added, not to plant a belt or clump of trees in too close proximity to the vines. The roots of the trees will soon find their way among the vines, and damage them greatly. We have seen instances where attempts were made to check this evil by opening trenches and cutting off the roots; but the check proved to be only temporary. If large trees surround the vineyard closely, ventilation is materially interfered with. There are other evils which we can not allude to here. The distance at which clumps and sheltering belts should be placed may be determined by the kind of trees and the distances at which they are planted apart. The proper distance for belts and clumps is about fifty feet from the vines. A hedge proper of Norway spruce, planted for a height of ten to fifteen feet, may be placed as near as twenty-five feet; but forty would be better, with the height of the hedge increased to twenty feet.

We must not be understood as saying that shelter is indispensable to all localities; we know of vineyards that yearly produce the best results that have no shelter; but, notwithstanding this, there are many places which, owing to their geographical position, are liable to sudden changes and violent winds; and for all such, protection of some kind is a matter of great importance.

CHAPTER III.

THE SOIL, AND ITS PREPARATION—MANURES.

Soil.—The soil may next occupy our attention. What is the best soil for the grape? This question has been variously answered. Those who live in a district where clay abounds say that a clayey soil is best; while those who live where sand prevails will tell you that a sandy soil is best, and so on. The solution of these answers may be found in the fact that good grapes are grown in both kinds of soil. Our own experience, and a pretty extended observation among vineyards, lead us to give preference to sandy or gravelly loams. It has been said that any soil that will grow good corn will grow good grapes. We have no doubt of the truthfulness of the remark; and we should not hesitate to plant a vineyard upon such a soil, if favorably located. But we may go further, and say that good grapes may be grown where good corn can not. Some of the best vineyards about New-York are planted in light sandy soils, to which muck has been added with a more or less liberal hand. There are many localities on Long Island and in New-Jersey, where light sands prevail, that could be converted into productive vineyards at a comparatively small expense. We have never seen better grapes than have been grown on similar soils properly treated. The vine has such a wonderful power of adaptability that the soil, whether light or heavy, becomes almost a matter of secondary importance.

Preparation.—Not so, however, its preparation for the reception of the plants. This should be most thoroughly done. In planting a vineyard, we are doing a work that is expected to last for generations; hence, every thing connected with it should be done in a manner to insure good and permanent results. Some soils will need more thorough preparation than others; but all will need more or less.

It may, or may not be, that some have recommended a more thorough and expensive mode of preparation than the case calls for. We leave each one at liberty to judge for himself, with the simple remark, that money spent in a judicious preparation of the soil is capital well invested, which is certain to return a good interest. A vineyard well prepared will pay better than one not so prepared: that may be received as an axiom in vineyard culture.

There are three principal methods of preparing the soil for a vineyard: *trenching*, *trench plowing*, and *subsoiling*. The first, except for small vineyards, and under peculiar circumstances, may be too expensive an operation for general adoption: it is chiefly confined to the garden. The second and third are exceedingly useful, and may be adopted wherever a plow can be run. We propose to give a brief description of each of the three methods above named.

Trenching is done with the spade. It consists in first removing the earth from a trench to the depth that it is proposed to work the soil, the trench to be of any convenient width, (say two feet wide,) and as long as the plot of ground to be trenched. To be a little precise, we will suppose the soil is to be trenched to the usual depth of two feet: the trench will then be two feet deep. With a line, mark off a slice two feet wide immediately adjoining the open trench; throw one foot of the *top soil* of this slice into the *bottom* of the open trench, and on the top of this throw the remaining foot of *bottom* soil. By this operation the trench has been filled, and the order of the soils reversed; the best, or surface soil, being at the bottom of the trench, and the poorest, or subsoil, on the top. We have at the same time opened a new trench. This is to be filled in the same manner as the first, and the operation repeated until the whole plot has been trenched. The last trench is to be filled with the soil that was removed from the first. If the plot of ground is large, some labor will be saved by making the trenches half the width of the plot, going down on one side and returning on the other. The last trench will then be on a line with the first, and there will be but little carting needed to fill it. This is a brief description of trenching, but we hope sufficiently plain to be understood. It will be observed that our operation has buried the good soil, and brought the poor or subsoil to the surface, which must be enriched with muck, manure, or good surface soil from some other place, and we shall have a soil that will bring any kind of plants to their highest state of excellence.

Trench plowing is much less expensive than spade trenching, and but little inferior to it, when well done, putting the ground in fine condition for growing grapes as well as other crops. In trench plowing, oxen are to be preferred to horses, their draught being steadier as well as more powerful. There is no plow in use at present specially adapted to this work, and we must therefore take the best we can get. The cylinder plow, on account of its easy draught, is perhaps one of the best. Two plows and two yokes of oxen are used; the work will be better done, however, if two yokes of oxen are attached to the second or following plow. The first plow opens a furrow as deep as the plow can be driven. The second plow follows immediately in the same furrow, and deepens it to the full capacity of the team. There must be no balks or jumps; the plow must be plunged in to the beam, and kept there. Men with spades should follow the second plow, to remove the stones, and keep the furrow open. The lot may be plowed round, or in lands; but we prefer to return without a furrow, so that the furrows may all be laid one way; the work will be more than enough better to pay for the additional labor. The work will be easier at the start, if both plows are run a second time in the first furrow, and the soil thrown out with spades; the plows will move easier in the subsequent furrows, as there will be less resistance to overcome. A common mistake in trench plowing, (and in all plowing, in fact,) is cutting the furrow slice too wide. It is true, that by cutting the furrow slice twelve inches wide we can get over the ground about twice as fast as when it is cut six inches wide; but in the latter case the work is more than twice as well done; and since we can not do it but once, let us do it well. Let the furrow slices, therefore, be narrow, and the furrows deep. The work will be all the better if the lot is cross-plowed in the same way. The plowing may be repeated with advantage as many times as can be afforded. This would very well meet our idea of *thorough* preparation with the plow. The manures used may be spread on the surface, and plowed in. The effect of trench plowing is not only to deepen the soil, but to mix the surface soil and subsoil together pretty thoroughly, and thus afford a deeper bed for the roots of plants to work in: but among its most important results is the protection it affords against the ill effects of sudden changes of the weather, drought and wetness, heat and cold, etc.

Subsoiling will next be described. This, for the vineyard, is the least thorough of the three methods named. It is but little, if any, less costly than trench plowing, and should not, therefore, except for very good reasons, supersede it. The process of subsoiling is very similar to that of trench plowing. Two plows are used, the common plow and the subsoil plow, which is simply a foot-piece in some wedge-shaped form, attached to a narrow upright shank. Of subsoil plows, there are only two or three in use, either of which will answer the purpose well enough if the furrow slices are made narrow. Mapes's has the lightest draught. In subsoiling, the furrow is opened with the common plow; the subsoil plow follows in the same furrow, and should be run up to the beam to make good work. The lot may be plowed round or in lands; sloping ground, however, should be plowed up and down the slope when the soil is at all heavy;

for the subsoil plow, in such soils, will leave an opening at the bottom of the furrow, which will for a time serve the purpose of a drain. There is this marked difference between subsoiling and trench plowing: the operation of the first is confined chiefly to loosening the subsoil, while the latter not only loosens the subsoil, but mixes it with the upper or surface soil. The value of trenching, trench plowing, and subsoiling, may be taken in the order in which they are named; and it is only the expense of the first which should prevent its general adoption for fruit culture.

Manures.—A few brief remarks may here be added on the subject of manures. The vine is said to be a gross feeder. To some extent this is true; yet there can be little doubt that the excessive application of gross manures is injurious to the quality of the fruit, and enfeebling to the vine, unfitting it, indeed, to withstand the changing rigors of our variable climate. All kinds of manures are said to be good for the vine, nothing coming amiss. If they are thoroughly decomposed, and have lost their grossness and unhealthful qualities, which produce distended rather than solid growth, we shall not object. Coarse, unfermented manures should not be applied to the vineyard, except when they can be thoroughly and evenly mixed with and through the soil. On the whole, we know of nothing so good as old, well-decayed barnyard manure, composted with muck. This, thoroughly worked in and through the soil at the beginning to the depth of eighteen or twenty inches, will leave little or nothing more to be desired. Ashes, bones, lime, poudrette, etc., have their value, but should generally be applied as a top dressing, though they may all be likewise mixed with the compost last named. In preparing a vineyard, the object to be aimed at is a thoroughly good, but not excessively rich, soil of considerable depth. Depth, indeed, is of more importance than great richness, though a pretty good degree of fertility may be considered indispensable for a productive vineyard. Where it can be done, a good plan is to place the materials of the compost heap in layers, and let them remain so for several weeks; then turn and mix them thoroughly, and repeat the operation every week or so till the compost is wanted for use. The oftener it is turned, the better it will be.

CHAPTER IV.

LAYING OUT THE VINEYARD.

Laying out the Vineyard.—Something may now be added, as to the best manner of laying out a vineyard. The directions which the rows should take is a matter of some importance, for we have no doubt that the thrift of the vines is sometimes more or less affected by it. Vineyardists are not quite agreed as to whether the rows should run east and west, or north and south. Local causes, no doubt, operate in some cases to affect the results; yet we believe the weight of authority preponderates in favor of running the rows east and west; and this agrees with our own most matured experience. It is not to be denied, however, that good grapes have been grown both ways, which will sufficiently account for any diversity of opinion. It must not be supposed, however, that there is really not, under given circumstances, some one way better than another, though we may not be able to state it in general terms. If circumstances permitted, we should by all means arrange the rows so that the morning sun should have free access to the vines: the nearer this point can be attained, the better. In the majority of cases, this point can be secured by running the rows more or less nearly east and west. On hill sides there is a necessity, arising from the situation, that the rows should run more or less nearly at right angles with the slope of the hill.

"Let every thing be well ordered" will apply to the vineyard, even in matters not affecting the health of the vine or the quality of its fruit. A man's nature and habits may be seen in the smallest matters of every day life; a man of refinement and taste may be as readily recognized by the arrangement of his trees and vines as by the neatness of his dress or the orderly disposition of the contents of his library or parlor. It may not enhance the value, but it clearly adds to the beauty of the vineyard, to have the vines planted in an orderly manner. Some find a difficulty in getting their rows at right angles; but there are two or three simple rules for doing this, which can be readily understood by any body. There ought to be no difficulty in getting one straight line to begin with. This ascertained, stretch a string along this line, and let it project about eight feet beyond the point or corner where it is proposed to form the right angle. See *Fig.* 1. Drive a stake at this corner, *a*, and eight feet from it, on both sides, drive two other stakes, *c*, *d*. With these two stakes as centers, take a string ten or more feet long, and describe an arc of a circle; a line drawn through the point, *b*, where the two arcs meet, will be a right-angled line. Tie a loop at the end of a string, place it over the middle stake, *a*, and stretch the string so that it passes directly over the point, *b*, where the two arcs meet, and you will have the desired line. By measuring off the distances on these two lines, the rows and the vines will be equally distant from each other. We have named eight and ten feet, but any distances will do, so that the last be greater than the first.

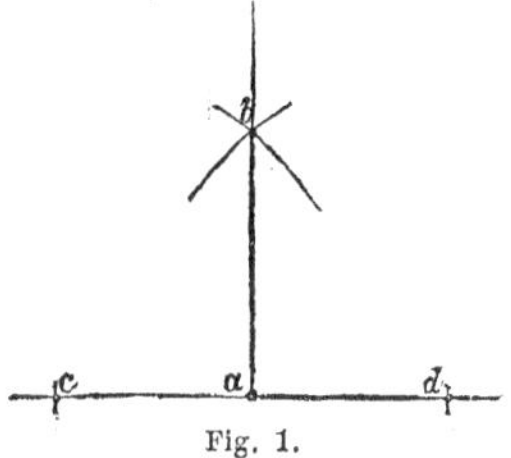

Fig. 1.

Another simple method is by the use of a ten foot pole. Ascertain one line as before, and drive a stake where it is proposed to have the corner. From this stake measure off eight feet on the line, and put a pin in it. With a loop attach another string to the stake, and measure off six feet on it, marking the point with a pin. Place one end of the pole on the first string at the point marked by the pin, and move the other string till the pin in it touches the other end of the pole, and a right angle will be formed. Both these methods are simple and of easy application.

Distances at which to Plant.—Something may also be said here in regard to the distances at which the vines should be planted, which vary, among different persons, from two to twelve or more feet. The discrepancies which exist among cultivators on this point may be referred chiefly to the different systems of training that have been adopted, and will disappear as uniformity becomes more general, which undoubtedly will be the case to a much greater extent than obtains at present. Vines of different kinds possess various degrees of vigor, and the inference is natural that some kinds should be planted closer together than others. The question to be decided is, not how far apart, but how close together vines may be planted consistently with the objects we have in view in growing them. We shall answer the question by saying, for general purposes, place the rows six feet apart, and the vines four feet apart in the rows, if two tiers of arms are contemplated. If only one tier, then the distance between the rows may vary from three and a half to five feet, and the plants may be five or six feet apart. For rank-growing kinds, a foot more may be added in each case. If the vines are to be trained on stakes, six by four is a good distance. The nature of the soil and the mode of training must have something to do with the decision of this question. The vines should be planted close enough to check redundancy of growth, but not so close as to impair their vitality.

CHAPTER V.

PLANTING THE VINEYARD.

Plants and Planting.—This part of the subject would seem to come in naturally at this point. We shall include under this head, the *Best Kind of Plants to Purchase, How to Plant, Best Time to Plant,* and *Time to Buy.* In regard to the first, vines are divided into, 1st, *Plants from Single Eyes,* of which *Fig.* 2 is a very fine specimen, and *Fig.* 3, on an enlarged scale, an extra fine one, as good, indeed, as it is possible to make; 2d, *Plants from Cuttings,* of which *Figs.* 4, 5, and 6 are good specimens of their kinds from two, three, and four eyes; 3d, *Plants from Layers,* of which *Fig.* 7 is one of the best examples; 4th, *Plants from Green Wood.* We present these engravings, in order that the reader may have the means of distinguishing vines of the best quality from those that are not. Further on we shall show how all these are made; at present we simply wish to indicate which are best to purchase. For general

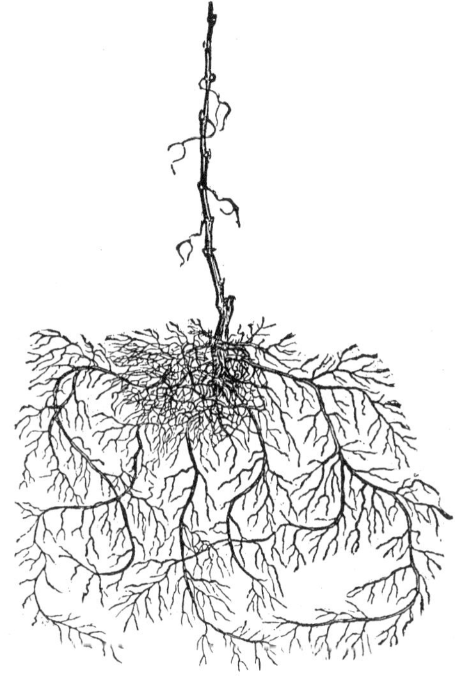

Fig. 2.

planting we recommend plants one year old from single eyes; next, plants from cuttings, and preferably those from two eyes, or at most three; for special purposes, the best form of layers; and last of all, but especially to be avoided for the vineyard, plants one year old from green wood.

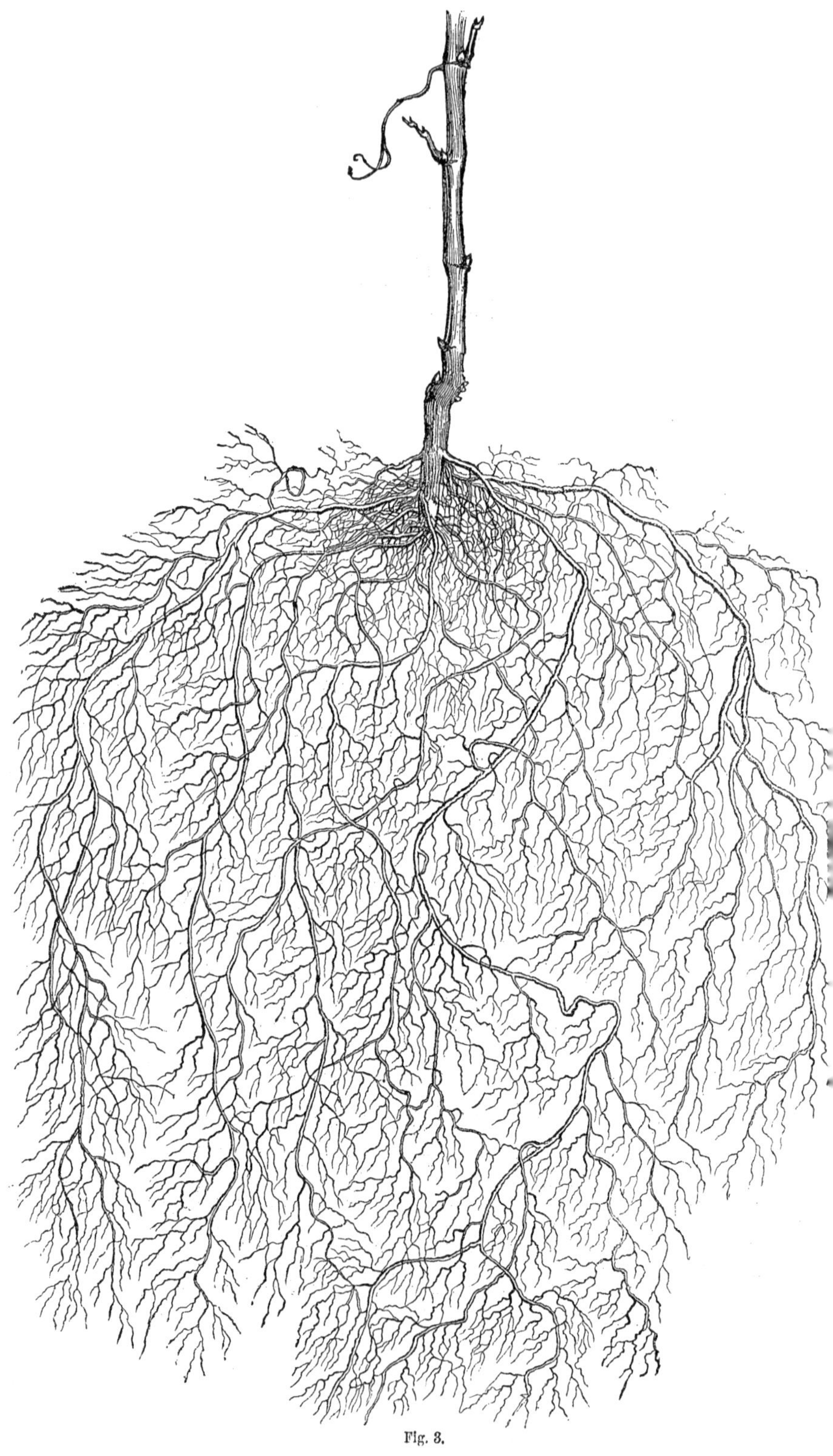

Fig. 3.

A few remarks may here be offered in regard to the relative value of vines one year or more old. There seems to be a prevalent opinion, at least among beginners, that, for planting, the vine increases in value with its age; whereas

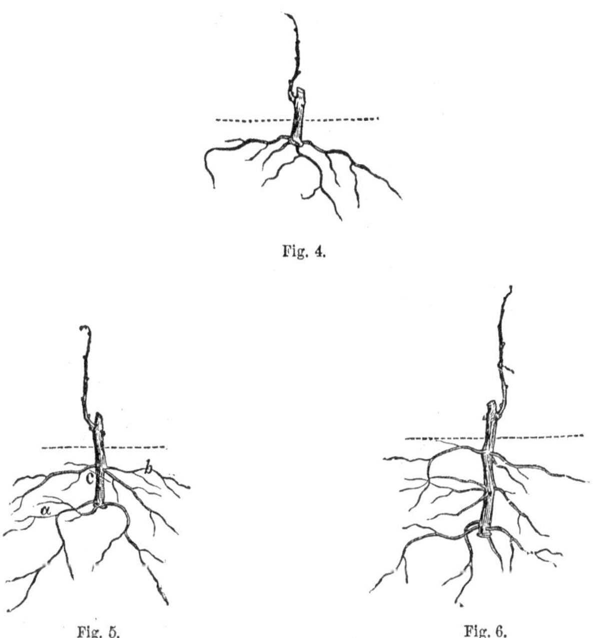

Fig. 4.

Fig. 5.

Fig. 6.

the very opposite of this is true. We lay down the general rule, that a well-grown vine is in its best condition for planting when one year old. There are but few exceptions to this rule, and some of these are only seeming exceptions. The real exceptions are vines that have been grown in large pots or tubs, and even these lose their value beyond the third year. The seeming exceptions consist of plants that have been root-pruned and transplanted when one year old; but these are substantially one year old plants, better if the work has been well done; but if not well done, they are not so good.

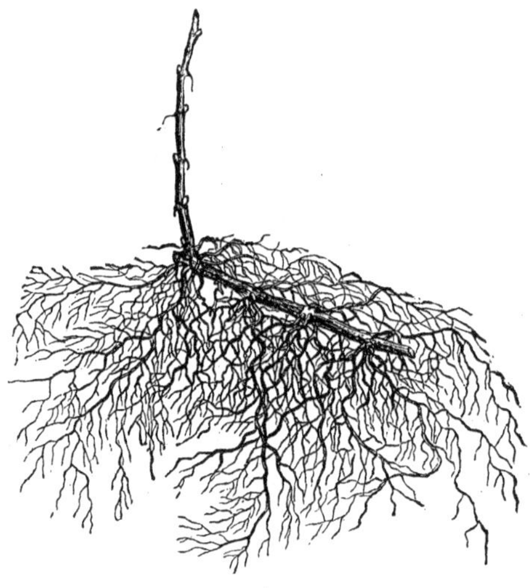

Fig. 7.

Skillful nurserymen can, if they will, make strong plants out of weak ones by root-pruning and transplanting; they can even make good plants exceedingly good in this way, at an increased cost; but they are still substantially one year old plants. *Fig.* 8 is an example of a root-pruned vine grown a second year in a large

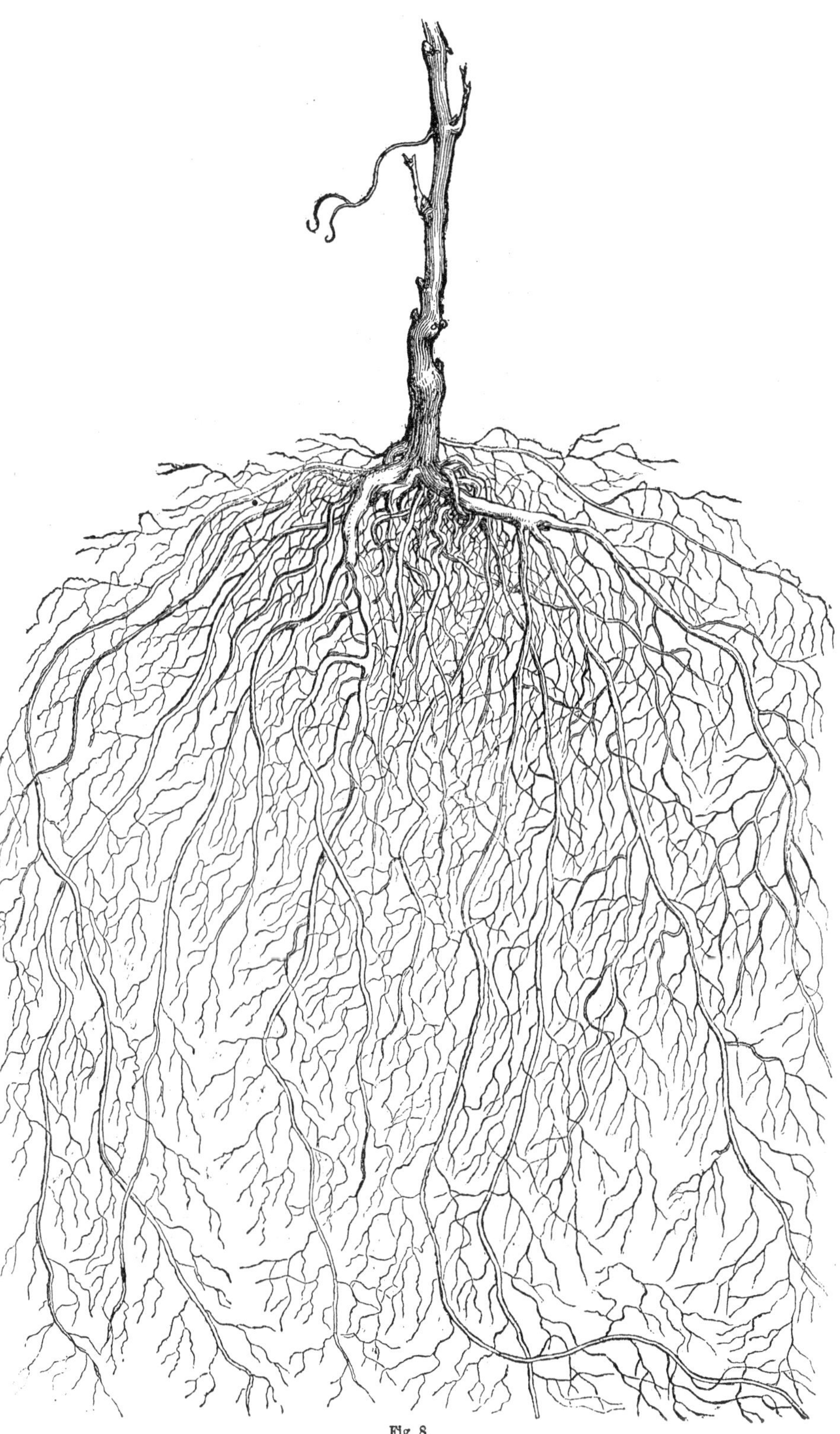

Fig. 8.

pot, and receiving special treatment, with a view of producing the best description of plant: nothing could be better. A vine three or more years old, that has not been transplanted, has generally but little value; and yet people very often pay as much for one such vine as would buy a dozen really good ones. They are generally bought under the supposition that they

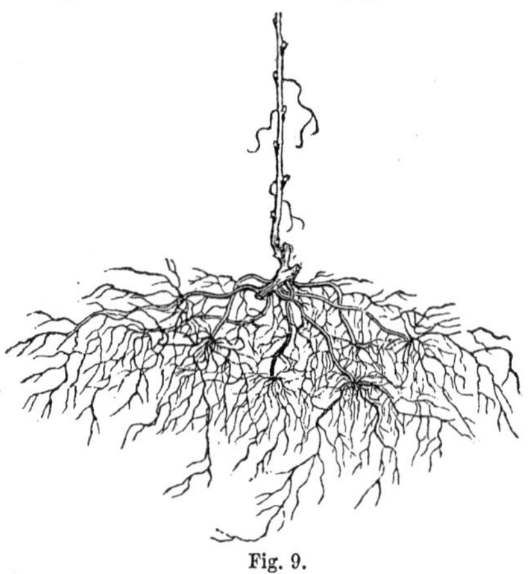

Fig. 9.

will get fruit from them sooner, and more of it; but they do neither. The results and advantages of root-pruning and transplanting are admirably shown in *Fig.* 9, a sketch from life.

These different kinds of plants are not all planted in precisely the same way, and our purpose now is to point out the difference. We must here make the preliminary remark, that the roots of the plants should not be allowed to get dry. The roots are furnished with many little mouths, and if these get dried up, they never reopen. The plant has then to spend a portion of its vitality in forming new ones, which sometimes so exhausts it that it remains feeble during the whole season. Every thing should be so ordered as to secure, as far as possible, the integrity of the vital principle of the plant. When the vines are taken to the vineyard to be planted, they should be covered with wet matting or cloths, and removed only one at a time.

First, let us take the *single-eye* plant. The ground having been already prepared, we have nothing to do but dig a hole of the proper size, and have at hand some good fine soil to place around the roots. It is a common practice among beginners to bed the roots in manure; a practice that is often fatal to the best of vines, but especially to those that are weak. We may remark, in a general way, that we aim to place the roots from four to ten inches beneath the surface, according as the soil is heavy or light. We may also add the caution, that the soil will sink, but the vines will not. This may be avoided, to some extent, by working the soil in firmly among the

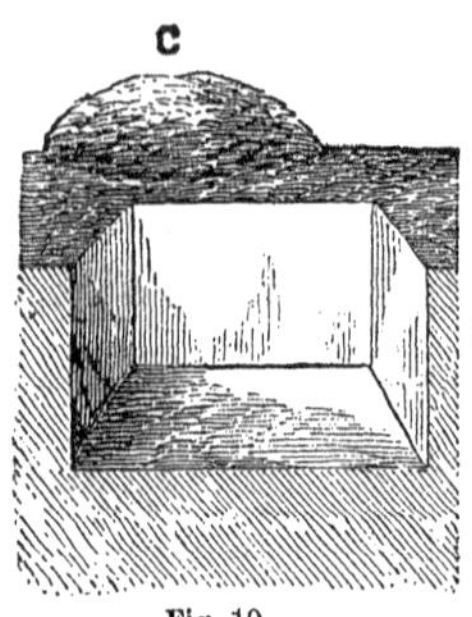

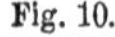
Fig. 10.

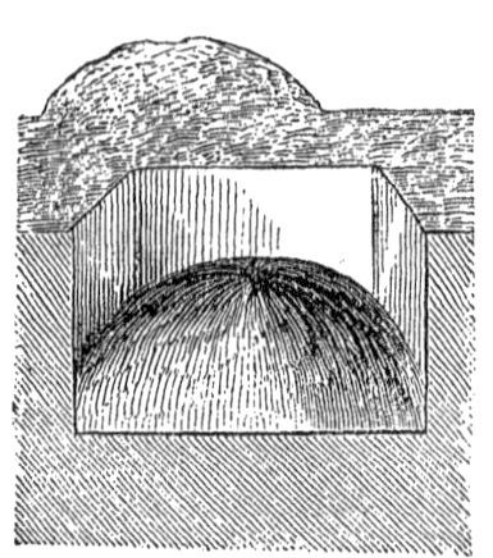
Fig. 11.

roots, but without packing it. Now dig a hole about eighteen inches wide and from six to ten inches deep, according to the texture of the

Fig. 12.

soil, the greatest depth being for light sandy soil. The hole will then be like *Fig.* 10, *c* being the heap of soil taken from the hole. Next, with the fine soil at hand raise a cone as shown in *Fig.* 11, so that the roots shall be about four inches from the surface. In the cut, however, the cone is too sharp, except for very small vines. Now prune or shorten the principal roots as shown in *Fig.* 12, and place the plant on the center of the cone. While the plant is held in its place with the thumb and forefinger of the left hand, the roots must be carefully spread out, ray-like, with the right; the assistant, with a spade, then sifts or shakes in some fine soil, which must be carefully and firmly worked in among the roots. By taking a portion of the roots at a time, and using the unemployed fingers of the left hand, a little practice will enable one to so spread out and cover the roots, that no one of them shall come in contact with another. If the roots are abundant, and overlap each other, as is the case with the best vines, the overlapping roots must be held up while those beneath them are being covered, so as to place a layer of soil between them. The hole is then to be filled up, and the cane cut down to three eyes or buds.

Another plan, well adapted to light soils, and also to prevent the ill effects of drought, is to make the hole about five inches deeper, and proceed in all respects as above, except that the hole must not be entirely filled up; an excavation of five or six inches being left, which may be filled up on the approach of winter. A vine thus planted is shown in *Fig.* 13. This is also a good plan for weak vines, which are very apt to die if the roots at planting are covered as deep as they should be permanently. As a rule, the roots, in such cases, should not be covered more than four inches when the vine is planted. If water is needed in time of drought, the hole gives the plant the full benefit of it, and prevents rapid evaporation. The hole should be filled in the fall, and the soil raised around the plant so as to shed water, but should be opened again the next spring if the growth of the vine has been weak. A feeble vine thus planted is shown in *Fig.* 14, B being the soil covering the roots, C the depth left unfilled, F the ground surface, and D the point at which the cane is to be pruned.

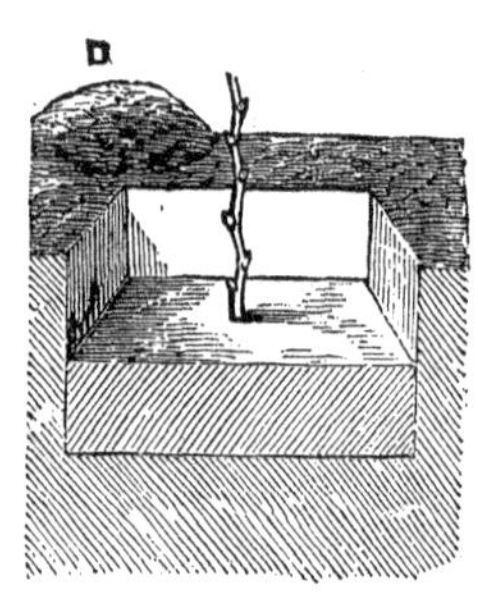

Fig. 13.

Some kind of protection often becomes necessary for the newly planted vine. This may be cheaply provided by nailing together two

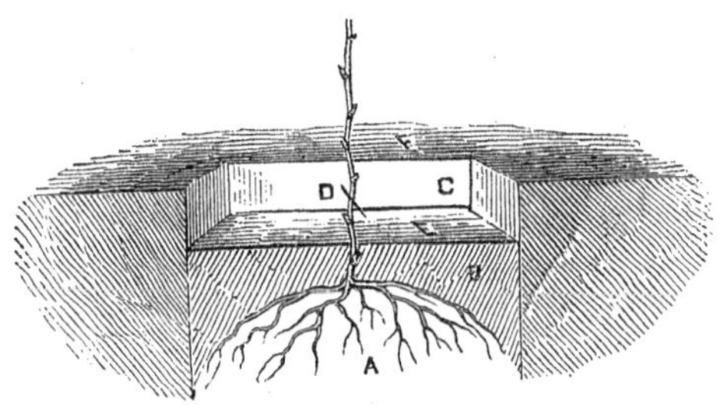

Fig. 14.

pieces of board one foot wide, and from eighteen inches to two feet long, as shown in *Fig*. 15. Place this so that the two boards run south and east, with the plant in the corner or angle. This will shelter the plant on the north and west, the points where shelter is most generally

Fig. 15.

needed. Another and better form of shelter may be made of three pieces of board, put together as in *Fig*. 16, and placed with the open side facing the southeast.

Next in order comes the plant made from a

cutting, which usually presents the appearance shown in *Fig.* 17, when grown from a long

Fig. 16.

cane. It will be observed that there are four tiers of roots. If the roots of the upper tier

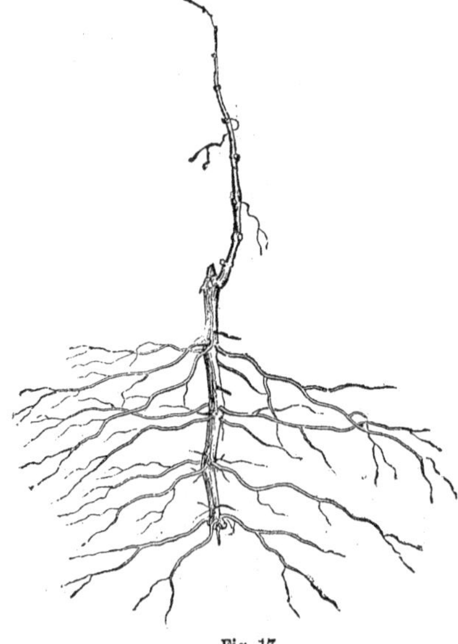

Fig. 17.

are good, the lower tiers may be cut away, and

the vine will in that case be planted as already described. If the upper roots, however, are few and feeble, the next tier must be retained, the upper one shaved off, and the two lower ones cut entirely away; for if they were retained and covered with soil, the lower roots would, as a general thing, be too deeply planted. If two tiers are retained, the upper must be held up by the hand while the lower are being spread out and covered; and then the same operation must be repeated with the upper. But there is no necessity for retaining two, since the lower roots usually die in consequence of being placed so deep in the ground. With the exception noted, the vine from a cutting is planted in the same manner as one from a bud. When the plant has been made from a cutting of two eyes, (*Fig.* 4, p. 37,) there is only one tier of roots, and the treatment, of course, differs in no respect from that first described.

Next in order comes the *layer*, which will need some special directions. The rooted portion of a layer consists of a piece of cane which has emitted roots from each joint. These roots are evenly and regularly disposed along each side, and overlap each other more or less. These roots should be pruned or shortened to about eight or ten inches in length. A layer thus pruned, and laid in the hole, with the roots spread out ready to be covered, may be seen in *Fig.* 18. *Fig.* 19 is a front view of the same vine. The hole should be dug some six or eight inches deep, as before directed, and twenty inches square, or large enough to admit

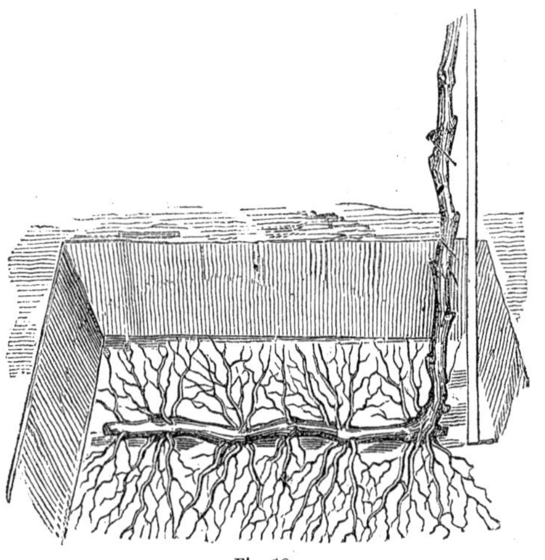

Fig. 18.

the roots when spread out. Proceed as follows: set a stake firmly, to support the vine while growing; then place the vine in position in the hole, and taking the roots on one side, spread out evenly all that will lie on the soil without overlapping each other, holding the rest up; cover them with an inch or so of soil, and then spread out the others in the same way, and cover with soil. Having finished one side, proceed with the other in the same way, and then fill up the hole. It must be borne in mind, that in all cases of planting, fine soil is to be well worked in among the roots.

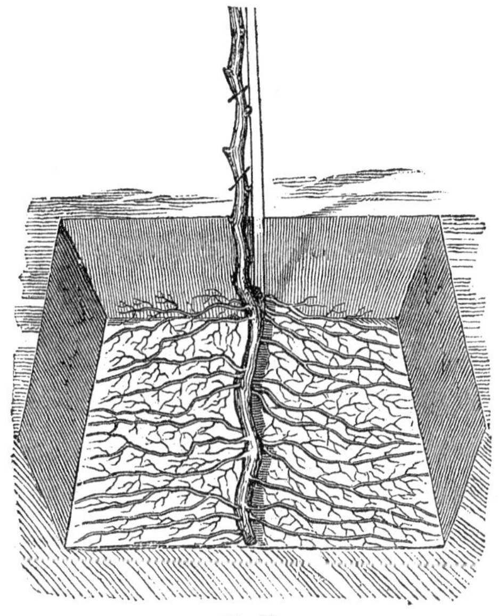

Fig. 19.

Lastly, we come to the plant from a green cutting. We would advise that this be left in the hands of the skillful nurseryman for a year or two more, to be manipulated by him into a tolerably good vine. It is his business, and he can do it cheaper and better than you can. At that time it may be planted in the manner first directed. As for buying the vine the first year—well, we would rather be excused.

We have cautioned the reader against putting manure in contact with the roots, and it will do no harm to repeat the caution. After the roots have been covered with two or three inches of soil, all the manure necessary may be added to the top. A finely prepared compost may in this way be added with good results, but care must be taken not to use stimulants too freely. We want a good healthy growth, commensurate with the vigor of the vine; but beyond this, what is called a "great growth" is generally an evil, for the wood is made soft, fails to ripen thoroughly, and is, in consequence, often winter-killed; besides, there are other and serious evils attending the too free use of gross manures.

Time to Plant.—In regard to the best time to plant, vineyardists are not all agreed, some favoring the spring, and others, and perhaps much the largest number, the fall. In some northern localities spring planting may have predominating advantages; but, as a general rule, we prefer to plant in the fall, and cover the vines. If done early, the roots have an opportunity of establishing themselves in their new quarters, and are ready for early spring work. We usually have more time in the fall, are less hurried, and do the work better. The vines in the fall are in their best condition for handling, and the buds receive less injury from the rough usage they generally meet with in being planted; in short, all the manipulations incidental to planting can be better done in the fall. In the spring the buds are soft, and many of them are rubbed off, leaving us dependent upon secondary buds and a smaller growth. Every thing seems to be "in a hurry," and most things get "a lick and a promise," the vines receiving their full share. A succession of fears worry us from morning till night; we are strongly tempted to slight our most important work, and only too often yield to the temptation.

Time to Buy.—Whatever may be said about the relative advantages of spring and fall planting, there ought to be no doubt about the great advantage of fall buying. The buds are then firm, and the vines can be handled without injury; the atmosphere is cool and moist, and the roots suffer but little from exposure; there is no danger of the buds swelling during transportation; every thing, in brief, is favorable to the lifting, packing, and shipping of the vines, and they are received in good order. In the spring, the very opposite of these conditions exist, and it is no uncommon occurrence to receive vines with the buds gone, bruised, or started into growth, greatly to the damage of the vines, and sometimes resulting in much loss. Our advice is, to buy in the fall; to plant as long as the work can be well done; to "heel in" the vines that are left over, and finish the planting early in the spring, or as soon as the ground has become warm. We should prefer to buy in the fall, even though we did not plant till spring. From what we have said, the reasons will be obvious.

The plants, when received, should be "heeled in" as follows: select a dry place, where water can not stand, and dig a trench eighteen inches deep and from twelve to eighteen inches wide, throwing the earth all on one side. In this trench the vines are to be placed close together in a slanting position, and the roots covered with soil to the depth of a foot. Where a large number of vines are to be "heeled in," the trench may be dug wider, and when the roots of the first row are covered, another row may be placed in front of them. Several rows may be placed together in this way. There is no danger of covering the vines too deep, if the soil is dry; the error of not covering them enough is often committed. The earth over the trench is to be rounded off, so as to shed water. If the canes are mostly covered, so much the better. For additional security, a little brush or coarse litter may be thrown on the top. Protected in this way, vines may be kept in good condition during the severest of winters.

Where a cool cellar is at command, the vines may be better kept with less trouble. In this case they should be bedded in clean coarse sand, that is just moist, but not wet. The vines may be placed close together on the floor of the cellar, and the sand worked in carefully among the roots, which should be covered from six inches to a foot. The vines may be packed in boxes in the same way. If the sand should get dry, it must be moistened a little, but not made wet. An advantage will be gained by pruning the roots before packing them away. The wounds will callus before spring, and be ready to emit new roots immediately after being planted.

Notwithstanding all the advantages of buying and planting in the fall, a large majority will probably continue, as at present, to purchase in the spring. They will perhaps be governed by a desire to save trouble, or the fear of losing their plants through some mismanagement of the details of "heeling in," or the trying alternations of winter. Under such circumstances, most of the advantages above named may be secured for spring by proper fall management of the plants on the part of the propagator. The plants should be "lifted" or dug up in the fall, and the unripe roots, if any, cut off, and the healthy character of the plants well ascertained. They should then be carefully "heeled in" in clean sand in the manner just described. Careful propagators have a cellar or pit specially prepared for this purpose, in which the plants keep admirably, the conditions of safety being well understood and thoughtfully provided. Where a cellar or pit is not possessed, recourse must be had to the open air. In this case, a place sheltered from the south should be selected, and the plants bedded in sand. This may be permitted to freeze a few inches, but the frost should not be allowed to reach the roots. The whole should then be covered with straw and evergreens, to prevent thawing till the plants are wanted in spring. In both these ways, vines may be kept from growing in the spring for a considerable time after vegetation has begun in the open air. In this manner good vines may be secured for late spring planting, after danger from late frosts has passed, and with a certainty of a good growth, if the vines are carefully handled, and the conditions of planting duly observed. Ultimate success depends so much upon securing a healthy, well-ripened growth during the first season, that we have dwelt somewhat at length upon this part of the subject.

CHAPTER VI.

TRAINING—FIRST AND SECOND YEARS.

Training.—If our directions thus far have been clear to the apprehension of the reader, and have been faithfully observed, we shall have a good and durable foundation upon which to build our superstructure. Unlike many other superstructures, this one must be built slowly; as it were, one stone at a time. The laws of vegetable growth are inexorable. By no skill of ours can we alter them; but by studying their nature and operation, we may gain as much knowledge as will enable us to apply them to certain given cases in such a manner as to produce their legitimate results with great uniformity; we may, by judiciously coöperating with them, and affording the ascertained requirements, enjoy these results in their most perfect form. It is our purpose now to state what these requirements are, so far as we have ascertained them by our own experience.

There are certain technical terms, the use of which it is hardly possible to avoid, even if it were desirable. The most of these will be readily understood; those that are obscure will be properly explained. There are a few, however, of such various and loose application, that their use necessarily begets confusion. Such, for example, is the word *lateral*, which is applied to any shoot growing laterally from another, such as an upright cane, a horizontal arm, etc.; it is also applied to the little green shoot which proceeds from the base of the leaves, and here it is simply meaningless. Dr. Grant has introduced the word *thallon* for use here. It is clearly from the Greek ϑαλλος, meaning a small branch, sprig, or little shoot, expressing precisely what we desire to say. By the aid of *a* privative, we naturally form *athallage*, *athallizing*, etc., words expressing an operation which has heretofore required an ungainly circumlocution. We dislike the introduction of new words as much as any body can; but new arts often demand, for the sake of precision and brevity, the introduction of new words, and their scholarly application, and there seems to be a necessity for it here; we propose, therefore, to adopt these new words, in the hope that their directness and conciseness will give them general favor.*

We will now proceed with the subject of *training* with all the brevity that is consistent with clearness. There are still not a few persons who doubt the necessity or utility of training the vine. Some will point with a scarcely concealed look of triumph to the wild vine clinging to some primeval denizen of the forest, and wreathing it with festoons. We are not insensible to the picturesque beauty of the vine as it lovingly clings to some noble old

---

* The following are the words, with their definitions, which we give in order that the reader may understand precisely how they are used: *Thallon, n.* (Greek, *θαλλος.*) A sprig or little shoot, especially one proceeding from the base or leaf, as in the grape-vine. *Athallage, n.* (*a priv.* and *θαλλος.*) The act or operation of removing or pinching off sprigs or little shoots, either partly or wholly. *Athallize, v. t.* To remove or pinch off sprigs or little shoots, either partly or wholly. *Athallizing, ppr.* Removing or pinching off sprigs or little shoots, either partly or wholly. *Athallized, pp.* Having the sprigs or little shoots removed or pinched off, either partly or wholly. Thus *thallons,* for our purpose, will mean the little shoots growing from the base of the leaf on the green cane; and *athallage,* the act or operation of pinching off the shoots at one leaf from the base, etc. Each time the thallon is *athallized,* an additional leaf will be left. In *Fig.* 21, p. 62, the thallons may be distinctly seen proceeding from the base of the leaves; and it may be further seen that they have been athallized a third time, the plant being a strong one. We venture to hope that we have made the application clear.

tree, and with its beautiful drapery strives to conceal the nakedness of its waning years; but we would respectfully suggest, that while it is a beautiful picture for some appreciative artist to copy, it is hardly a fit subject for the vineyardist to follow as a model. So, too, of vines more properly located, and growing unpruned on apple and other trees. They will produce some good fruit, but not as good as it might be, and by no means as good as is grown on vines judiciously trained; the fruit fails in quality, and dwindles away, from year to year, becoming at last almost as hard and indigestible as that grown in the woods. Besides, the practice, if adopted, would be found an exceedingly wasteful one. The fact should be accepted, that training is a necessity to all who aim at economy and the best results. It has the great value of systematizing all our labors, placing the vine within easy reach, and reducing the necessary manipulations to their lowest terms.

By way of introduction, it will perhaps enable the beginner more readily to understand the details of practice, if we first give him a general idea of the vine. The vine is composed of different members or parts, known to cultivators by names that have a more or less technical application. These will be understood by an inspection of *Fig.* 20, the left-hand side of which is a vine pruned for fruit. The part D, proceeding from the ground, is called the *stock* or body of the vine. The horizontal part, C, growing at right angles from the stock, is called a *horizontal arm.* A, A, A, on this arm, are *spurs:* B, B, B, are *canes.* There are other parts, which the reader will learn as we go along;

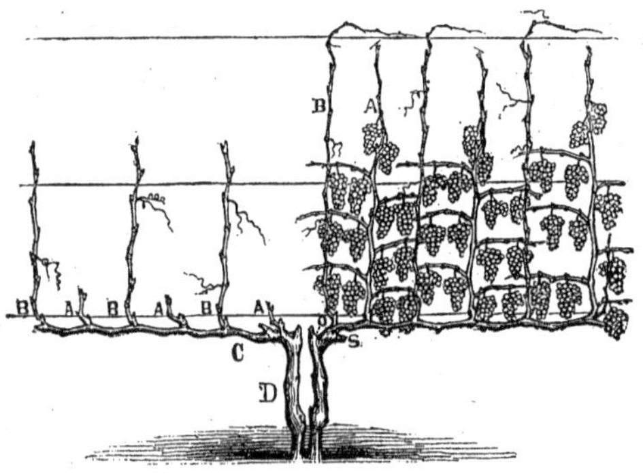

Fig. 20.

but these are the principal ones, and the engraving shows their relation to each other. The right-hand side of the engraving shows the vine in fruit on the *renewal* system, with the canes unpruned, which will be explained in its proper place.

Double Horizontal Arms—First Year.—There are many modes of training, some of the best of which we shall explain; but all good ones start from one and the same point. We therefore ask the reader's particular attention to what we shall say of the vine during the first three years of its life. That part of the subject being well understood, the rest becomes comparatively easy. We propose now to take a single vine, and carry it through the first year of its growth. At the time of planting, we directed the vine to be cut down to three eyes or buds. From these eyes three shoots will grow. When they have reached the length of three or four inches, the strongest must be selected, and the other two rubbed off. It is an object, however, to have the selected cane as low down as possible; if, therefore, the three are nearly of the same strength, rub off the two upper ones. The one selected must be tied to a stake, and the tying repeated from time to time, as growth progresses. It is an essentially bad practice to let the canes grow on the ground.

We propose the first year to grow one strong healthy cane, like that shown in *Fig.* 21. This can only be done by tying the cane to a stake, and having recourse to athallage. We thus secure large and durable foliage, fitted to withstand changes in the weather and the attacks of disease; better and more enduring roots; and a

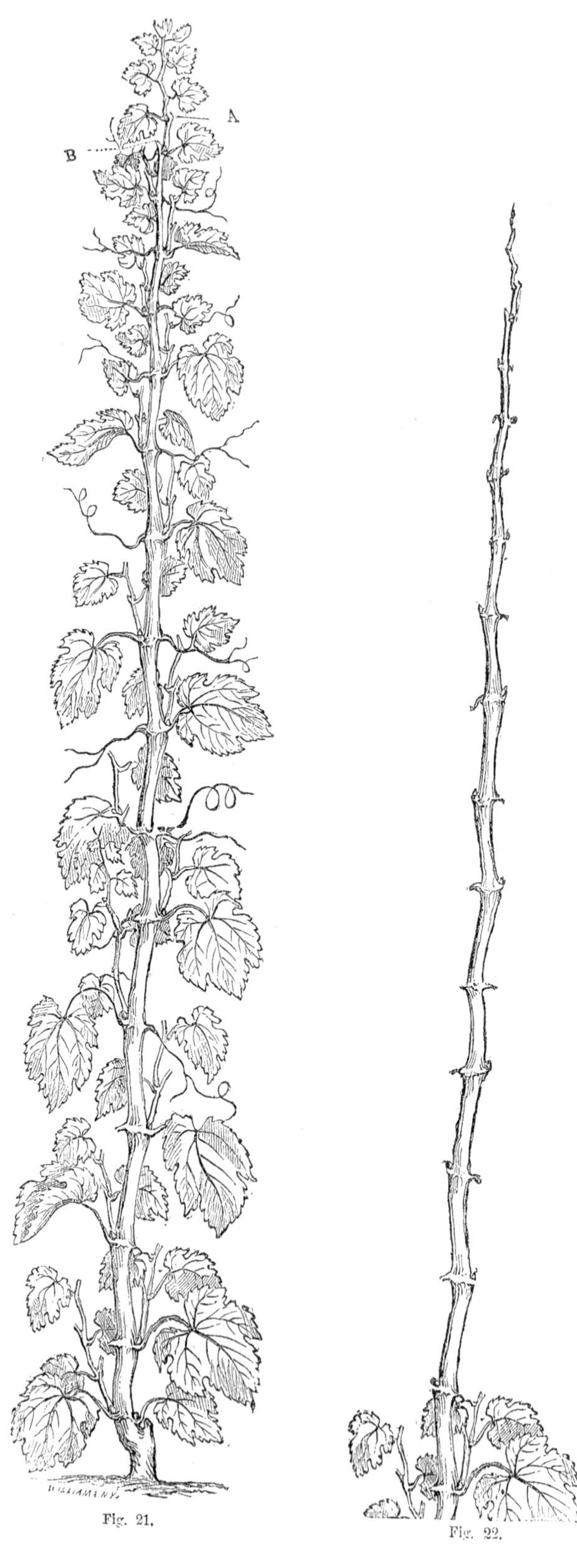

Fig. 21.

Fig. 22.

healthy, well-ripened cane. As the young shoot progresses in growth, the thallons (C, C) make their appearance, and must receive our attention. To secure the full benefits of athallage, it must be performed at the right moment; this is when the first leaf on the thallon has reached the size of a half-dollar, (if the reader can remember how large that was; to the best of our recollection, it was over an inch in diameter;) the end must then be *pinched* off, (not *cut*,) so as to leave only the single little leaf. By athallizing at this early stage, we avoid that shock to the action of the roots which takes place when it is performed after the thallon has made a considerable growth. There is scarcely any check to the growth of the plant; the vital force, or action, which would otherwise have gone to the extension of the thallon, is now directed in part to the little leaf and the bud at its base; the leaf increases in size and improves in texture; becomes, indeed, much larger than it would otherwise have been; the bud also increases in size, and finally bursts into a new shoot. All this has taken many days, but the thallon has not increased in length. After the bursting of the bud, the thallon is allowed to grow till the first *new* leaf has reached about the diameter of an inch, when it must be athallized precisely as before. If the vine is growing strongly, it may be necessary to repeat the operation a third time, after which the thallons may be allowed to take care of themselves. We have spoken of one thallon; but there will be one at the base of nearly every leaf, and all must be treated alike. This is clearly shown on the vine in *Fig.* 21, where the first thallon has been athallized three times, and the others twice, with the exception of one on the left, about half-way up. We have said above that the vital force is directed in part to the little leaf and the bud at its base; the rest goes to increase the size of the cane and its proper leaves, as well as the buds at their base. The whole vine has thus been benefited, both above and below ground.

The young vine, treated as above, is allowed to grow till about the beginning of September, when the extreme end of the growing cane is to be pinched out. This will materially help in ripening the upper portion of the cane and buds, especially if the operation is repeated at the end of two or three weeks. On the vine in *Fig.* 21 this has been done twice, as may be seen at A and B. With the exception of tying up, the vine will need no further care in the way of training. When the leaves have ripened and fallen off, the vine will have the appearance presented in *Fig.* 22. It may be regarded as an example of a first-class vine. Let *Fig.* 23 be taken as the same vine on a reduced scale. In November, or before the ground freezes, the cane must be pruned to three eyes, as indicated by the cross mark. It may then be bent down, and an inch or so of earth thrown over it, and thus left for the winter. *Fig.* 24 shows how vines may be prepared for laying down and covering. Cedar brush may be thrown over the plants instead of earth, or the covering may be omitted altogether in favorable localities, though it is always a safe and prudent course to give some kind of protection to young vines. The pruning may be left till spring, but it is far better to do it in the fall.

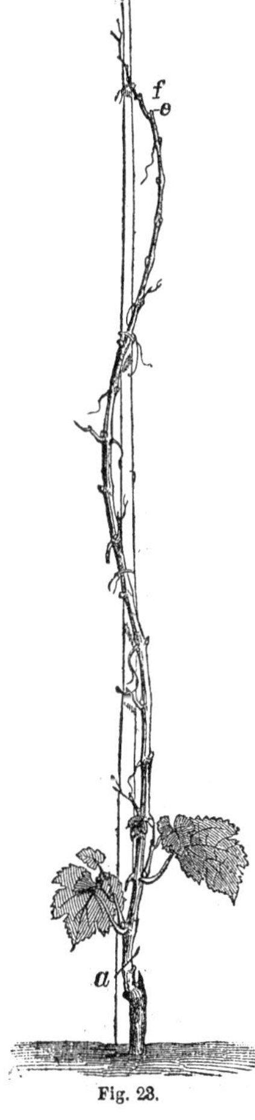

Fig. 23.

Second Year.—In the spring the first thing to be done is to uncover the vines. There is danger of doing this too soon. In northern and exposed localities, the vines should remain covered till danger from late frosts is past, for vines that are covered will not begin growing

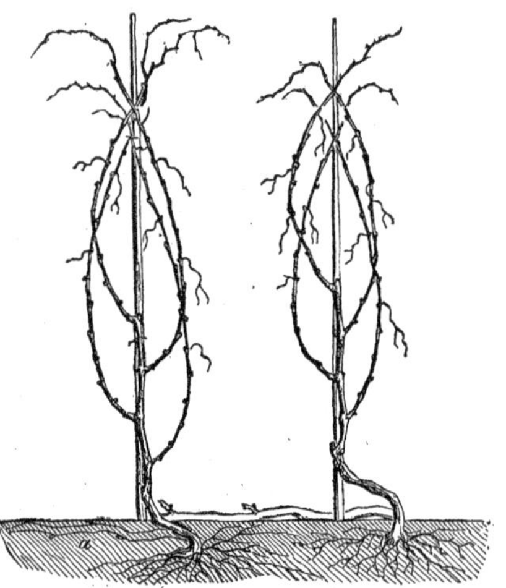

Fig. 24.

as soon as those that are uncovered. If the pruning was neglected in the fall, it should be done as soon as the vines are uncovered. We shall say nothing here about cultivation, reserving that for another place, but we shall suppose that the ground has been plowed or spaded, and the pruned vines tied to the stakes, ready for growth. We propose to grow two good canes this year. We left three buds at the time of pruning, but one was simply intended to insure against loss by accident. When the young canes have grown about three inches, one of them must be rubbed off, and that should be the weakest; yet it is desirable that the two that remain should be on opposite sides. Usually, in good vines, the three start about equally strong, and no difficulty is presented; but when it is otherwise, we must either take both on the same side, and submit to a little present deformity, or we must endeavor to restore the equilibrium by bending the strongest cane toward a horizontal position, and growing the weak one upright. In a large vineyard this would involve considerable labor and skill, and the reader may determine for himself what he will do under the circumstances. Having selected the two canes, they should be tied up to prevent their accidental loss. These canes must be tied to the stake from time to time during the whole season of growth. One bunch of fruit may be allowed to grow on strong canes, but the vines, on the whole, will be better if all the fruit is removed. When the thallons make their appearance, they are to be athallized precisely at the time and in the manner directed for the first year. The ends of both canes should also be pinched out as was then directed. The whole routine of training, indeed, is the same for the first and second years, the only difference being, that during the second year we have two canes instead of one.

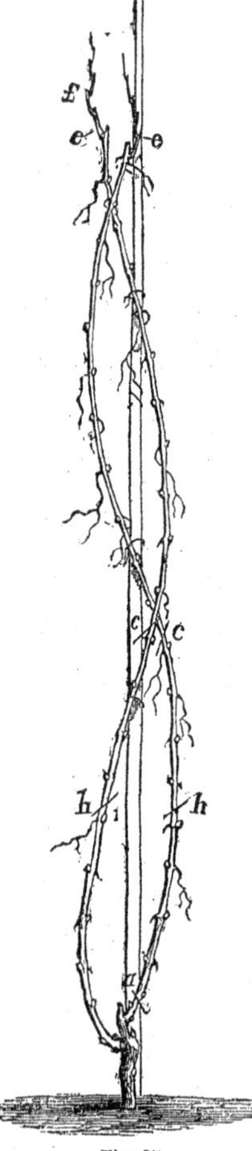

Fig. 25.

If every thing has gone on nicely, as it should, at the end of the season, when the leaves have fallen, we shall have a vine with two good canes, like that in *Fig.* 25. It will occasionally happen that a vine here and there will be weak, and not able to produce two good canes. In such cases, the proper course is to grow only one cane the second year. If, however, two are grown, they will be too weak to lay down for arms, and they must therefore be cut back to two eyes each, and only two canes grown the third year. Nothing will or can be gained by attempting to keep weak vines up to the advanced stage of growth of strong ones. It will also happen that some vines will make too coarse or rank a growth. When this rank growth takes place, the wood is coarse and spongy, and the buds that are chiefly wanted for future use are imperfectly developed. In such cases it will be well to let three canes grow instead of two, which will have the effect of preventing this grossness, and improving the quality of the wood. A vine grown with three canes is shown in *Fig.* 26. At the time of pruning, the middle cane is cut entirely out at the cross mark. If the trellis has been put up, it is a good plan to lay the canes down horizontally about the first of August; it is still better to begin to bend them to a horizontal position early in the season. The result is a better development of the buds near the stock of the vine.

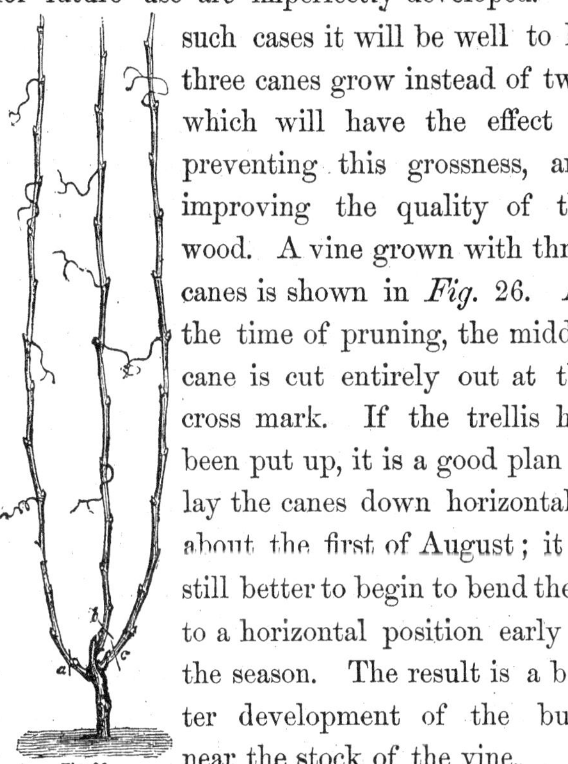

Fig. 26.

Our next labor will consist in pruning, and putting down the vines for winter; but, before doing this, it becomes necessary to determine what particular mode of training shall be adopted; for our pruning now must give shape to this. There are several good methods of training the vine, the best of which we propose to explain. We shall begin with the *double horizontal arm* system, since a good knowledge of that will pave the way to an easy understanding of the rest. Our pruning at the close of the second year will have in view the beginning of the arms. We say the beginning, because, if we should form or lay down the whole arm at one time, the lower buds, or those nearest the body of the vine, would break feebly, and either remain weak, or disappear altogether. The vital force, or action, tends so strongly to the end of the cane, that we must in some way control it, in order to fill up the entire length of the arm with fruitful spurs. This can be done with certainty only by a gradual extension of the arm; but even then the arm must not be extended beyond a certain length, or the vital force will overcome the restraint put upon it, and defeat our purpose. As a general rule, arms four feet long should not be increased more than one third of their length at a time, and that only when the canes are good.

We will suppose our vines are four feet

apart for a double tier of arms; each vine will then have about seven feet of horizontal arm, or about three feet six inches on each side of the stock. In this case, the arms may be laid down from a third to half their length, or from fourteen to twenty-one inches. There will, however, be here and there canes not stout enough to lay down as much as one foot. From such vines as may have three canes, the middle one must be cut through the old wood below the cross mark in *Fig.* 26, which will make the vine like *Fig.* 25; the canes must be cut at *h*, or from fourteen to twenty inches long. The canes are now to be placed in a horizontal position, and tied there, as shown in *Fig.* 27. The

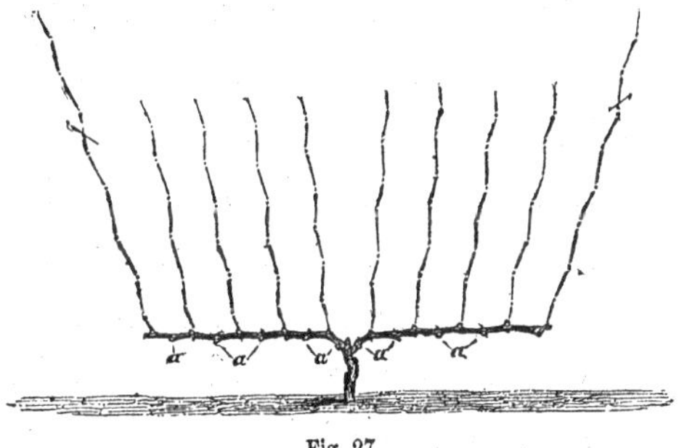

Fig. 27.

dotted lines show where the upright canes will grow from the upper buds. If all the lower buds, *a*, are rubbed off, the upper ones will place the spurs at about the proper distance from each other, except in a few kinds making very long joints; in these it may be desirable to retain both the upper and the lower buds for making spurs. The canes just bent down may or may not contain the exact number of buds represented in the figure; that will depend partly upon the kind and partly upon circumstances. The spurs should be from six to twelve inches apart, according to the kind of vine. The smaller distance will generally answer for the Delaware, Rebecca, and kinds of similar growth; while the longer distance will suit the Iona, Allen's Hybrid, etc. It may be reduced to a rule, thus: the distance between the spurs must be determined by the habit of the kind. The object is, to have the arms of about equal length, the same number of spurs on each arm, and the distance between the spurs just sufficient to accommodate the foliage. The reader must keep this object constantly in view in forming the arms. The two years' growth previous to the formation of the arms will give him a good idea of the habit of the kind; but he must make proper allowance for the greater vigor of the vine during these two years. *Fig.* 27 is a Delaware vine, and the portion of arm laid down is pretty nearly two feet long.

CHAPTER VII.

TRAINING—THIRD, FOURTH, AND FIFTH YEARS.

Third Year.—We will suppose that the vines have been wintered as heretofore directed, and proceed with the training for the third year. The upper eyes on the arms in *Fig.* 27 will each produce a cane, as indicated by the dotted lines, and each cane will set two or three bunches of fruit. Just here it becomes necessary to decide how many bunches shall be left to mature. The temptation to leave all is very great, and it is often done, to the great and permanent injury of the vine; in this way, indeed, it is sometimes tasked so much beyond its power, that the fruit not only fails to ripen, but the leaves fall off prematurely, the roots and wood in consequence fail to ripen, and the vine often dies, or is winter killed. It is not necessary here to state the physiology of the case, or to present an array of reasons; it will be sufficient to say, that, as a rule, not more than one bunch to each shoot should be left this year, and on weak shoots none at all. A very strong cane, however, may have two bunches.

We propose this year to grow a certain number of upright canes with well-developed buds at the base for spurs, and two good canes to extend the arms. The cane which proceeds from the bud on the end of the arm is for the extension of the arm. It may be grown at an angle of about forty-five degrees, or, better still, when from eighteen inches to two feet long, it may be bent toward a horizontal position, and tied securely to the trellis from time to time as it increases in length. All the canes intended for the extension of the arms must be athallized as directed for the first year's training. The upright, or fruit-bearing cane, must be treated as follows: as the thallons make their appearance, they must be athallized, and the operation repeated two or three times, or as often as may be necessary. We repeat here the injunction, not to fail in doing it at the right time. When the upright cane has reached a length of about two feet, pinch out its *extreme end*, and no more.

And just here let us say that it is a great fallacy to suppose that we wish to check the force of the vital principle; on the contrary, we believe that all checks are injurious, and just in proportion to their violence. Our object is not to check action, but to convert it all to use, with as little loss as possible; to concentrate it, in short, upon those parts that are to produce useful results, such as the fruit and buds. To check the growth of the vine at this time, would be like spending our labor and skill to collect its vital forces, and then, just as they were ready to perform their allotted office, to take the readiest means to destroy them. That summer pruning, or pinching, as generally performed in the vineyard, does check the vital force, and inflict more or less injury, there can be no doubt; but if summer pruning is performed at the right time, and in a proper manner, it is an exceedingly useful operation, and almost indispensable to the production of the best results. If we should allow this cane to grow five or six feet long, and then cut or break off two or three feet of it, as is commonly done, we should undoubtedly do great violence to the vitality of the vine; but if we pinch out the extreme end, the loss amounts to almost nothing. There is no interruption to the action of the plant; the vital force that would have gone to the extension of the cane finds more useful employment in improving the quality and size of the fruit, developing and maturing the fruit buds, and increasing the size and hardihood of the leaves. Nothing has been lost, but very much gained.

In course of time the buds at the ends of the canes that have been pinched will begin to grow. The young canes proceeding from these end buds may be allowed to grow from six inches to a foot long, when their ends must be pinched out. The operation may be repeated even a third time with advantage. Practice will in no long time give considerable expertness in matters pertaining to the summer treatment of the vine, and its labor will thus be considerably reduced.

Fig. 28 is a beautiful and truthful representation of an Israella vine in the third year of its growth, taken from life. Some of the lower leaves have been removed to show the fruit, of which there is rather more than a vine at this age should generally bear. The thallons are omitted, so as to give a better idea of the character of the leaves. The fruit canes are longer than they should be, but the wood was wanted for a special purpose. The pinching of

c
b
B
A
a
a

the fruit canes is not shown for want of room on the page.

At the end of the season we shall have a vine with several upright fruit canes, and two canes at the ends of the arms for their extension. The arms, as we have already said, should be extended very gradually. The second and subsequent extensions should be even more gradual than the first; if the arms are carried out too rapidly, there is danger of weakening the action of the part first laid down. As a general rule, one foot will be enough for the annual extension of the arms. In some cases it may be more; in others less. We have already pretty clearly indicated the nature of both these cases. We shall suppose that about one foot is to be added to each arm. The end canes must then, of course, be cut to the required length. The upright canes now remain to be pruned. These we propose to convert into *spurs*. This is done by cutting these canes down to two eyes each. *Fig.* 29 shows the appearance of the

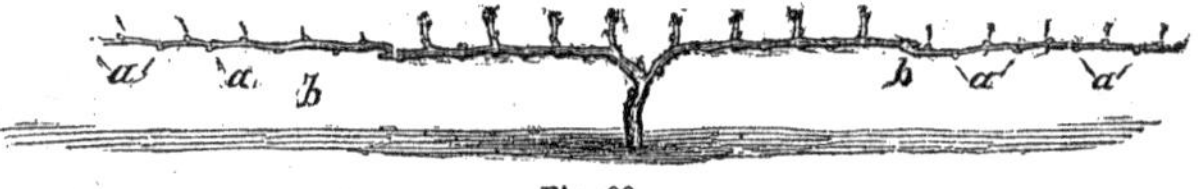

Fig. 29.

vine when pruned and the addition made to the arms, except that the addition in the cut is longer than it should be. The letter *b* shows the point at which the addition was made to the arm; and the letter *a* the buds on the under side which are to be rubbed off.

To make the matter plainer, we introduce *Fig.* 30, a piece of an arm, with its cane, on a full scale. *a* is the point at which the cane is cut to make the spur; *e* and *f* are the two principal or primary buds; *b* and *c* are base buds, so called because situated at the base of the cane. These base buds vary greatly in number, and in some cases are not apparent. All the spurs on the arm are sometimes formed to produce two canes, and sometimes only one; at others, again, these two kinds of spurs alternate. If we wish to grow two canes, the cut is made at *a*; if only one, the cut is made about half an inch above the bud *f*. To save repetition, we will alternate the spurs in the vine we are growing, pruning every other one for two canes; the canes, therefore, will be cut alternately at *a* and about half an inch above *f*. We shall thus illustrate the

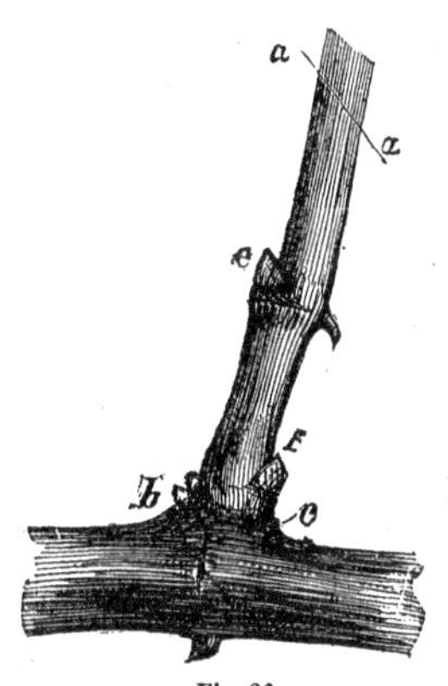

Fig. 30.

double and single spurs at one and the same time. The vines having been pruned, will now be put down and covered for the winter.

Fourth Year.—We have now a vine with one portion of the arms spurred, and another portion newly added. Let us first follow out the spurs with two buds. The buds *e* and *f*, in *Fig.* 30, will each produce a cane, and each cane will set two or more bunches of fruit. That from *e* may be allowed to mature two bunches of fruit; the cane from *f* should not be allowed to bear any, all its strength being reserved for fruit the following year. The base buds *b* and *c* must be rubbed off. They would have been very valuable, however, if the buds above them had been accidentally lost. We could, indeed, have pruned this cane just above the bud *f*, and taken the lower cane from one of the base buds; they are not always strong enough, however, to be depended upon; but when they are, it is a good practice to use them, as the spur will then be a little shorter. We have reserved the lower cane for next year's fruit spur, not only because it is best situated for this purpose, but also because the upper one will produce the largest and best bunches of grapes. If the upper cane were reserved for next year's fruit, the spur would soon become inconveniently long.

When the growing canes have reached the length of some two feet, pinch out the extreme end, as above directed. Repeat the operation when the additional or new growth has reached the length of six inches to a foot; and still a third time, if the action is very strong. Watch the appearance of the thallons, and athallize them at the proper moment. It will be understood that these directions apply to all the spurs having two canes. The treatment of the spurs having single canes is not materially different. These may carry two bunches of fruit; when the canes have grown about two feet long, the ends must be pinched out, and the operation repeated, in all respects, as above. Athallage must likewise be attended to as above. This will complete the treatment of the spurs. *Fig.* 31 represents a portion of an old arm with its spurs, and the new canes growing on them. It is a beautiful and truthful portrait, taken from life. In this example, the canes and thallons are ready for the operations of pinching and athallage.

In regard to the new portion of arm laid down, the cane from the end bud must be grown at an angle for further extension of the arm next year. The buds on the lower side must be rubbed off; and the canes from those on the upper side are to be grown upright for future spurs. The ends are to be pinched out at the time and in the manner before directed. Athallage, also, must be promptly and faithfully attended to. We have said nothing about tying up; but it will be understood that the canes are to be tied as they lengthen; some care must be used, however, that the strings

Fig. 31.

do not cut and injure the canes: they should always be loose.

These details will carry us through the season, up to the period of pruning. In the best vines the arms may now be completed. Lay down the end cane, therefore, and cut it so that there shall be an interval of about a foot between the ends of the arms of adjoining vines. If the ends of the arms should meet, there would be no space for training the last fruit canes. Passing along to the portion of arm laid down last fall, the canes must be pruned

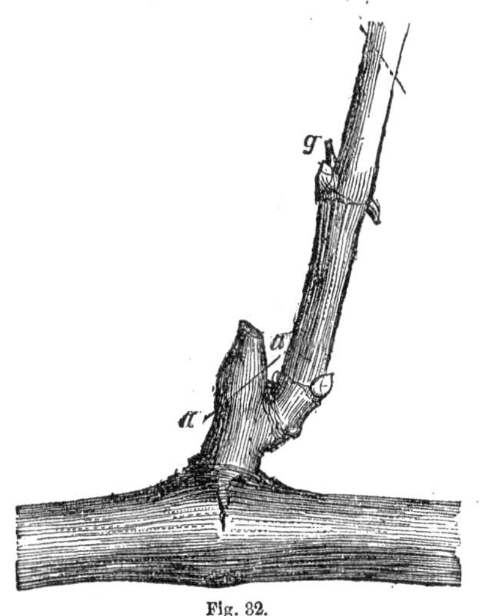

Fig. 32.

to one and two eyes alternately, in the manner before described. Next will come the spurs.

An example of those having one cane is shown in *Fig.* 32. The pruning consists in cutting off the cane just above the bud *l.* The stump of the old spur may be cut at *a*, *a*. All the spurs with single canes are to be pruned in this manner. A spur having two canes is shown in *Fig.* 33. This must be pruned by first cutting the left-hand cane entirely away at the mark *a*; the

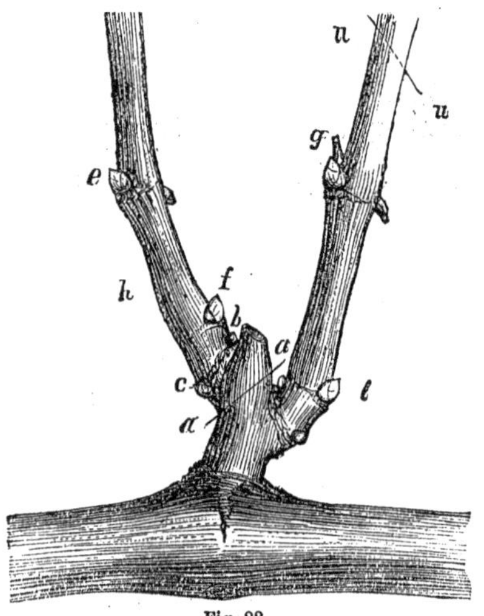

Fig. 33.

right-hand cane is then cut at the mark *u*, which leaves two buds for the two new canes. The reader will observe that two simple cuts complete the pruning even for a spur of two canes, and will no doubt be impressed by the fact, that *system* not only simplifies labor, but divests it of much of the forbidding hardness that results from the constant exercise of perplexing thoughts where system is not observed. Our vine is now ready to be laid down for the winter.

Fifth Year.—With our good vine, we shall this year fully establish the arms and complete the system of training. The arms are now all furnished with fruit spurs, except the small piece at the ends just laid down. The training is now only an extended repetition of the routine pursued last year. Beginning at the end of the arms, we must rub off the lower buds from the part last laid down; the upper buds will produce the usual canes for fruit spurs. These canes may carry one bunch of fruit each; the ends must be pinched out, and the thallons athallized, as heretofore. The remainder of the arm is furnished with spurs, which are to be treated precisely as was done last year. The canes growing from these spurs (except the lower cane, where there are two) may now carry two bunches of fruit. If, however, there should be any weak ones, the bunches must be reduced, or removed entirely. The reader must learn to exercise his judgment in regard to this and other matters that must necessarily vary somewhat in their treatment, as they may be affected by circumstances. If every thing has gone on favorably, at the end of the fifth year we shall have a perfect specimen of double horizontal arm training. The pruning may now be done as directed last year, and the vine laid down for the winter.

Fig. 34 will give a good idea of the appear-

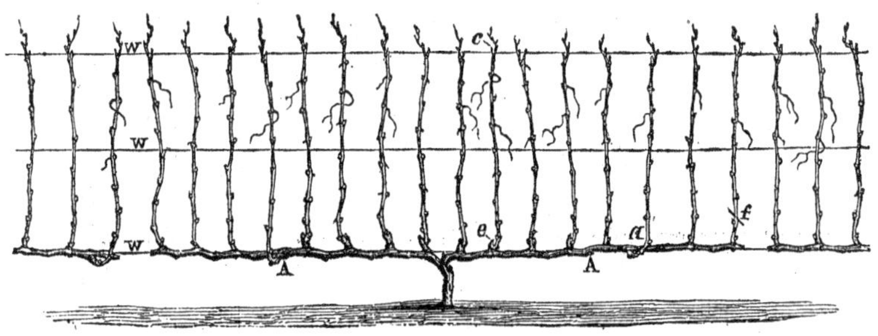

Fig. 34.

ance of the vine at this time, except that the fruit canes are all single, whereas we have made part of them double. It will be observed, too, at *a*, that a bud has "missed," and its place been supplied by a cane from a bud beneath. This and other methods of replacing spurs will be described elsewhere.

Double Horizontal Arms, with two Tiers.—We have alluded to the double horizontal arm system with *two tiers* of arms, one above the other. This is formed as follows: in pruning at the end of the first year, *every other vine* is cut to the three lowest eyes, as described at the time. The intermediate vines are pruned about three feet six inches long, the canes from the two upper eyes being selected to form the arms for the upper tier. All the other buds are to be rubbed off. It will sometimes happen that a vine is not sufficiently strong to grow two canes at this height. In that case it must be cut lower for the canes, or even cut to three eyes, and another year taken to grow a

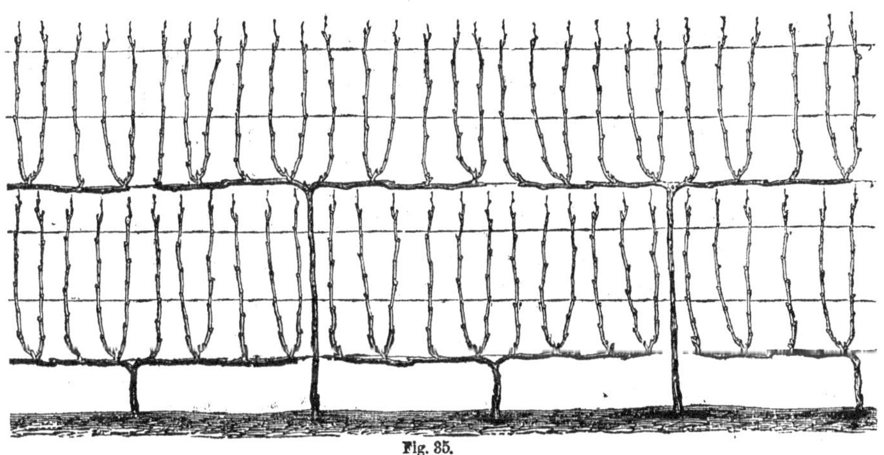

Fig. 35.

cane that will be stout enough. There should be no hesitation in pursuing this course. With the exceptions here noted, the training is in all respects like that for a single tier of arms. *Fig.* 35 gives a good idea of the system when complete, except that the arms are too short for our description. In this figure the spurs are shown as carrying alternately one and two canes. The end vines must have only one arm each, in order to fill up the trellis, as shown in the engraving. The single arms will be on the upper or lower tier, according to the number of vines in the row. It is better to have both the single arms on the upper tier, where it can conveniently be done. The trellis for this system should be six to seven feet high from the ground. The first tier of arms should be from twelve to fifteen inches from the ground, and the second tier midway between the first tier and the top of the trellis. The intermediate spaces should be filled by two or three rows of wire. The manner of making a trellis will be described hereafter.

CHAPTER VIII.

TRAINING—GUYOT—GUYOT IMPROVED—UPRIGHT STOCK WITH ALTERNATE SPURS—BOW SYSTEM—THE JURA.

System of Guyot.—Inventions are sometimes brilliant, and nearly perfect at the moment of leaving the brain; but often they result from the long-continued study of rude examples of the principle involved, and are only made perfect by gradual improvements; and the transitions are so simple and natural that we wonder they were not made before. The plan advocated by Dr. Guyot seems to be a case of this kind. *Fig.* 36 may be taken as one of its original forms. It is an old one, and consists in taking, at the beginning, a fruit cane from a bud on an upright stock, and bending it in a curve to the ground, where the end is secured. This cane is renewed each year. The whole arrangement is rude, the vine having no support; in fact, it is left to take care of itself.

Fig. 36.

The attentive observer, however, could not fail to see how evenly the bending of the cane set

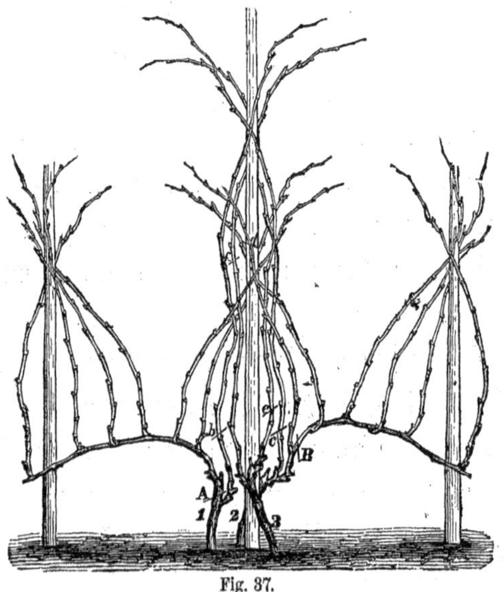

Fig. 37.

the fruit along its whole length; and this naturally led to the next step in advance, that of giving some kind of support to the vine, while substantially the same mode of training was observed. (See *Fig.* 37.) To save expense, no doubt, three vines were planted to one stake;

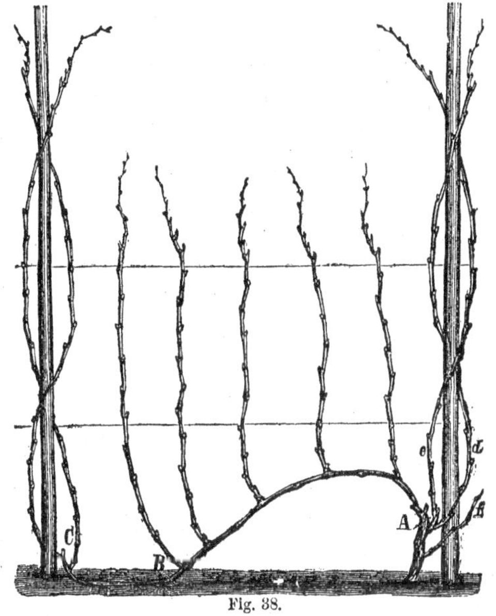

Fig. 38.

(clearly a mistake;) but an improvement was made in adding a spur for renewal, instead of appropriating the cane nearest the stock.

A still further improvement in time followed, as shown in *Fig.* 38. Here the vines are supported by stakes and wire, and only one vine planted at the stake. System and order have now made their appearance in the vineyard; let us hope, to abide there; for it is a good place for them. In the engraving, the end of the fruit cane has been "layered" to make a new vine; a practice hurtful to the bearing vine, and not to be commended in ordinary circumstances. Yet another step forward, and we have the plan of Dr. Guyot, properly so called, into which he has introduced the greatest degree of precision of which the case seems to be susceptible, in so training the vines on a wire trellis as to employ a system

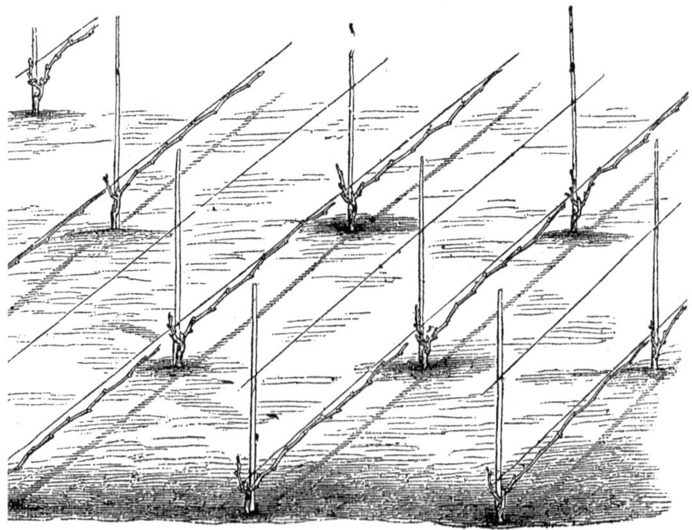

Fig. 39.

of movable shelters, by which he claims to have secured such a degree of *certainty*, as re-

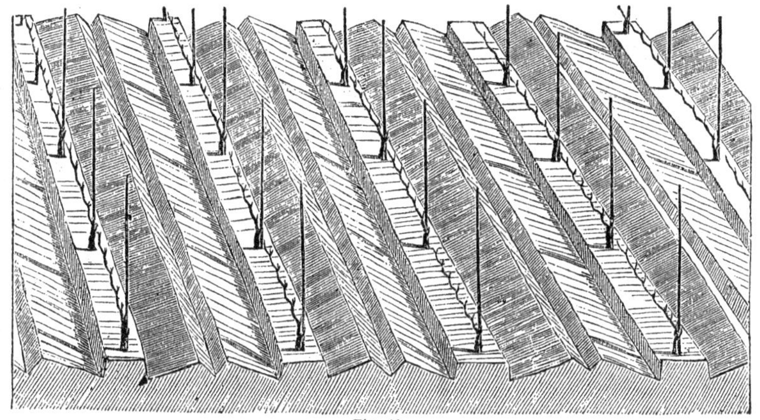

Fig. 40.

gards both the excellence and abundance of the crops, as to place them beyond the fear of fail-

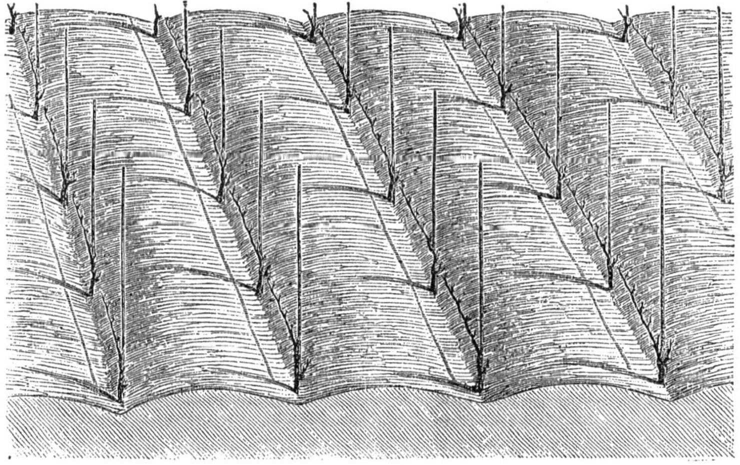

Fig. 41.

ure. The statistics which he presents, as the results of trials continued during a series of years, and on a large scale, would seem to warrant his conclusions. The system of Dr. Guyot may be understood in a good measure from an inspection of *Figs.* 39–44. He has shelters to

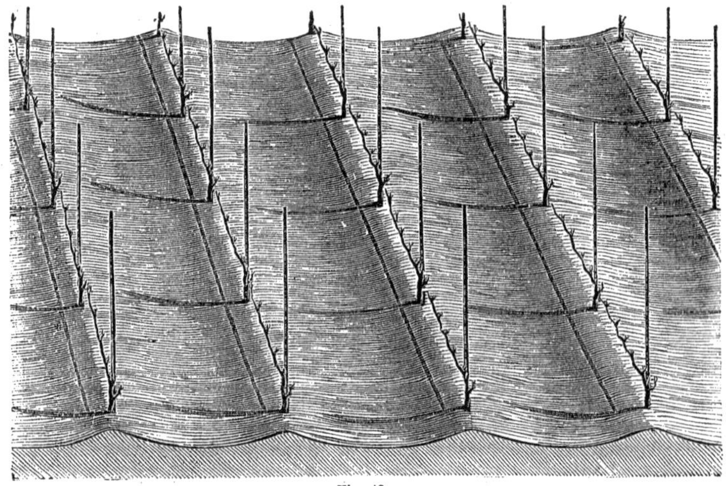

Fig. 42.

be used at different seasons of the year, which would require quite a number of engravings to illustrate fully. Dr. Grant, however, just before the appearance of Guyot's work, suggested

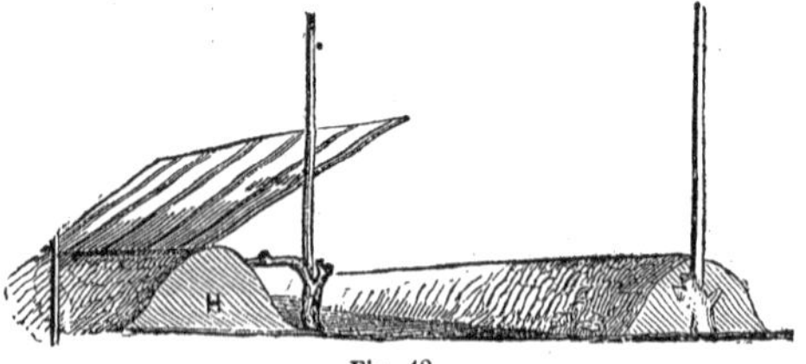

Fig. 43.

a form of shelter having considerable resemblance to his, and which is shown in *Figs.* 43, 44. On the right, in *Fig.* 43, the vine is covered for the winter. In the spring the soil is removed from the vine, and placed as seen on the left. The bottom of the shelter rests on the raised earth, and is supported just above the middle by wooden pins on the trellis. A front view is given in *Fig.* 44. A vineyard shel-

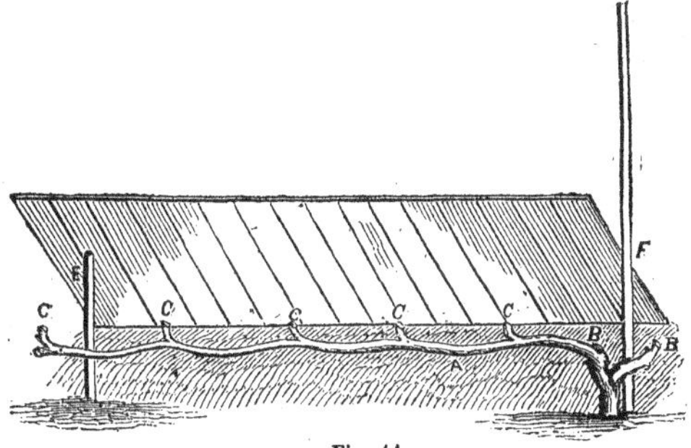

Fig. 44.

tered in this way is almost as well protected as if the vines were under glass, and it is easy to perceive with how much certainty the crop may be secured. There can be no doubt that this system of shelter possesses great advantages for many portions of our own country, liable as we are to sudden and sharp changes of weather; but there are few, perhaps, who will for some time yet be willing to incur the additional labor and expense. We may remark that it is the system of Guyot without the shelter that is practiced among us. In this system, also, in its earliest forms, may be seen the germ of the horizontal arm, which is the horizontal renewal made permanent, and in that respect an improvement, especially where excellence of fruit is concerned.

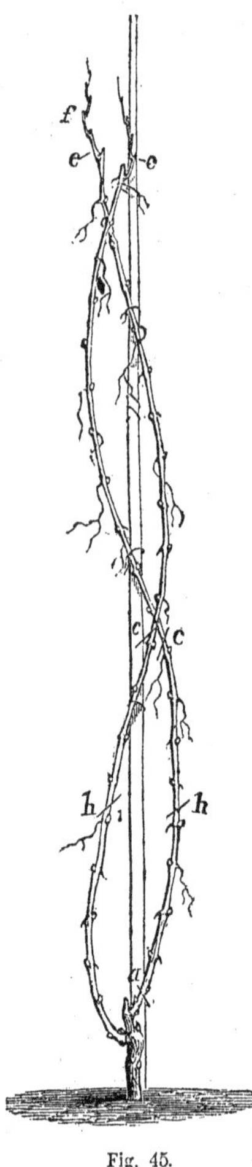

Fig. 45.

We propose now to describe the training of Dr. Guyot. This, for the first two years, is like that already described for horizontal arms, and need not, therefore, be detailed here. At the end of the second year we have two upright canes, as in *Fig.* 45. The cane on the left must be cut at the two lowest buds, to form a spur; and that on the right at the mark *h;* it should not, however, this year be more than two feet long. The cane on the right is for bearing fruit, and must be bent to a horizontal position, as shown in *Fig.* 46. From the spur on the left two canes must be grown. The upper cane may carry one bunch of fruit this year; the lower one, none. The thallons on both these canes must be athallized as directed for the horizontal system. When about five feet high, pinch out the ends of both canes, and repeat the op-

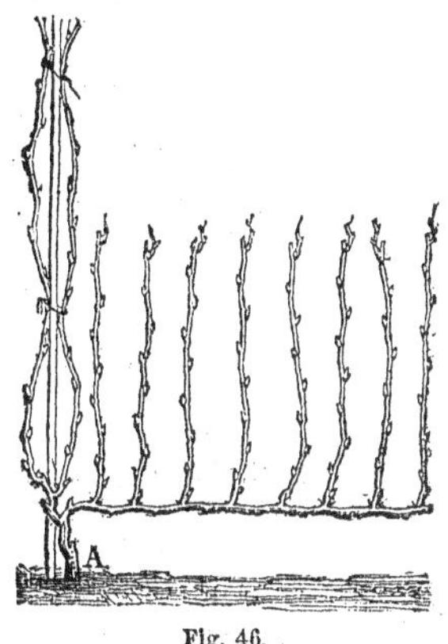

Fig. 46.

eration, in the manner before described. There is a necessity for economizing action at all points; we want especially to ripen the lower upright cane in the most perfect manner, as we expect it to carry a large crop of fruit next year. The two feet of cane that was laid down horizontally must have all the lower buds rubbed off; the canes from the upper ones may carry one bunch of fruit each. More would be an injury to the vine at this time. When these fruit canes are about two feet long, pinch out the extreme end, as before directed for fruit canes. The thallons must also be treated in the usual manner.

In the fall, the pruning will be as follows: the arm on the right, that has borne fruit, must be cut entirely away; the lower cane on the spur must then be cut about four feet long, and laid down horizontally, to take the place of the arm just cut away; the upper cane must be cut to the two lowest buds, for producing two more upright canes. The reader will now doubtless perceive a necessity for keeping this spur as near as possible to the stock, since it must annually furnish a cane for laying down.

Fourth Year.—This system may now be considered as complete. The treatment this year is only a repetition of that of last year, including pinching and athallage. The fruit canes may now be allowed to carry two bunches each, if the vine is in good healthy condition. The upper cane on the spur may also carry two bunches, and none of the canes, as a general rule, should exceed this number. The lower cane on the spur should never be allowed to carry fruit. As the vine gets older, three canes may be allowed to grow from the spur, but two are generally much better. The pruning hereafter will be the same as last year: the arm is cut off, the lower cane on the spur cut to four feet and laid down, and the upper cane cut to the two lowest buds for a spur. *Fig.* 47 shows an old vine in fruit on Guyot's plan.

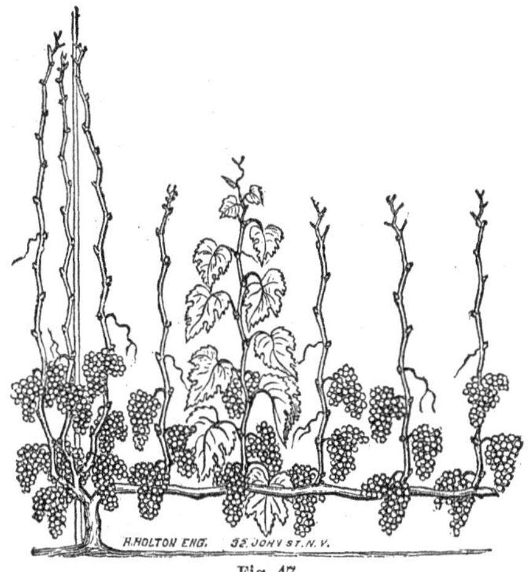

Fig. 47.

There are three canes from the spur, however, and too much fruit, at least for ordinary vines. Two bunches are quite enough.

Guyot's Plan Improved.—We say improved, because, in our hands, it has yielded better results. The improvement consists chiefly in making the arm *permanent*, instead of renewing it annually, and was suggested by Dr. Grant. It is one of the best systems for the vineyard.

After what has been said above, the manner of doing this will be easily understood. There is no difference in the plan up to the third year, when the cane is laid down for the arm. The spur is already pruned to two buds. The portion of arm laid down, however, should be only about fourteen inches long, or about one third the length of the arm when complete. Let us first look after the renewal spur. If the base buds break nicely, select two of them in preference to the buds left above them, which should then be rubbed off. The object is to get the spur as close as possible to the stock.

The arm is treated as follows: the cane from the end bud is to be grown at an angle for the extension of the arm, and should be pinched when about four feet long. The canes from the other buds must be grown upright, and may carry one bunch of fruit each. When these canes are about two feet long, pinch out the end, and otherwise treat them as directed when growing horizontal arms. The thallons must have proper attention, and at the right time. The treatment here, indeed, is just the same as was given for fruit canes on a former page, and we may therefore pass on to the end of the season, and explain how the vine is to be pruned.

The upper cane on the renewal spur is to be cut off at *c*, (*Fig.* 48,) the cut being made through the old wood; the lower cane is to be cut at *d*, or the two lowest buds. The cane at the end of the arm is to be cut about fourteen inches long, and laid down for the extension of the arm. The upright fruit canes are to be cut about an inch above the lowest bud; or, to prevent accidental loss, cut above the second bud, and if every thing is safe in the spring, rub the upper one off.

The next year two canes are to be grown from the renewal spur, and may carry two bunches of fruit each. The cane from the bud at the end of the arm must be grown horizontally for the extension and completion of the arm. The buds must be removed from the under side of the portion of cane just laid down, and the canes from the upper buds grown upright. These canes may carry one bunch of fruit each. The rest of the arm is spurred; a cane must be grown from the lowest bud on each spur, and may carry two bunches of fruit each. The pinching, athallage, and general treatment will be like that of last year. Where the spurs are not too close together, they should have two canes, the formation and treatment of which the reader already understands.

The next pruning will be as follows: the upper cane must be cut entirely away from the renewal spur by cutting through the old wood, and the lower cane cut at the two lowest buds. Passing to the arm, cut all the canes on the spurs at the lowest bud, if single spurs are adopted, and at the second bud, if double spurs. The arm is now laid down its full length, and

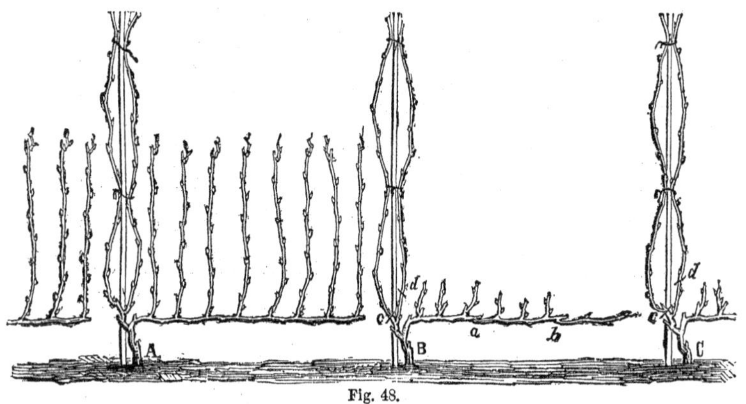

Fig. 48.

the system is complete. The pruning, pinching, athallage, etc., will be the same each succeeding year. The spurs may hereafter carry two bunches of fruit, but more than this will not be consistent with the permanent welfare and duration of the vine, as a general rule. The exceptions to the rule must be determined by the kind of vine and its native disposition to bear. In *Fig.* 48, the vine on the left shows the system of Guyot; that on the right, Guyot's system as improved, *a* and *b* indicating the points where the arm was lengthened, the last addition not being yet spurred. *Fig.* 49 shows the same vines in fruit and leaf.

Fig. 49.

The improved Guyot system is one of the best, both for the amateur and the vineyard. Its safety-valves give us a control over the vine which no system can possess without them. In practice we have found them a valuable aid, and in that light they are regarded by those who have adopted them. They are valuable in

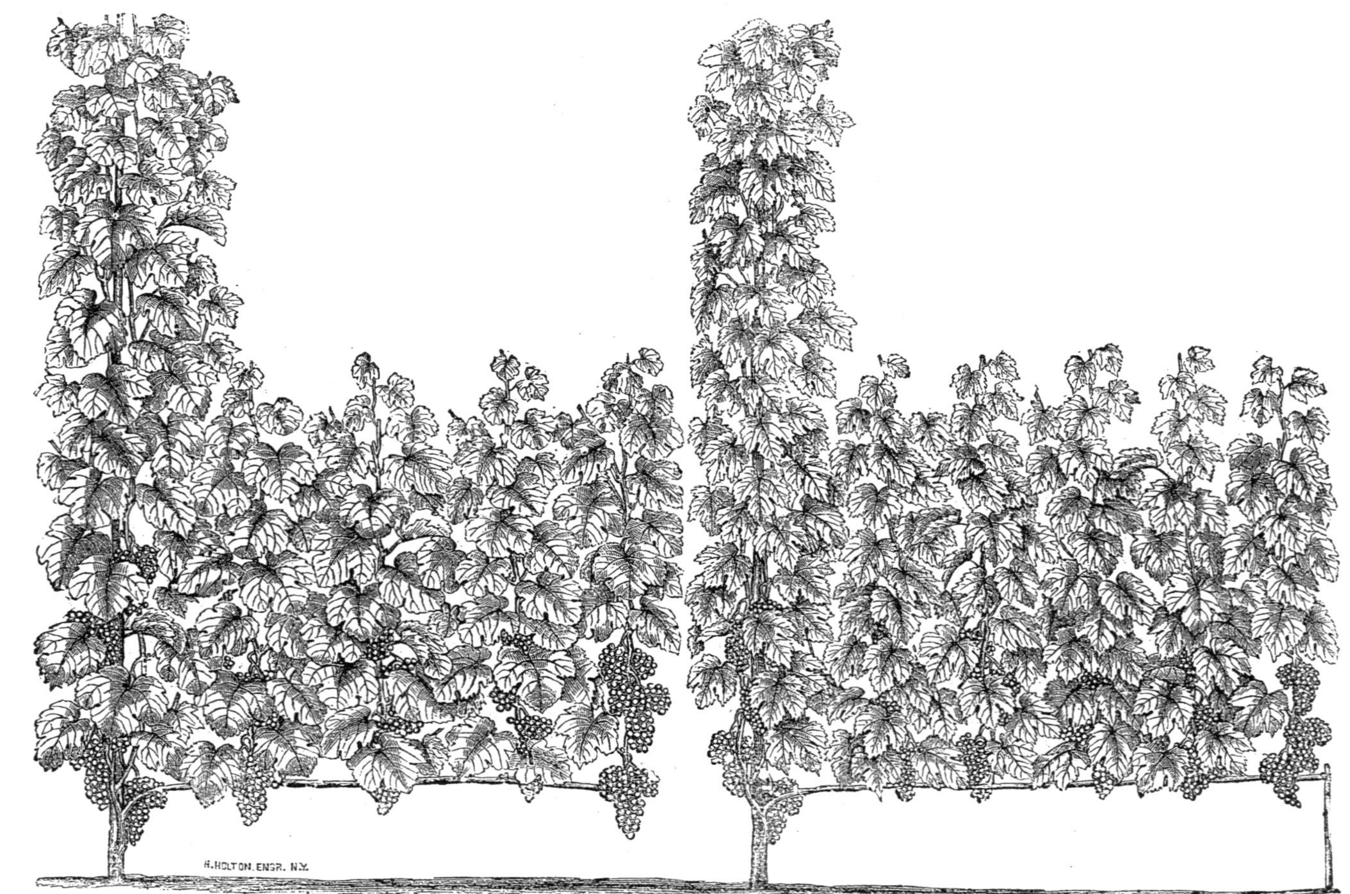
H. HOLTON. ENGR. N.Y.

other respects when understood, an important one being the facility they afford for replacing an arm without loss of fruit. The permanent arm, in place of the annual renewal, yields a better quality of fruit, which should be considered of some importance, whether for wine or the table.

In this connection we introduce *Figs.* 50, 51, the most beautiful and perfect portraits of the kind ever presented to the public. The vine on the left is the *Iona;* that on the right is the *Delaware,* the characteristics of each being finely shown. The lower leaves have been removed from one cane of each, to show the fruit.

This system may be used with a double tier of arms, as shown in *Fig.* 52. In this case, the vines must be planted at equal distances, and the stocks buried and brought up together as shown by the shaded lines in *Fig.* 53, which is an example of the renewal system, which the reader can study till we find time to explain it.

Upright Stock with Alternate Spurs.—This is a neat and pretty mode of growing the vine for the amateur and the garden. It has a look of simplicity about it which will commend it to many. The reader perhaps thinks he has only to grow an upright

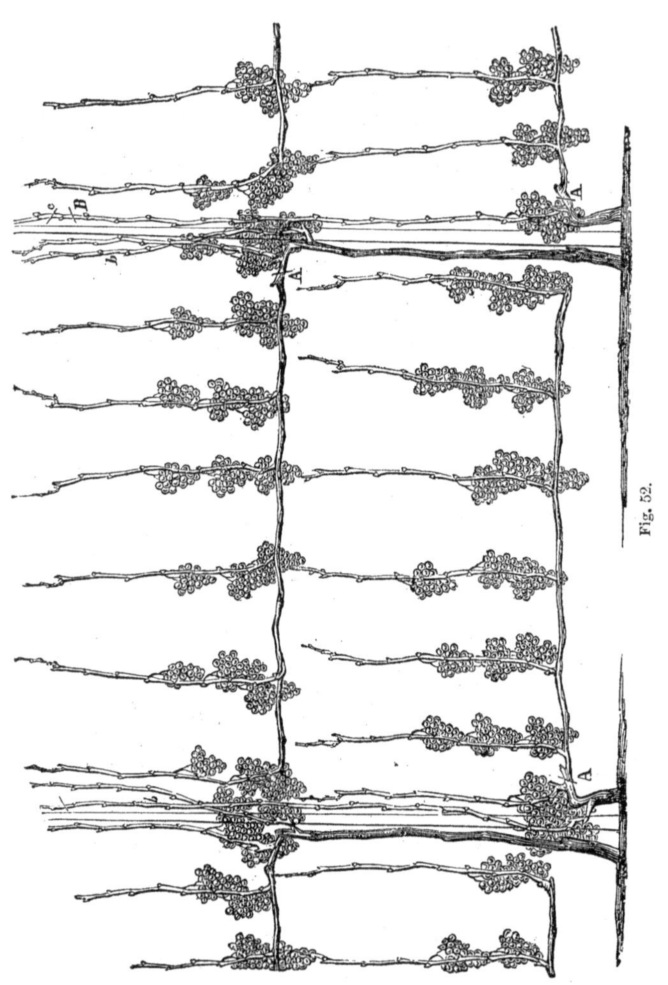

Fig. 52.

cane, cut off the top, and the thing is done. We shall probably undeceive him when we state, that to grow the vine successfully in this way is a rather tedious process, requiring several years for its completion. The form is pretty, and it presents a good example of how subservient we can make the vine to our purpose. If we should form it from a cane of one year's growth, it would soon become bare at the bottom, yielding its fruit only at the top, and giving us a great deal of trouble to control it; in short, it could not be done. We have elsewhere explained that the action of the vine tends strongly to the top. The position of the vine in this case strongly favors this tendency, and it is our purpose now to show how it may be measurably overcome or held in check.

We shall take a vine that has been planted and grown one year, as described elsewhere. If the cane is not strong, it must be cut to the lowest bud, and grown another year; for we shall have poor success here without a good cane. The cane is to be cut about two feet long, and tied to a stake. From the end bud a cane must be grown for extending the stock. The next bud below this must be selected for

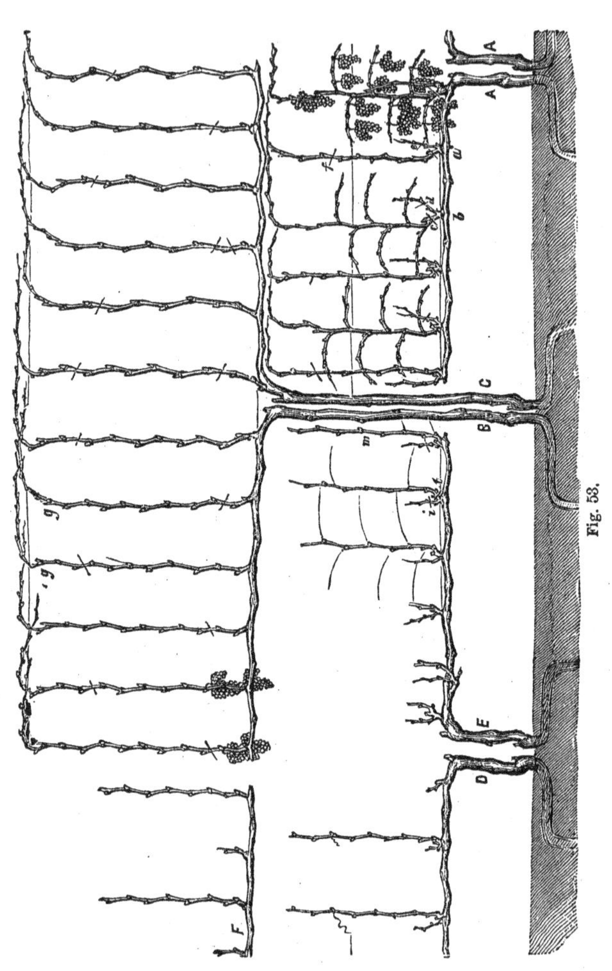

Fig. 53.

a fruit cane, and grown at an angle. Six inches below this, but on the opposite side, select another bud for the same purpose. Select another six inches below, and on the same side as the first, the object being to have the canes alternate on opposite sides, with about one foot between those on the same side. All the other buds are rubbed off. The lateral or side canes may carry one bunch of fruit each. The upright cane and the side canes must be pinched and athallized as usual; the upright cane, however, must not be pinched till it has grown about four feet. In the fall, the upright cane must be cut about fifteen inches long, which will allow of two additional side canes, one on each side. The side canes must then be spurred by cutting them off at the two lowest buds, and the vine is ready for winter.

The next season, grow an upright cane from the end bud for extending the stock. On the newly added stock select two buds for the two new spurs on opposite sides. From the spurs grow two canes, using a base bud wherever it is strong enough. The upper canes from the spurs may carry two bunches each, and the two new canes one bunch each. Pinching and athalliz-ing must be attended to as usual. The appearance of the vine at this time may be seen in *Fig.* 54. X is the point where the vine was cut

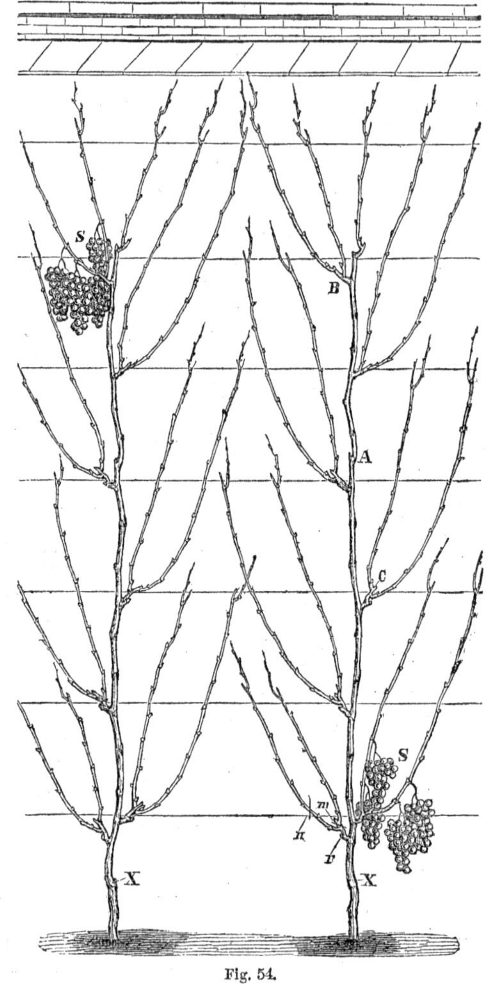

Fig. 54.

at planting; and A, where it was cut at the

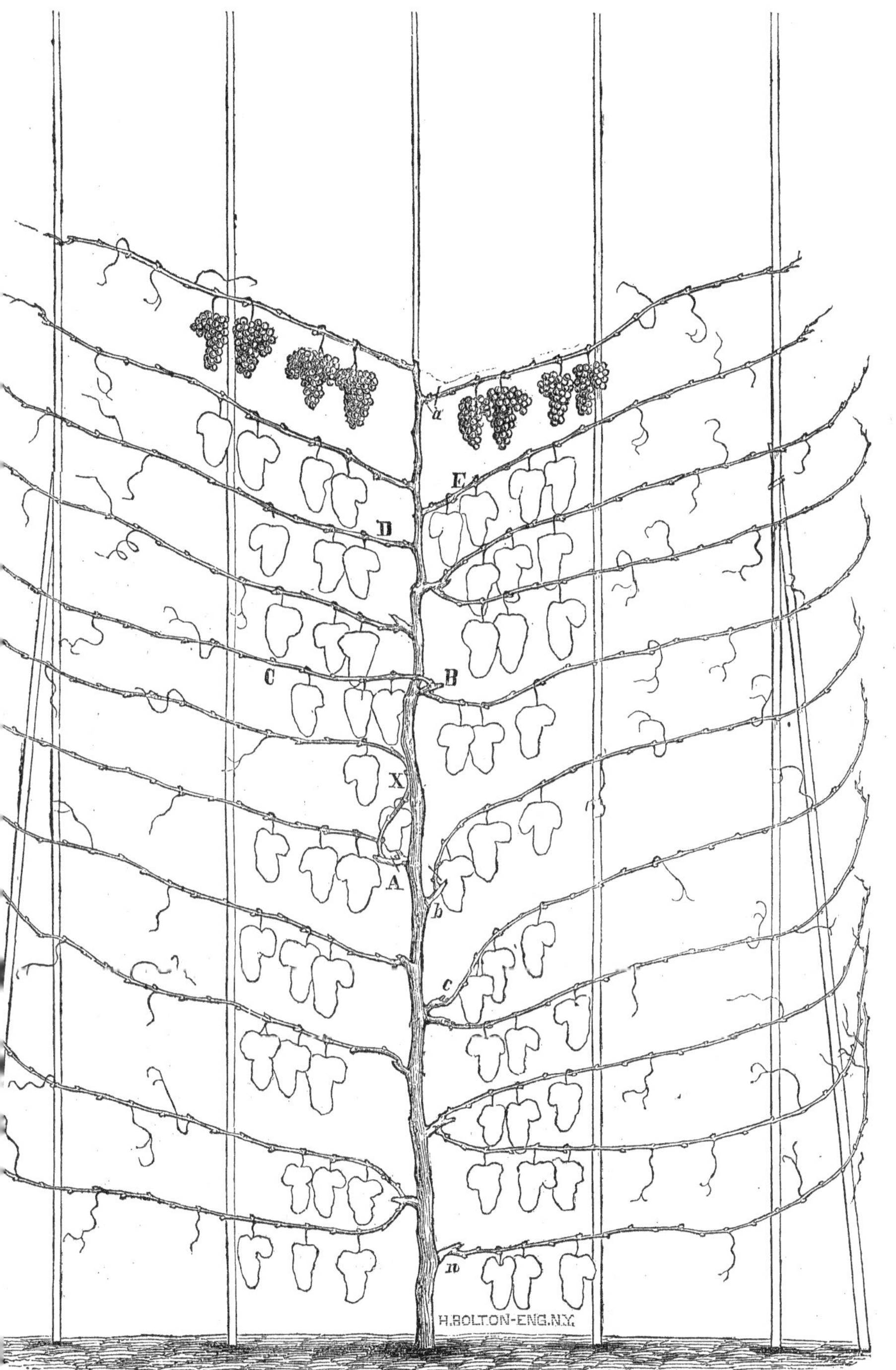

Fig. 55.

end of the first year. The pruning will be as follows, beginning at the lowest spur on the left: the upper cane is to be cut off at *m* through the old wood, and the lower cane cut at *n*, or the two lowest buds. (The spurs on this vine, in fact, are two years old, and the stump made by last year's pruning is seen at *r*.) All the spurs are to be pruned like this one. The two upper canes are to be cut to the two lowest buds for spurs. The treatment in succeeding years is only a repetition of this. The stock may be extended to the height of five feet; if carried much beyond this, the vine soon gives out at the bottom. With a stock four feet high, like that in *Fig.* 54, the vine may be kept in full bearing many years. When fully established, all the canes may carry two bunches each.

Fig. 55 is a Delaware vine trained in this way, engraved from a photograph taken by Mr. Morand at Iona. At X may be seen one method of replacing a spur. The vine carried just the number of bunches seen, but not without injury. *Fig.* 56 is the same vine in leaf. *Fig.* 57 shows how this system may be applied for covering a trellis or wall from eight to ten feet high. The inter-

8

Fig. 56.

mediate vines, X, are grown with naked stocks up to the point A, and thence spurred to the top of the trellis. In this way any amount of surface may be covered.

The Bow System.—This system, as practiced at the West, was introduced by German emigrants, and in Ohio and other places is more or less common, but seems now to be giving way to other and better plans. *Figs.* 58, 59, 60 will make it quite plain to the reader. The first year one good cane is grown, which is cut down to the two lowest buds, from which two canes are grown the following year. One of these canes is pruned to a spur with three buds, and the other shortened to about two feet, as shown by the cross marks in *Fig.* 58. The cane is bent and tied to a stake as seen in *Fig.* 59. Usually, this cane is allowed to fruit its whole length. From the spur three canes are taken, which are also allowed to fruit. The appearance of the vine at this time is shown in *Fig.* 60. The pruning consists in cutting away the bow or bent cane. There are three upright canes left, the lowest of which should be cut to a spur of three buds, to produce three new canes. Of the two remaining canes, one is cut off, and the other bent

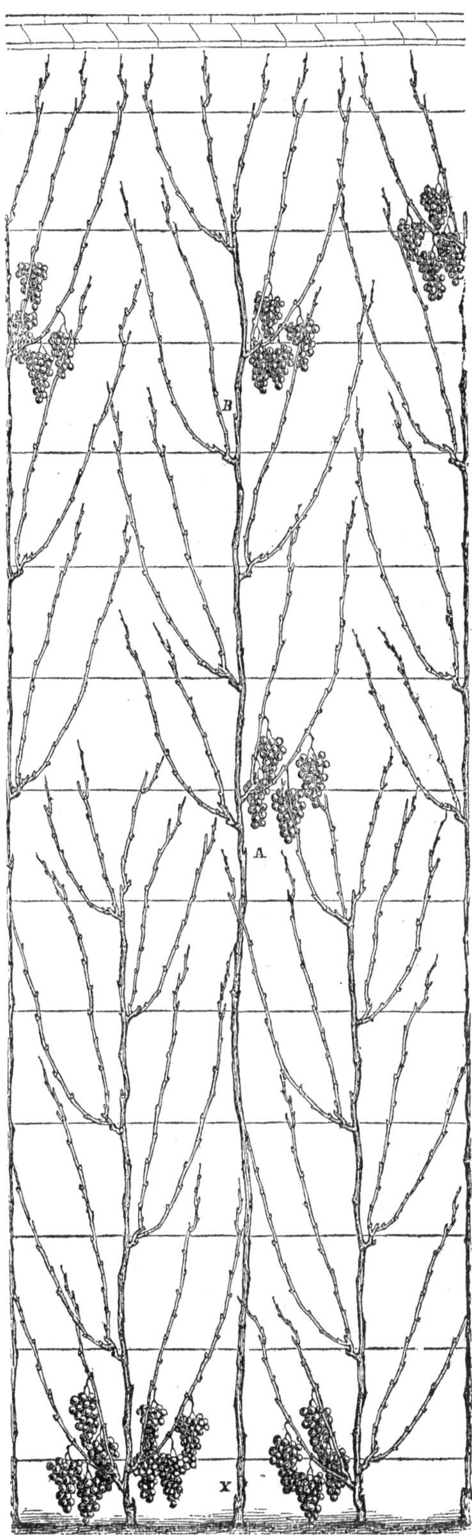

Fig. 57.

or bowed, and tied to a stake. The same treatment follows year after year.

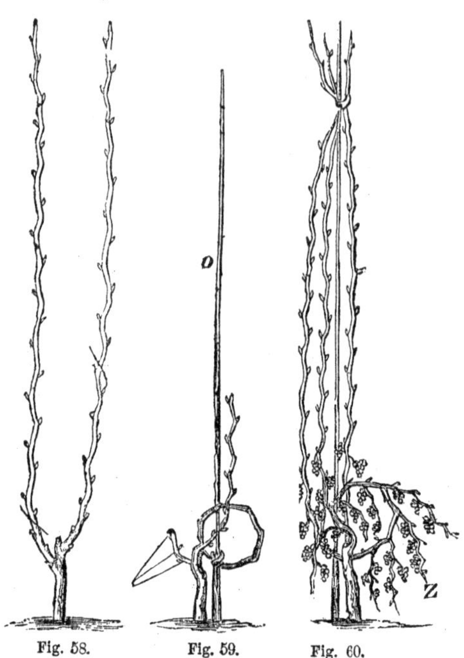

Fig. 58. Fig. 59. Fig. 60.

Figs. 60 and 61 show a better form of the bow system. In this the two canes, at the close of the second year, are both cut to spurs, each having two buds. From each spur two canes are grown, and fruited. The next pruning is as follows: the lowest cane on each spur is cut to two buds for a new spur, and the remaining canes shortened to about two feet, and bent as in *Fig.* 61. The bows are fruited their whole length, and the canes from the spurs are allowed two bunches each. The appearance of the

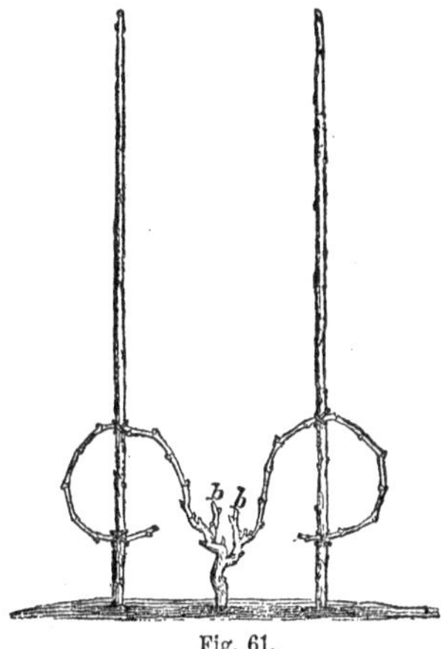

Fig. 61.

vine at this time is shown in *Fig.* 62. Two courses may now be pursued: first, to cut off the end of the cane *b* at the lowest point

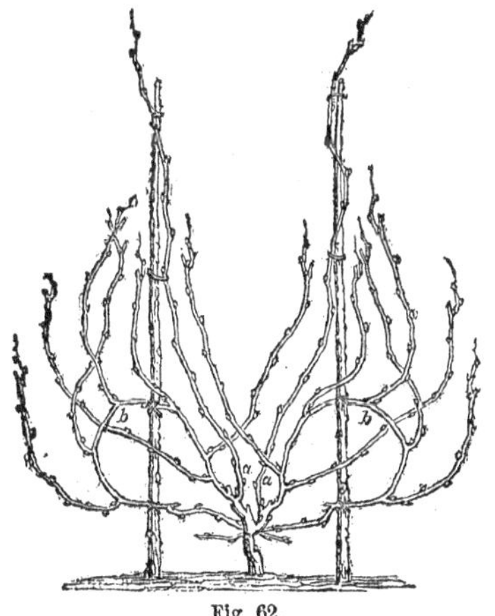

Fig. 62.

where it is tied to the stake, and prune the lateral or fruit canes into spurs of one bud each; in which case the cane *a* should be cut to its lowest bud for a single cane, to be treated as a safety-valve. Second, (if this course is pursued, the spurs should have *two* upright canes instead of one,) cut the cane *b* entirely

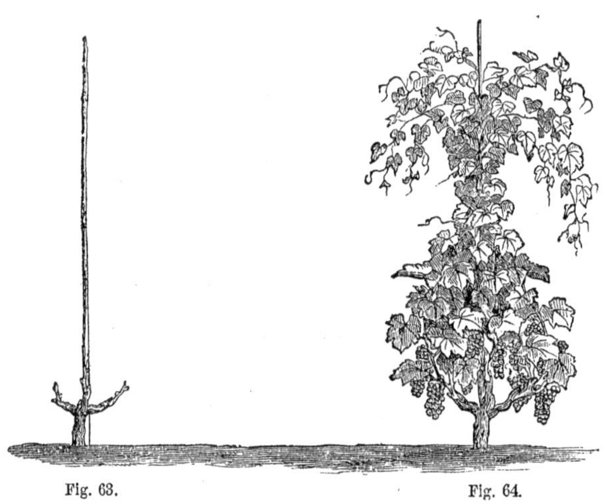

Fig. 63. Fig. 64.

away, bow one of the upright canes, and cut the other to the two lowest buds for a spur.

Figs. 63 and 64 are examples of growing the vine from spurs on low stocks.

A little study of *Figs.* 65 and 66 will show how they may easily be converted into the bow, Guyot, or horizontal arm system.

The Jura Plan.—This is very simple, and

will afford the reader a good subject for experiment as well as amusement. For the vineyard, too, we prefer it to the bow system, as it is even

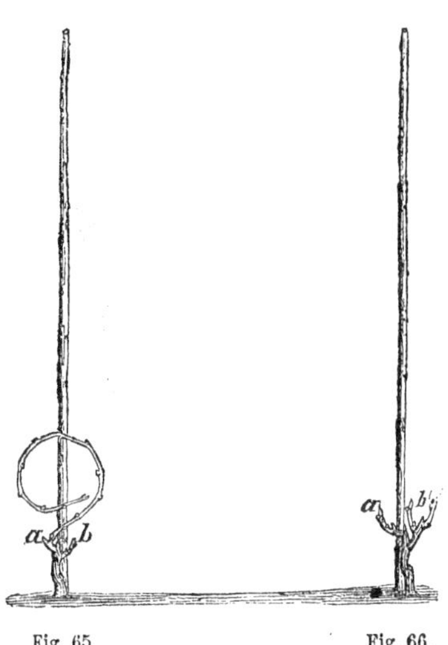

Fig. 65. Fig. 66.

more simple, and will produce better fruit. The vines may be planted three or four feet apart. An inspection of *Figs*. 67, 68 will make the treatment very plain. The first year a good cane is to be grown, and in the fall cut down to about two feet. The second year four fruit canes are to be grown, as shown at *a*, *b*, *c*, *d*, in the vine in *Fig*. 67. These are to be converted into double spurs in the usual way at the next pruning, and the system is complete. The pruning thereafter will consist in cutting away the upper cane, and pruning the lower cane to the two lowest buds. The stock is not to be

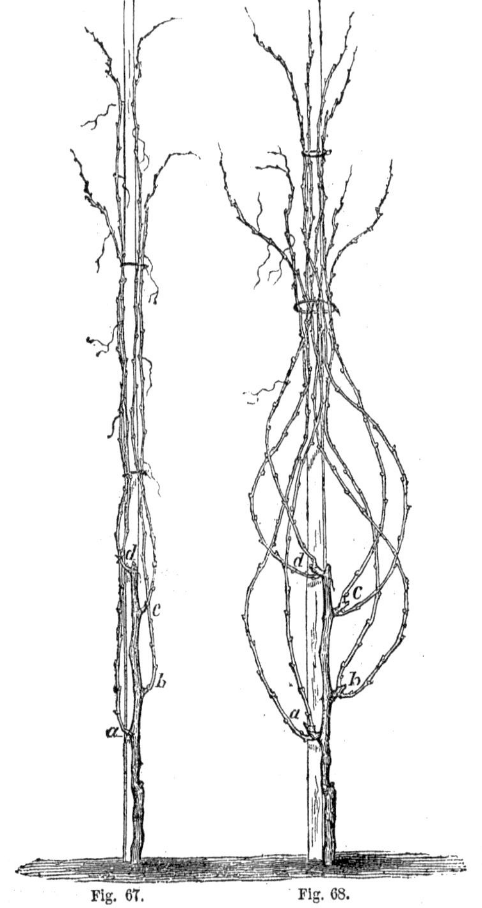

Fig. 67. Fig. 68.

lengthened. This plan admits of a variety of modifications, which the general principles we have given will enable the reader to study out for himself.

CHAPTER IX.

TRAINING—THOMERY.

Thomery.—Notwithstanding all that has been said and written about the Thomery, there are few who have any just conception of what it really is. There has been a failure to understand its details, or to comprehend it as a whole. One thinks it consists in growing vines in successive tiers, one above the other; another supposes that it is some peculiar manner of planting the vines; still another has an idea that it is some special or peculiar mode of pruning, and so on *ad infinitum.* It is simply no one of these, but all of them, and more besides. The Thomery, in brief, consists mainly of a happy selection and combination of the best features of prevalent modes of training, and their successful application to overcome local difficulties of a trying nature. This system takes its name from a little village in France, called Thomery, where the system had its origin, and where it still finds its best exemplification. We hope, by giving an illustration, to make the system understood. In all that has gone before we have relied upon our own experience; we shall still rely upon it here, and also call to our aid some of the best French authors, as well as the account of a friend personally cognizant of the details practiced at Thomery.

To Dr. C. W. Grant belongs the merit of having brought the Thomery prominently before the American public. It was he who first studied and mastered it as a system, and successfully worked it out in practice; and it is not too much to say that he has furnished the chief part of the material for nearly all that has been written upon the subject in this country. Candor and the amenities of literature demand the acknowledgment of this much, and we do it most cheerfully.

This method of training, and its appliances, need careful study preparatory to undertaking it. No part of it is obscure or difficult of execution; but inasmuch as it is an extended system, each step of which, in its progress toward completion, prepares the way for the next, it is important that the whole should be clearly seen from the beginning. The success and permanence of the result depend upon having each step well taken.

The ground should be prepared in the best manner, and the plants be uniformly of the best quality. When plants of only moderate quality can be obtained, they may be improved by planting them two or three feet from the wall, and bringing them to it by one or more "*beddings*," as represented in *Fig*. 69. Each bedding will delay the beginning of training one year; but, if well done, will secure plants of the requisite character. It is much better, however, to be provided with suitable plants at the beginning, and avoid the delay. *Fig*. 3, p. 36, represents a vine of the best possible character and quality one year old. *Fig*. 8, p. 39, represents one of the best quality two years old. These may rank as nearly equal in value for our purpose.

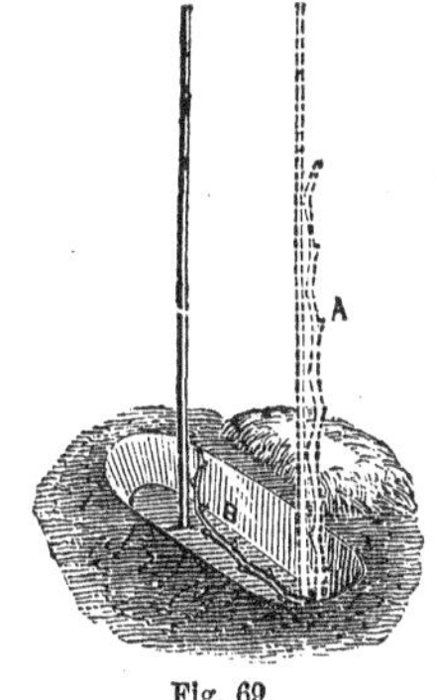

Fig. 69.

As we proceed, each vine with its arms is subjected to the same treatment as that for the formation of double arms, (p. 60, *et seq*., and *Fig*.

25,) or in the two-tier system, (p. 86, and *Fig.* 35 ;) but, having greater regard to permanence, from the greater disappointment resulting from any degree of failure in the present case, we proceed rather more slowly in forming and lengthening the arms. While that is in progress, more regard should be had to securing a perfect bearing condition than to getting a great quantity of fruit early. The former being well done, the latter follows in due course. *Fig.* 70 is drawn from life, and is a very good representation of well-managed Delawares in process of formation, only the stopping of the canes, by which they were brought to the proper length, is not shown, in consequence of the small scale which the comprehensiveness of the engraving required. For this, see *Double* and *Single Arm Systems*, pages 86 and 87.

Although it is desirable to form all the arms at the same time by equal steps, it is scarcely to be expected. Some difference of growth will take place, and the highest arms in the system will ordinarily require one year more of growth of stock than the lowest, before being ready for the first laying down. Thus *D*, *Fig.* 70, will require one year more than *A*, for the formation of its greater length

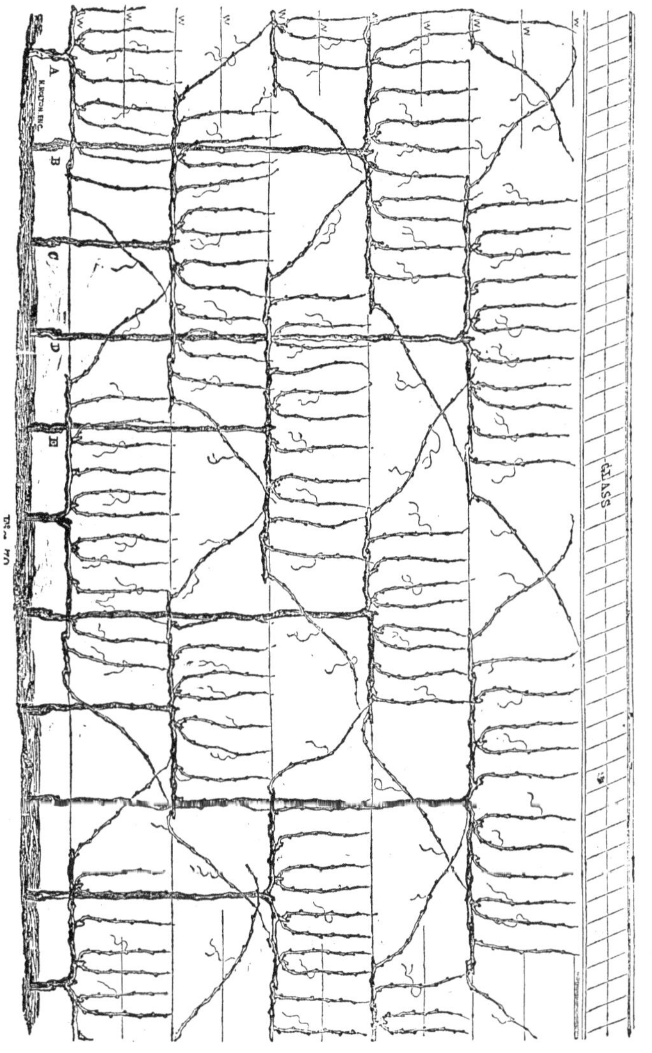
A
B
C
D
E
GLASS

of stock. In this matter the vigor and ability of the vines must regulate the rate of progress, according to the directions already given. The vines with longest stock, although later at the beginning, eventually become disposed to the most vigor, and this must be regulated, as before stated, by the quantity of bearing, according to general principles.

Fig. 71 represents that part of the Thomery system that is the most immediately related to the main wall, which is all that we can consider at present, leaving the full exposition of the whole system for another occasion.

This suite consists of five rows, the first and most important one of which we have just reviewed; but the first row here differs from that in having only four instead of five tiers of arms, and, consequently, allowing one fifth more for length of cane for a wall of the same height. This should be at least ten feet from the ground to the top of the cap.

The first trellis stands about twelve inches from the wall, and the vines are planted two feet apart in the rows; this, it will be seen, gives eight feet to be occupied by the arms of each vine, the arms being made a little shorter than the space, so that their ends may not touch.

Fig. 71.

The distance between the tiers of arms is about two feet, affording room for canes of that length.

The next row is seven feet in advance of the first, and the plants two feet apart in the row, as before; this leaves seven and a half feet space for the arms of each vine, with their tiers. The next row stands five feet in advance of the last; and the vines being set three feet apart, gives six feet in length for the arms of each vine. The fourth row has the vines trained on a different plan. See *Fig.* 45. It is four feet in advance of the last, and the vines are set three feet apart. The fifth row is three feet from the last, and is trained on the single arm plan. The vines in this also are three feet apart. This might with about equal propriety have been with double arms at the same distance, with the vines four or five feet apart in the row.

The object of this graduation, which has probably been already anticipated in the mind of the reader, is to accommodate the vines to the lessening influence of the shelter as the distance from the main wall increases.

Fig. 72 was taken from life at different periods, to represent different stages of prog-

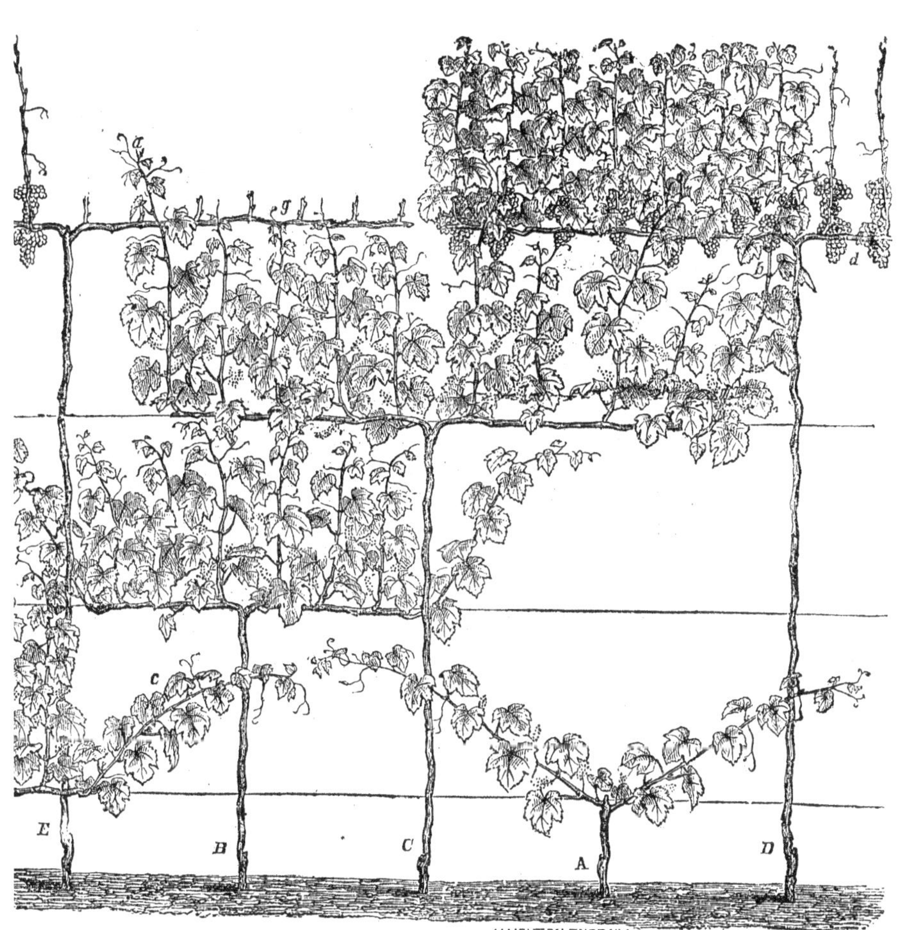

9

Fig. 72.

ress during the season in one engraving. A, B, C, and F represent the vines as they appeared in June at the time for first pinching. D represents a vine at the first maturity of fruit, on which all of the proper summer operations have been well performed. Some of the leaves have been taken away at *d*, to show the canes and the fruit as it is borne uniformly throughout the vine. E is one like it late in the fall, with some of the bunches still hanging at *f*. The canes of the arm *g* are properly pruned, as may be done in November; but, for safety, it is well to leave one bud more on each spur, to be rubbed off at starting in the spring.

At A is shown a vine that has been delayed two years in its progress by having had layers taken from it. The canes *a* and *b*, on the vine C, are ready to be depressed (like *c* on F) toward the horizontal position, to finish their growth for the beginning of arms. The student who has followed us attentively thus far has found that this system is no more difficult of comprehension than any other, except that there is more of it. It is not so well adapted for the vineyard as some others that we have described, except where high and extended walls or close fences are its attendants; but it is very advantageous for making the most of the shelter afforded in yards, gardens, and by the sides of buildings, and especially for arbors, on which the ordinary efforts always fail.

Fig. 73 is part of an arm of a large vine

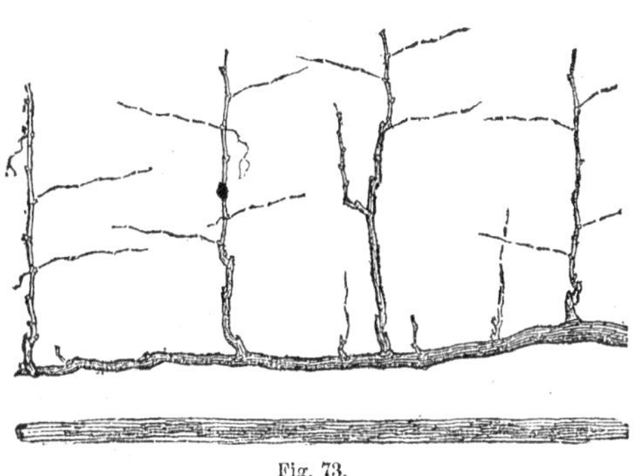

Fig. 73.

trained with the aim of covering a high trellis like *Fig.* 74. It has been planted twelve years, and has already been cut back twice in impracticable efforts to cover the whole elevation of about nine feet with bearing wood. Four feet of elevation is about the limit to which this can be done by ordinary means from one vine. *Fig.* 74 represents the trellis covered, which is quite practicable by the Thomery system, and easily maintained.

In *Fig.* 75 is represented a vine that has been trained to cover a trellis twelve feet high. The bearing wood, it will be seen, is all near

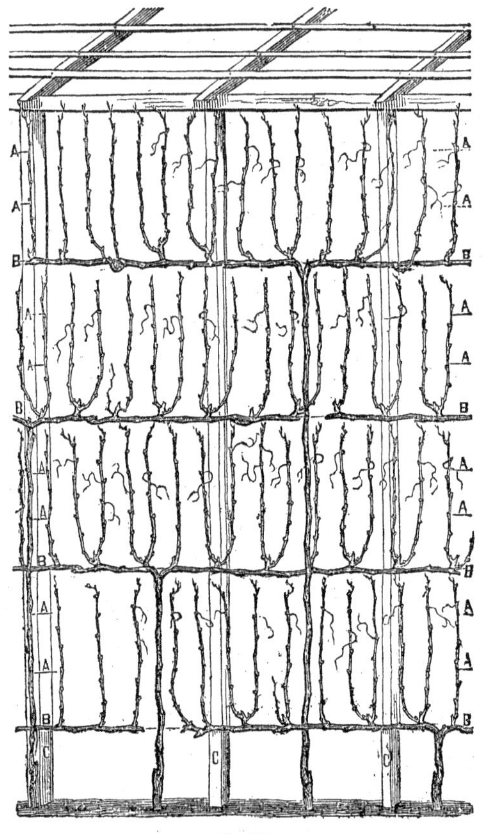

Fig. 74.

the top. If pruned for next season at the cross marks, which is the usual course, the bearing portion will be moved one step higher,

Fig. 75.

leaving another equal distance below unproductive. "Cutting back" down to A, B, C, D, E, would only be attended with the loss of one season's fruiting, to go the same course over again. This does not come from faulty pruning, but from a radically defective plan.

The principal objection to the Thomery plan for high trellises is the slowness with which it is necessary to proceed, six or seven years being required for its establishment in full bearing. There need be, however, but little if any delay in getting fruit beyond that of any other permanent system, and none at all when proper vines are obtained.

In *Figs.* 45 and 48 a more expeditious way of covering a wall or arbor is shown, but one promising less permanence. *Fig.* 76 is a modification of the same, making it a renewal plan, for which canes are provided as at P, to be pruned at the cross mark, and laid down to take the place of the arm O, which is to be cut away. It may also be made a system of permanent arms by pinching the canes grown for renewal like the others, and then pruning all the canes on the arms to spurs.

Vines are very picturesquely grown on the

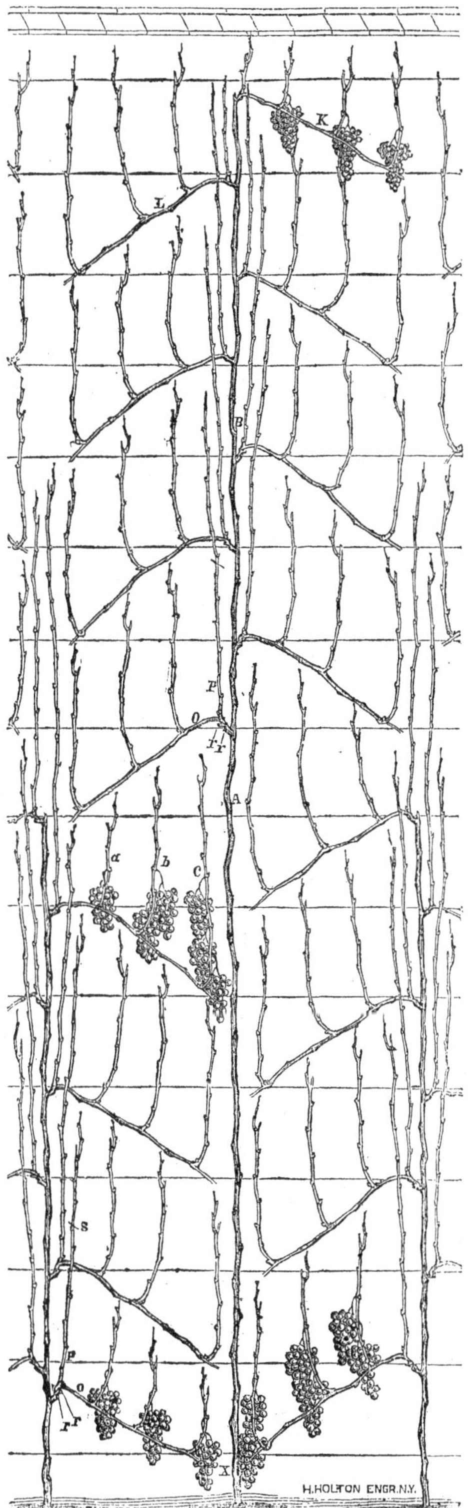

Fig. 76.

sides of houses in a sort of fan method, as represented in *Fig.* 77, and at first are remarkably productive; but they soon nearly cease to bear, except at their upper and most distant parts. This vine has been a European

Fig. 77.

celebrity of sufficient notoriety to attract visitors from a distance, one of whom (Mr. Hay of Edinburgh) has recorded his disappointment at the smallness of its crop by the accompanying drawing, which he affirms is truthful.

Grapes may be easily grown in abundance and perfection on the sides of buildings which are exposed to the sun two thirds of the day. The sides which have the morning portion are the most advantageous. The shade of the vines of a well-covered trellis, standing about two feet from the sunny sides of dwellings, is most grateful in summer, and, unlike that from trees, brings no dampness or unwholesomeness of atmosphere with it. Well trained vines are not only admissible, but highly pleasing in almost every style of building, from the cozy cottage to the elegant mansion. *Fig.* 78 represents a small cottage with its southeasterly and southwesterly sides sheltered by bearing vines. Those only who have made trial of them on small buildings can form an idea of their comfort, aside from their fruit, in the hot days of summer. This detail of the southeasterly side will soon be made clear to the careful student of the Thomery.

Fig. 79 shows a more commodious dwelling with vines on the side that is almost fully exposed to the east, but inclining a little to the south. There is an iron trellis on its southerly side, made of gas pipe, that is admirably adapted, by its neatness of appearance as well as by its cheapness, for the purpose. Some wire is needed to make it complete for the occupation of the vines. The side occupied by the vines is 36 feet long and 24 feet high, 18 of which are covered with vines in six tiers,

Fig. 78.

the first beginning three feet from the ground, and all of them being three feet apart. Twelve vines were set in a row two feet from the house and three feet apart. The second season these vines made a growth of eighteen feet and upward. At the time for pruning, the canes were bent along near the ground, and, being gathered together, were bent upward through the little pedestals, three of which are shown in the engraving. Four canes were passed through each, trained up perpendicularly, and cut off at points one foot above the height at which each was destined to furnish arms for the four upper tiers. The excess of one foot was to be used the next season in burying the horizontal portion six inches deep, when little disposition to put forth roots would exist.

Six feet further from the house another row, containing six vines, was planted, and grown two seasons to stakes. At the end of that time they were led along the ground and up through the pedestals, to form the two lower tiers, in the same manner as those above. Three vines occupy each tier; consequently, each vine has twelve feet for the length of its arms.

Fig. 79.

Figs. 80, 81, 82, are on so small a scale that the intricacy of the training will require

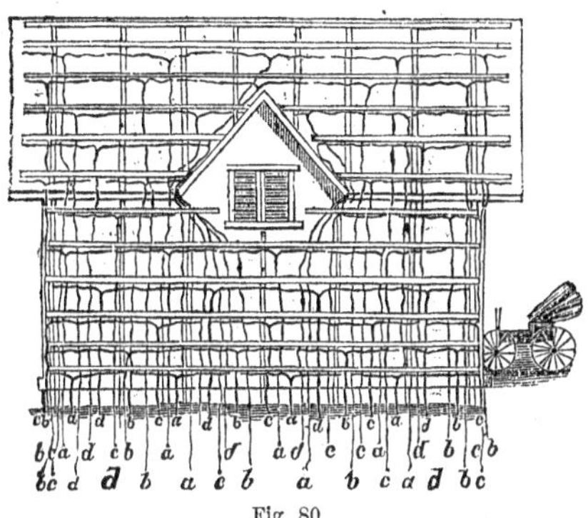
Fig. 80.

attention to follow it. The stable is 24 feet long, and the height to be covered, including

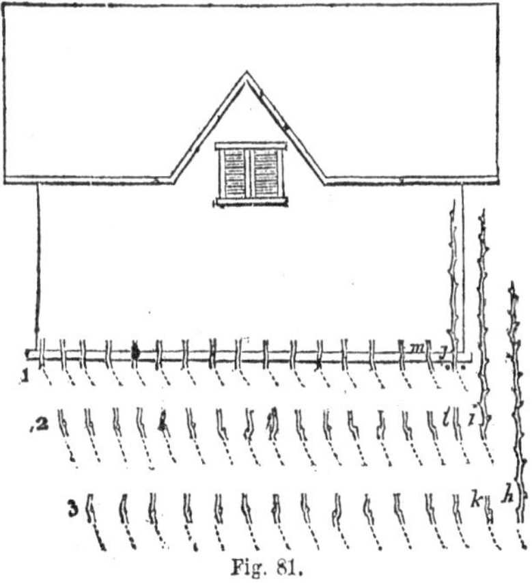
Fig. 81.

roof, about 30 feet. For this purpose, eleven tiers on the Thomery principle were required. Three rows of vines were planted, each row two feet from the position it was intended to occupy. The vines were all bedded once, as represented by the dotted lines in *Fig.* 81. The rows were six feet apart at the beginning, and still maintain that relative distance. That

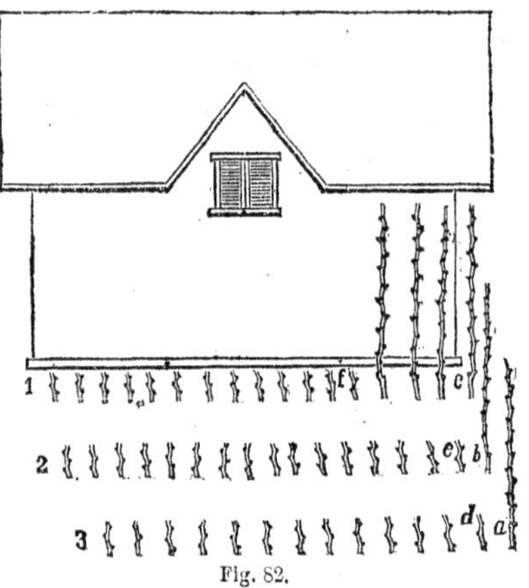

Fig. 82.

is their present condition. It is now proposed to establish all the tiers as nearly at the same time as practicable. The first row will therefore be trained for the highest part of the roof, the next following, and the third nearest the ground. The second row must be trained on stakes one year where the vines now stand, to be led along the ground the next year, and be turned up perpendicularly as their length will permit. The third row will follow in the same order. The manner of forming the arms has been already fully described. The letters in *Fig.* 80 will enable the reader to trace the course of every vine from the ground to the arms. All of those in the second and third rows are to be buried about six inches deep as fast as the two year old wood is formed, so that all will stand in one row along the side of the building. This will be more clearly exhibited on a larger scale elsewhere; but the present will be found sufficient to enable any one who has mastered the general principles to perform all the operations successfully.

CHAPTER X.

TRAINING—VARIOUS FORMS.

The Renewal System.—This was so earnestly advocated many years ago by Mr. Clement Hoare, as to have had his name associated with it ever since. It consists of two horizontal arms, from which upright canes are grown in a serpentine course, the canes being alternately fruited and renewed. Some have misunderstood it, or modified it by growing the canes straight, and thus destroyed its best feature. Mr. Hoare understood how the action of the vine tends to the ends of the canes, and advocated the plan of growing them in a serpentine form to equalize it. To take away this feature, therefore, is to damage the system.

The reader now so well understands the formation of horizontal arms, that we can pass at once to the peculiar treatment of the spurs and canes. There should not be more than four spurs on each arm. Let us suppose that half the arm has just been laid down. Two buds are selected for upright canes, and one at the end

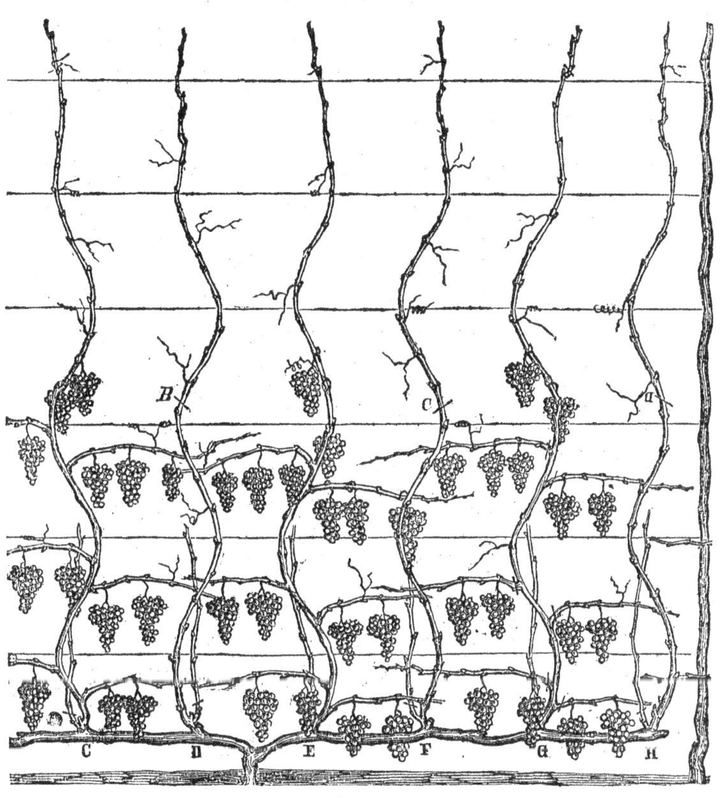

Fig. 83.

for the extension of the arm, all the others being rubbed off. The two upright canes must be grown in a serpentine form, like B, C, in *Fig.* 83, and the end cane, for the extension of the arm, must be grown straight, and all pinched and athallized in the usual manner. In the fall, the end cane must be cut of the proper length for completing the arms, and the upright canes pruned, one to the lowest bud, and the other, this year, not more than two feet long. In the spring, from each of the spurs grow a cane for renewal, and also a small cane from one of the base buds. From the alternate canes pruned two feet long, grow as much fruit as the vine is able to ripen, and no more; and from one of the base buds grow a small cane for a spur. From the portion of arm newly laid down grow two upright canes. The canes, in all these instances, are to be grown in serpentine form. The fruit canes are to be pinched two or three leaves above the fruit, the renewal canes pinched about the first of September, and athallage attended to in the usual manner. The reader must, by this time, so well understand these operations that it is not necessary to repeat them in detail.

In the fall we shall have, beginning at the stock, first, a cane that has fruited, with a small cane at its base; the old cane must be cut entirely away, and the small cane cut to its lowest bud; secondly, we have from the spur a long, or renewal cane, which must be cut three or four feet long; and also a small cane from a base bud, which must be cut low enough to get another small cane from a base bud; thirdly, on the part of the arm newly laid down we have an upright cane, which must be pruned to the lowest bud; last, we have another cane, which must be pruned about two feet long. The other arm must be pruned in the same way. The reader will get a good idea of the system from an examination of *Fig.* 83.

In the spring the treatment will be as follows, beginning at the stock, as before: from the first spur grow a cane for renewal; on the cane on the second spur grow fruit, and take a small cane from a base bud; on the third spur grow a renewal cane, and also a cane from a base bud; on the cane at the end grow fruit, and also a small cane from a base bud. The summer treatment will be the same as before. The pruning and treatment in subsequent years will be only a repetition of what has now been described, each alternate cane being annually fruited, and the others renewed. *Fig.* 84 shows a section of the system complete, as arranged for covering a wall six or seven feet high. This system, though written about by almost every body, is very rarely comprehended, and it must be admitted to be a somewhat difficult one to maintain in perfect order through a long series of years. It is far less satisfactory in its results than others that are much more simple.

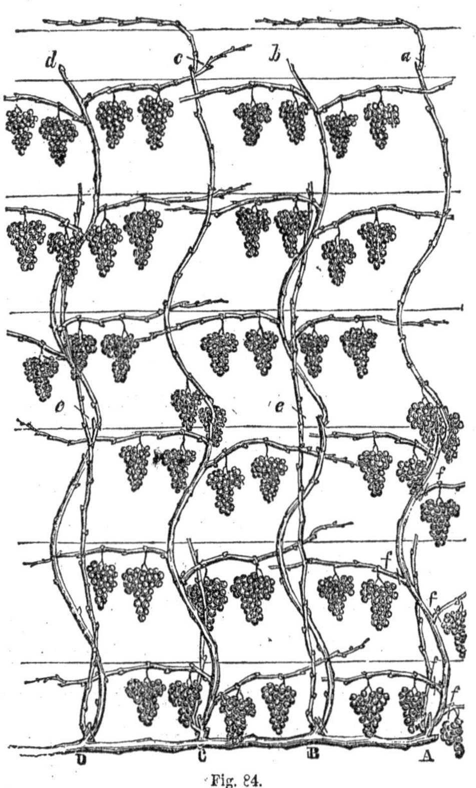

Fig. 84.

Some depend for renewal upon the buds at the base of the canes on the spurs, instead of providing a small spur; but the spur then soon becomes inconveniently long, and the buds often fail. As between the renewal and spur systems in all their various forms, the latter are much to be preferred, both on account of their greater simplicity, and the better quality of the fruit.

The Oblique System.—The French are ingenious as well as prolific in the forms which they give to fruit trees. The "cordon oblique" had hardly been worked out on the peach and the pear, when it was also applied to the grape, as

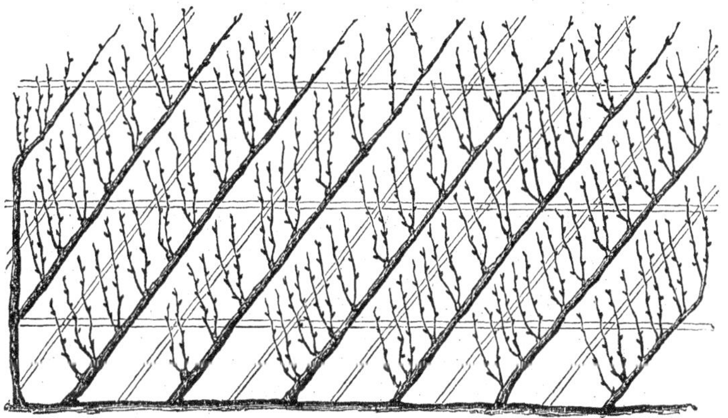

Fig. 85.

may be seen in *Fig.* 85, which is a copy from the work of M. Forney, 1862. It has such a look of the Frenchman about it that one would suspect its origin at first sight. Our engraver has followed the original literally, instead of making grape wood of the stocks, as he knows how to do better than any body else. The system is very simple, and the engraving shows quite plainly how it is formed. The vines are planted two or three feet apart, and grown obliquely at an angle of about forty-five degrees, the spurs being all on one side. With this exception, it is precisely like the *Upright Stock* described at p. 107, and the directions there given may be followed here. The two end vines, it will be seen, are somewhat modified to fill up the trellis; the one on the right being made shorter, and the one on the left having two oblique arms. Any body but a Frenchman would have left out the two end vines; but he understands the value of space too well, and, besides, brings his good taste as well as judgment to bear upon every thing he does, always striving to unite the beautiful with the useful. The trellis, too, it will be observed, is a little peculiar. The uprights are oblique as well as the vines, and do not stop at the horizontal top piece, but extend above it, so that the canes from the upper buds may have something to be tied to. Every thing necessary seems to be provided in the engraving. We do not present the system as being at all suited to the vineyard, but as something that may gratify the amateur in the garden, where it would have a pretty effect. The only improvement we would suggest would be to bend the arms to a horizontal position, and grow them in tiers.

Something like this was done by Dr. May, of Warsaw, Ill., several years ago. He has two systems, the double horizontal arm, and the Guyot, with permanent arms. Beginning at the ground, he takes the arms up to the wire at an angle of about forty-five degrees, and then horizontally along the wire. His idea was, that he could in this way bend his arms down easier for winter covering. *Figs.* 86 and 87 are from a drawing furnished by Dr. May.

Reversed Horizontal Arms.—This plan consists in bending the arms in reversed order in the first stage of formation. The ends should be bent to the ground, and pegged there. Reversing in this way tends to equalize the action of the plant, causing the buds near the stock to grow much stronger than they otherwise would. To secure its full benefits, the end should remain pegged down during a portion of the season, or until the action of the plant has well developed the canes near the stock. If they are at the beginning well established in this way, or by laying down a portion only of the arm at a time, they will remain good pretty nearly as

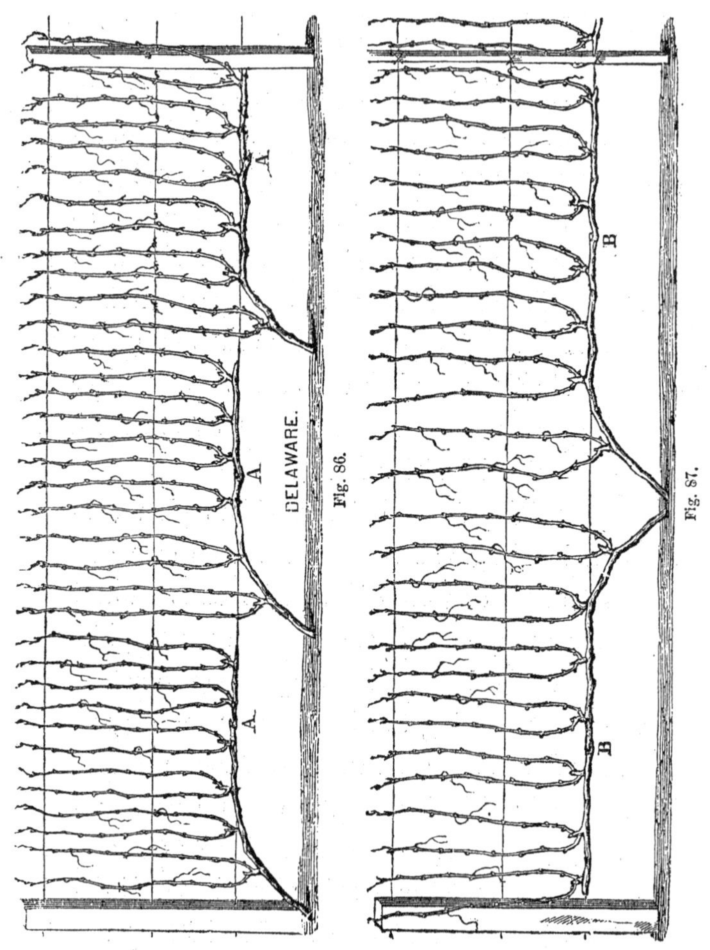

Fig. 86.

Fig. 87.

long as any other portion of the arm, except the extreme end. If they are weak at the start, they will speedily decline. The reader will comprehend this better when he has acquired a knowledge of the physiology of the vine.

The Fan System.—If not complicated by the addition of too many spurs, this system may be neatly worked out on a small trellis. It is easily formed, and will be readily understood

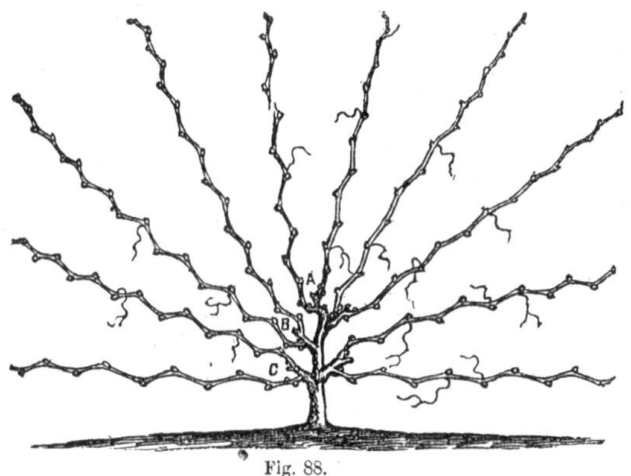

Fig. 88.

by referring to *Fig.* 88. The spurs should be formed in two successive years, so as to secure strength for the lower ones. The form is maintained by repeated pinching, so as to restrain the strong and encourage the weak. The pruning is the same as in the plan on p. 155.

Goblet, and other Forms.—This (*Fig.* 89) is a very ornamental form in which to grow the vine, and is presented to the novice as an exercise or "study," that will give a good direction to his taste. It would form a pretty feature on a well-shaven lawn, where we have seen a similar form used with pleasing effect. The frame should be made of stout iron wire, and braced with cross pieces, as seen in the engraving. The fruiting canes are grown from four spurs. A

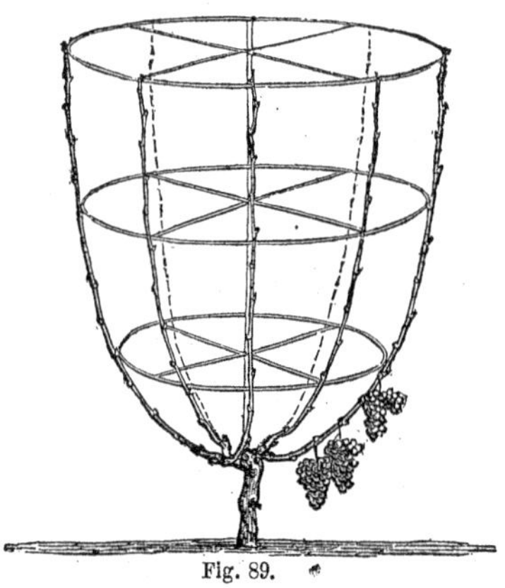

Fig. 89.

brief description will assist the novice in working his "study" out. The first year a single cane is grown. In the fall this is cut down to the height at which it is desired to form the goblet. Two canes are grown the second year, and in the fall each of the canes is cut down to the two lowest buds. This will give four canes the third year. These four canes must next be cut so as to form four double spurs, which will give eight canes. *Figs.* 90, 91, will show how this is done. The principle understood, the reader can have

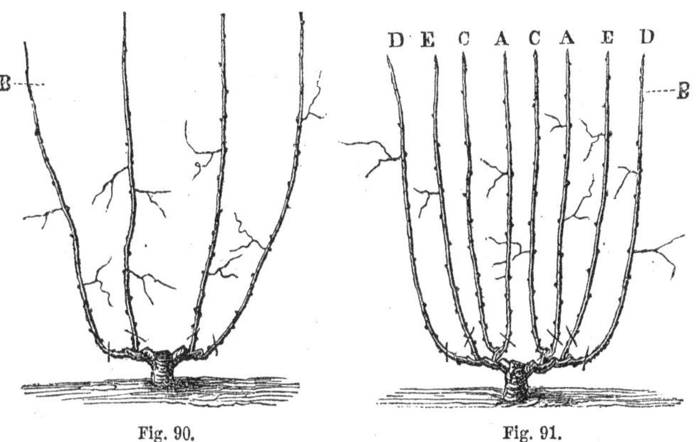

Fig. 90.

Fig. 91.

goblets, globes, urns, or any other form which his fancy may suggest. *Fig.* 92 is an illustration of the *globe* form. It may be remarked that pretty constant pinching and athallizing will be necessary to keep the form in its proper shape.

Fig. 92.

Trouillet's Plan.—In the East it has been the practice from time immemorial to grow the vine without stakes, and we have accounts of very old stocks of almost fabulous dimensions. It is done by spurring, and M.

Trouillet's plain, shown in *Fig.* 93, will give the reader a very clear idea of the principle.

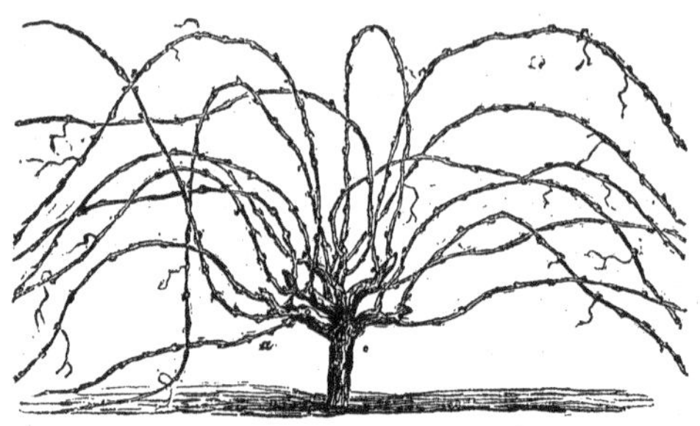

Fig. 93.

The Hermitage Plan.—"Hermitage" wine is famous wherever good wine is known. It may

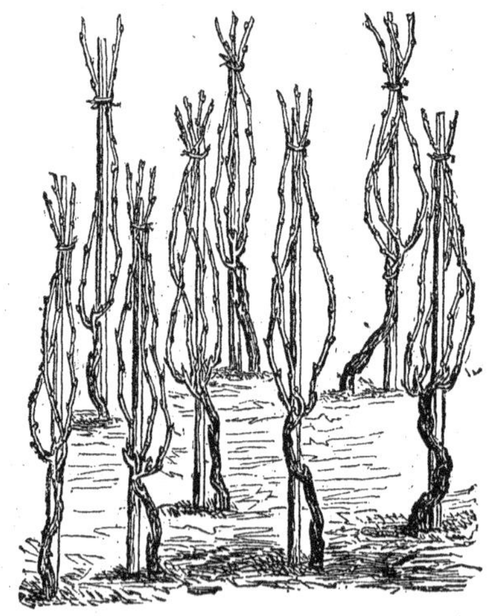

Fig. 94.

interest the reader to know how the vines are grown. The "system" is shown in *Fig.* 94. It

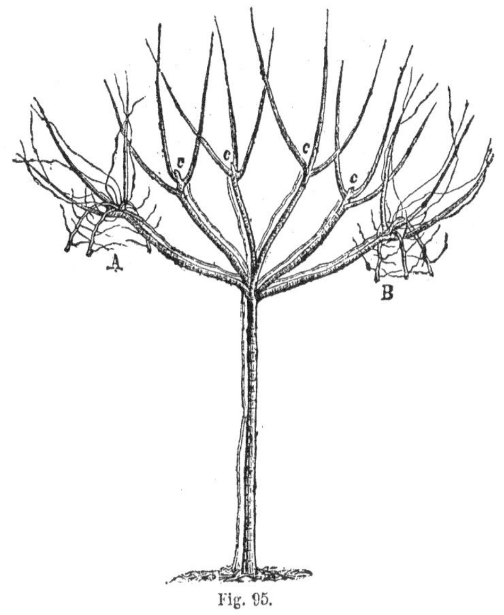

Fig. 95.

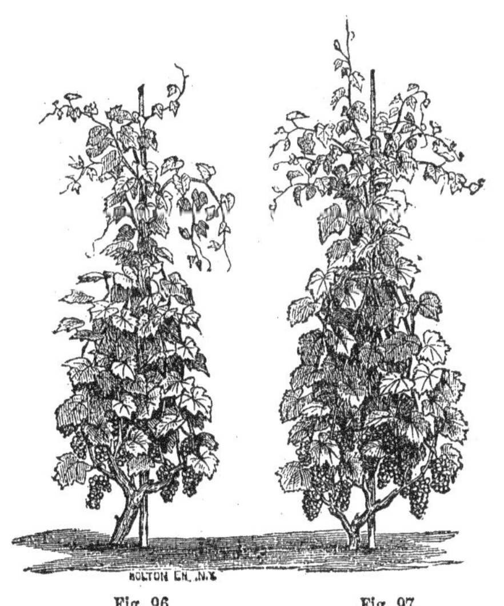

Fig. 96. Fig. 97.

might characteristically be called the "irregular" system, so far as the planting is concerned, for no order is observed in this respect.

Training on Trees.—Where vines are grown on trees as a practice, it is usual to train the trees into such form as will admit also of training the vines. A good example of this is shown in *Fig.* 95.

Training on Stakes.—The manner of training on stakes from three or four spurs is prettily shown in *Figs.* 96, 97. It needs no explanation.

CHAPTER XI.

DESCRIPTION OF VARIETIES—ISABELLA GROUP.

In an elementary work like this, it is not desirable to give a full descriptive list of the numerous varieties of the native grape. A large portion of them have no value whatever, and others are confined chiefly to the garden or the curious amateur. We shall confine our descriptions principally to such as are generally grown in the vineyard. A full list, with elaborate descriptions, is reserved for another place.

The Isabella Group. — For present purposes, we shall divide our principal vineyard grapes into two groups, the *Isabella* and *Catawba*, the last group being distinctively vinous grapes. The characteristics of the *Isabella group* are, a thick and acrid skin, a tough, acid center, and a peculiar "foxy" odor. We shall begin with the first group, in which will be included the *Isabella*, *Concord*, *Hart-*

ford Prolific, *Creveling*, *Adirondac*, *Israella*, and *Ives's Seedling*.

ISABELLA.

Description of Varieties.—The Isabella, of southern origin, may be said to be the mother of American grape culture. She performed her

Fig. 98. Leaf of Isabella.

work faithfully and well, and we would therefore speak tenderly of her faults. A generation has grown up around her, some of them far less comely than she, but others of great delicacy, refinement, and beauty. The Isabella is a good grower, hardy, and submits pretty well to treatment. The bunches are large, compact, and shouldered. The color is dark purple, with a light bloom. The berries are large, and oval in form. The flesh is neither melting nor tender, except near the surface, and has a tough, acid center, that always remains, and must either be rejected, or swallowed whole. The skin is thick and rather tough, with a certain acridity which produces soreness of the mouth when the grapes are eaten in quantity. Between the skin and the tough center there is a sprightly, sweet juice, that is really good. This goodness is increased in quantity in the most favorable localities, for the center then becomes somewhat broken down. The Isabella has the "foxy" odor peculiar to the native grape. It will not ripen generally in the New-England States, except in sheltered places. There is only one way of eating the Isabella and similar grapes, that yields much enjoyment, and that is, to break the skin, and place the berry at the lips so that the juice can be sucked in, while the skin and tough center are thrown away.

CONCORD.

The *Concord* is only one remove from the

wild native, and, with the native vigor and hardiness of its parent, possesses also its strongly marked faults. It originated with Mr. Bull, of Concord, Massachusetts. The vine is hardy, vigorous, and early, ripening its fruit over a wide extent of country, which alone would give it value, if we had not much better grapes ripening about as early. The bunch is very large, compact, and shouldered. The color is dark purple, with a light bloom. The berry is large, round, and has a thin skin. The flesh is soft or buttery, with the fibrous, acid center characteristic of this class of grapes, and which only disappears when the fruit has passed the period of maturity. The juice is sweet, but without that vinous spirit that gives so much enjoyment in the use of the grape. In quality, it bears a close resemblance to the Northern Muscadine. The fruit, even in its best condition, has a strong "foxy" odor, which is very offensive, and only becomes more so by use; this, added to its peculiar buttery flesh and want of spirit, renders it any thing but an agreeable fruit to tastes that have been cultivated by the use of good grapes. It owes its popularity to its vigor and productiveness, and not to its goodness. When mature, the berries often drop from the bunch, and are disposed to crack; hence it requires to be sent to market, in common with some others, before it is fully ripe. Its tenderness of skin also unfits it for distant transportation or close packing.

HARTFORD PROLIFIC.

The *Hartford Prolific* is a seedling from the woods. It is hardy, a vigorous grower, very productive, and very early, ripening nearly two weeks before the Concord. The bunch is large, and shouldered. The color is dark purple, with a light bloom. The berries are large, somewhat oval, with a thick skin. The flesh has the usual tough, acid center of this class. The juice is rather sweet, with more sprightliness than the Concord, but has little or no vinous flavor. The fruit is somewhat less "foxy" than the Concord. When ripe, the berries often drop from the bunch. It has been popular on account of its earliness and large yield.

CREVELING.

The *Creveling* had its origin in Bloomsburgh, Pennsylvania, and is no doubt a seedling of the Isabella, which it resembles. It has about the same degree of hardiness and vigor as the Isabella, but ripens about two weeks earlier, or nearly at the time of the Hartford Prolific. The bunch is large, tapering, and generally loose, with a small shoulder. The color is dark purple, with a light bloom. The berry is large, oval, with a thick skin. The flesh has the usual tough, acid center. The juice next the skin is sweet, and more sprightly than either the Concord or Hartford. The fruit, also, has less of the "foxy" odor. It has a habit, however, of setting its berries very thin, owing to imperfect fertilization.

ADIRONDAC.

The *Adirondac* was introduced in 1863, and had its origin among the Adirondac Mountains, N. Y., whence its name. It is no doubt a seedling of the Isabella. In favorable localities it is a good grower, but with us, and in many places where we have seen it, it drops its leaves early, and hence ripens imperfectly, and gets winter-killed. How far this is owing to imperfections in propagation, remains to be seen. The bunch is large, compact, and shouldered. Color dark purple, with a light bloom. The berry is large, roundish oval, with a thin skin. The flesh is tender, with very little unripe center. The juice is sweet, with a pleasant, but not strongly marked flavor. In the Adirondac we see the first decided step in the breaking down and ripening of the tough, fibrous center, and the disappearance of the offensive "foxy" odor, more or less characteristic of the Isabella group. The skin, too, has become thinner and more tender. In quality, it is much the best grape thus far mentioned. It ripens early, or soon after the Hartford Prolific.

ISRAELLA.

The *Israella*, also lately introduced, was originated by Dr. C. W. Grant, of Iona Island. The vine is vigorous, hardy, and productive. The bunch is large, compact, and shouldered. The color is dark purple, with a light bloom. The berry is large, roundish oval, with a moderately tender skin. The flesh is tender, and ripens fully, quite to the center. The juice is sweet and sprightly, with a pleasant flavor. In the Israella we have another step in advance. One great desideratum in the grape, in common with all fruits used as food, is thorough ripe-

Fig. 99—Israella.

ness in all its parts. Nothing less should satisfy us in the grape, any more than in the apple or the pear. In this respect, the Israella stands at the head of the Isabella group. The disagreeable "foxiness," too, has mostly disappeared, and the fruit may be eaten without offense to the taste or smell. It ripens quite early, or about the time of the Hartford Prolific. It is a long keeper, the berries adhering well to the bunch.

IVES'S SEEDLING.

Ives's Seedling, just now becoming known at the West, originated with the Hon. Mr. Ives, near Cincinnati, something more than twenty years ago, by whom cuttings were liberally distributed. Dr. Kittredge was one of the early growers of it, and for a time it took his name. It is probably a seedling of the Isabella, which it somewhat resembles. Its chief recommendations are its hardiness and productiveness; its prominent defects, a large, tough, acid center, and very "foxy" odor. Since the marked failure of the Catawba in the vicinity of Cincinnati, for which neither soil nor climate is well adapted, the Ives has been gaining favor, and Col. Waring, with whom the Catawba will not thrive, has pretty extensive vineyards of it. It has not even the remotest value as a table grape, but it is claimed that good wine may be made from it. We think that attempts to make *real* wine from any "hard-hearted" member of this family must end in a small measure of success.

Comparison of Varieties.—We have now noticed such of this group as are prominently before the public. We propose next to group them together for certain purposes of comparison.

1*st.* *Quality.*—If we compare them in *quality*, they will arrange themselves in the following order: *Israella, Adirondac, Isabella, Creveling, Hartford Prolific, Concord, Ives's Seedling.* The difference between some is quite trifling, while between others it is very marked.

2*d.* *For the Table.*—If we compare them for the *table*, as articles of food, goodness must take precedence, and they will assume the same order.

3*d.* *For Market.*—If we compare them for *market* purposes, we must consider something besides goodness; because, if a grape, however good, will not "carry" to market, it loses its market value: it may be the best grape for wine or for the table, for home consumption, but it is clearly not the best for market, however much it ought to be so. That is a rare grape which possesses in itself all these qualifications. We must look for it outside of this group. We may, notwithstanding, find here a grape that is best for both market and the table. In time our group will no doubt settle itself in this wise: Israella, Concord, Isabella, Hartford Prolific, Creveling. We omit the Ives, since it is clearly not a table grape. We are at a loss how to place the Adirondac, because we have seen it winter kill so badly. If this is only a temporary fault, its excellence must give it a place far in advance of the Concord. We think the Hartford a better grape than the Concord; but, though both have the vice of dropping their berries, the Hartford is much the greatest sinner, and we therefore place the Concord in advance of it for market. If, however, we add that the berries of the Concord crack pretty badly, it will reduce their vicious habits pretty nearly to a level. The Israella is as hardy as either of them; ripens before the Concord, is as early as the Hartford, infinitely better than either, and free from their vice of dropping the fruit. These qualities give it the first position in this group as a market fruit. We place the Isabella after the Concord, only because it can not be ripened over so wide a surface; but where it will ripen, it ought to take precedence of it. So, too, of the Creveling. We make no comparisons for wine, because we do not consider this group true wine grapes.

CHAPTER XII.

DESCRIPTION OF VARIETIES—CONTINUED.

The Catawba Group.—We now pass to the *Catawba* group, which is composed of grapes that are distinctively vinous. It must not be understood, however, that all the grapes of this group are of the Catawba family. Allen's Hybrid, for example, clearly is not; but it is placed here for our present purpose, since it is a truly vinous grape, and has but little affinity with the Isabella family. The leading characteristics of this group are, a flesh more or less tender, with a sweet juice having a vinous flavor. It is here that we find our best table as well as wine grapes; some, indeed, of such excellence as to elevate the native grape to a very high position by the side of the best varieties of Europe. We shall include in this group the *Catawba*, *Diana*, *Allen's Hybrid*, *Delaware*, and *Iona.*

CATAWBA.

If the Isabella was the mother of American grape culture, the *Catawba* may be regarded as the mother of American *wine making.* It has performed its mission equally well; it has done, indeed, all that it is

Fig. 100. Leaf of Catawba.

capable of doing, and might now very well be laid aside as a pleasant memory, while its place is filled by others better fitted to perfect the work it so well began. The Catawba had its origin in the South. Whatever of goodness the Isabella may have is found in the Catawba in a greater degree. The Isabella has sweetness nearly in its simplest form, and, consequently, only a feeble or low degree of vinous flavor, suited to tastes that are satisfied with sweetness chiefly, and look for little more. The Catawba has more sweetness, but added to it, enough of the acid of the grape to produce spirit and animation. It is also less "foxy" than the Isabella. The Catawba, though very far from faultless, is altogether a better grape than the Isabella. It is hardy, and a good grower. The bunch is large, moderately compact, and shouldered. The color is a dark claret, covered with a fine light bloom. The berry is large, round, with a thick skin. The flesh has a large tough, acid center, between which and the skin is a sweet juice, having a spicy, vinous flavor. In the Catawba the "foxy" odor has lost a considerable degree of its offensiveness. The skin, however, is acrid, and often produces soreness in tender mouths. There is always some astringency, and often also a peculiar bitterness, in the Catawba, very unpleasant to the taste. The acid center disappears more or less, according as the grape is grown in localities more or less favorable to its ripening, but is never wholly absent. There is a considerable degree of vinous spirit in the juice of the Catawba; but, on the whole, there is a want of purity that detracts greatly from its excellence. The Catawba is so subject to mildew, sun-scald, and especially rot, both black and bitter, as to make its culture precarious, except under favorable conditions of soil and climate. It ripens too late for the New-England States.

DIANA.

The *Diana* originated with Mrs. Diana Crehore, of Milton Hill, Massachusetts. It is a seedling of the Catawba. It is hardy, and a rank grower. The bunch varies from below to above medium size, is very compact, and usually shouldered. The color is a pale or tawny claret. The berry is of medium size, round, with a thick skin. The flesh has a small fibrous center, becoming sweet when ripe, and considerable toughness near the skin, which, however, becomes pretty tender and good when fully ripe. The flesh, indeed, is somewhat meaty; hence it is a good keeper, and will make a tolerable raisin. The juice is sweet, with a high vinous flavor. The Diana is sweet some time before it is ripe; in-

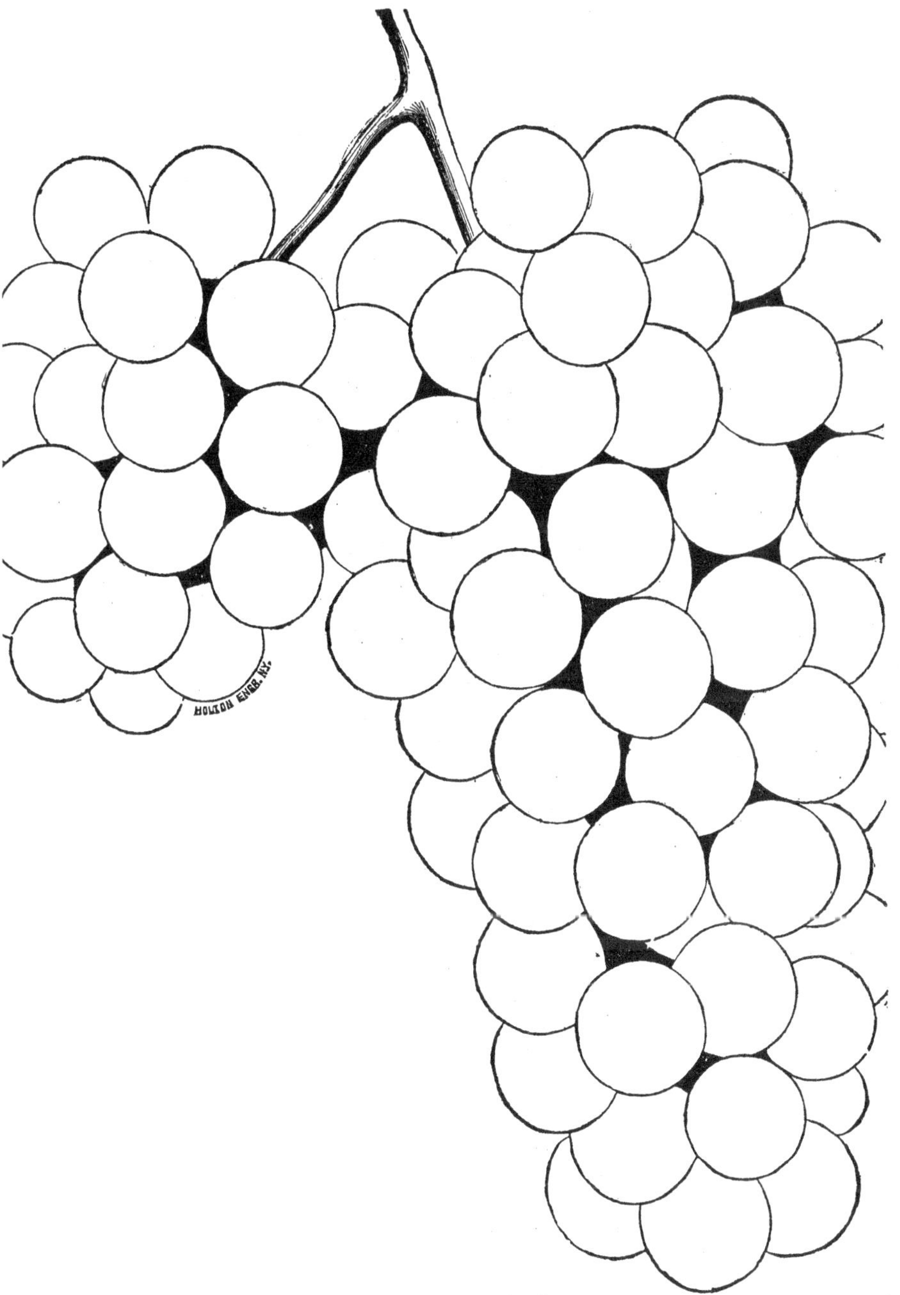

Fig. 101—Diana, from a specimen bunch.

deed, it is often sweet when not colored. It has a peculiar animal odor before ripe, which has been variously characterized, and sometimes rather too broadly for good taste. This odor, however, gradually disappears as the fruit approaches full maturity, and almost ceases to be offensive. When young, the vine is disposed to overbear, and hence ripens its fruit imperfectly. It is only as the vine acquires age that the sugary sweetness and high vinous flavor of the Diana are fully developed, and then we see its great superiority to the Catawba. It requires peculiar treatment, however; and this is so little understood that it has been a great drawback to its cultivation. It will ripen in a considerable portion of the New-England States, in well-chosen and sheltered positions. We have said that the Diana is hardy, but this is true only when its wood is mature. In a soil too rich it makes a very rampant growth, that is neither very hardy nor productive. It needs a deep, dry, but not rich soil.

ALLEN'S HYBRID.

Allen's Hybrid originated with Mr. J. Fisk Allen, of Salem, Massachusetts, a gen-

Fig. 102—Allen's Hybrid.

tleman to whom grape culture is largely indebted. It is a hybrid between the native and foreign grape, its mixed character being plainly seen both in the fruit and the leaves. It is the first example of the kind of which we have any knowledge, and in this respect is one of our most interesting grapes. Mr. Allen raised other seedlings at the same time, but this is the only one that proved to be valuable. The vine is not very hardy, but a good grower, and yields readily to treatment. The leaves are well marked, having a peculiar crumpled appearance not common to any other variety. The bunch is large, compact, and shouldered. The color is amber green, with a translucent pearly bloom, and here and there dots of claret. The berry is large, nearly round, and has a thin, tender skin. The flesh is tender. The juice is sweet, rich, and spirited, with a pure vinous and mild muscat flavor. The Allen is one of our best table grapes. The flesh matures uniformly, and the skin is tender and good. It is free from "foxy" odor. The vine is not sufficiently hardy to adapt it to cultivation in the vineyard, except in sheltered localities. When exposed, it is apt to mildew and be winter-killed. For the garden, and places where shelter and ventilation are provided, it is one of the best grapes we have. It ripens nearly three weeks before the Isabella.

DELAWARE.

The origin of the *Delaware* is wrapped in mystery. That it is a native grape, there should be no more doubt than there is in regard to the Isabella and Catawba. The leaves on young vines often show the characteristic furziness; but seedlings which we and others have raised from it show the native character in fruit and foliage too broadly to be mistaken. The question of its origin would never have been raised, but for the excellence of its fruit. It was thought to be too refined for a native; in fact, the native grape had become, in our minds, so almost indissolubly associated with the "fox," that we had learned to recognize a native by its offensive smell and tough center. Happily, the Iona, which more than one old grape grower has pronounced to be a Frontignan, and which it certainly resembles very closely, has stepped in to spoil the logic of this kind of argument, and we may now claim to have at least three natives free from this offensive taint. The Delaware is hardy, a vigorous but compact grower, and few kinds yield so readily to treatment. The bunch is small, very compact, (the berries being often compressed in consequence,) and has a small shoulder, very much like a little bunch. The color varies from bright to pale claret. The berry is small, round, with a thin and rather tender skin. The flesh has only a very small fibrous center, but quite sweet when ripe. The juice is sugary and sweet, with a pure, delicate, but spirited vinous flavor. The berry is sweet some time before it is ripe. This sweetness of the berry before maturity is characteristic of the Diana, Delaware, and Iona. The early ripening and hardy character of the Delaware fit it for general cultivation.

The Delaware has taken, and will always maintain, a high rank among American grapes. It was the first to give us a true idea of purity, delicacy, and refinement, almost its only fault, besides its want of size, being its small fibrous center, which prevents it from being tender in all its parts. That little center, however, is sweet when ripe. It must be admitted, also, that the bunch is too compact; so much so, often, as to prevent the interior berries from becoming fully ripe; it makes it difficult, too, to pick the berries to eat. These faults conceded, it still remains a delicious grape. It has performed the great and invaluable office of educating the American taste up to the standard of European kinds; it has at least done this with a portion of the public, and prepared others for a truer appreciation of real excellence in the grape. The mass are already beginning to perceive the difference between a grape that must be shot down with closed eyes and wide open mouth, and one that may be deliberately eaten as food.

IONA.

The *Iona* originated with Dr. C. W. Grant, of Iona Island, N. Y. The vine is hardy, a vigorous grower, and yields readily to treatment. The bunch is large, moderately compact, and distinctly double shouldered or winged. The color is a bright claret. The berry is large, round, with a thin skin. The flesh is meaty, melting, and tender all the way through. The juice is sugary and sweet, spirited and vinous, with a pure but delicate muscat flavor. Just after "stoning," the berry becomes so transparent that the seed may be distinctly seen. The flesh is sweet enough to be eaten nearly two weeks before it is perfectly ripe.

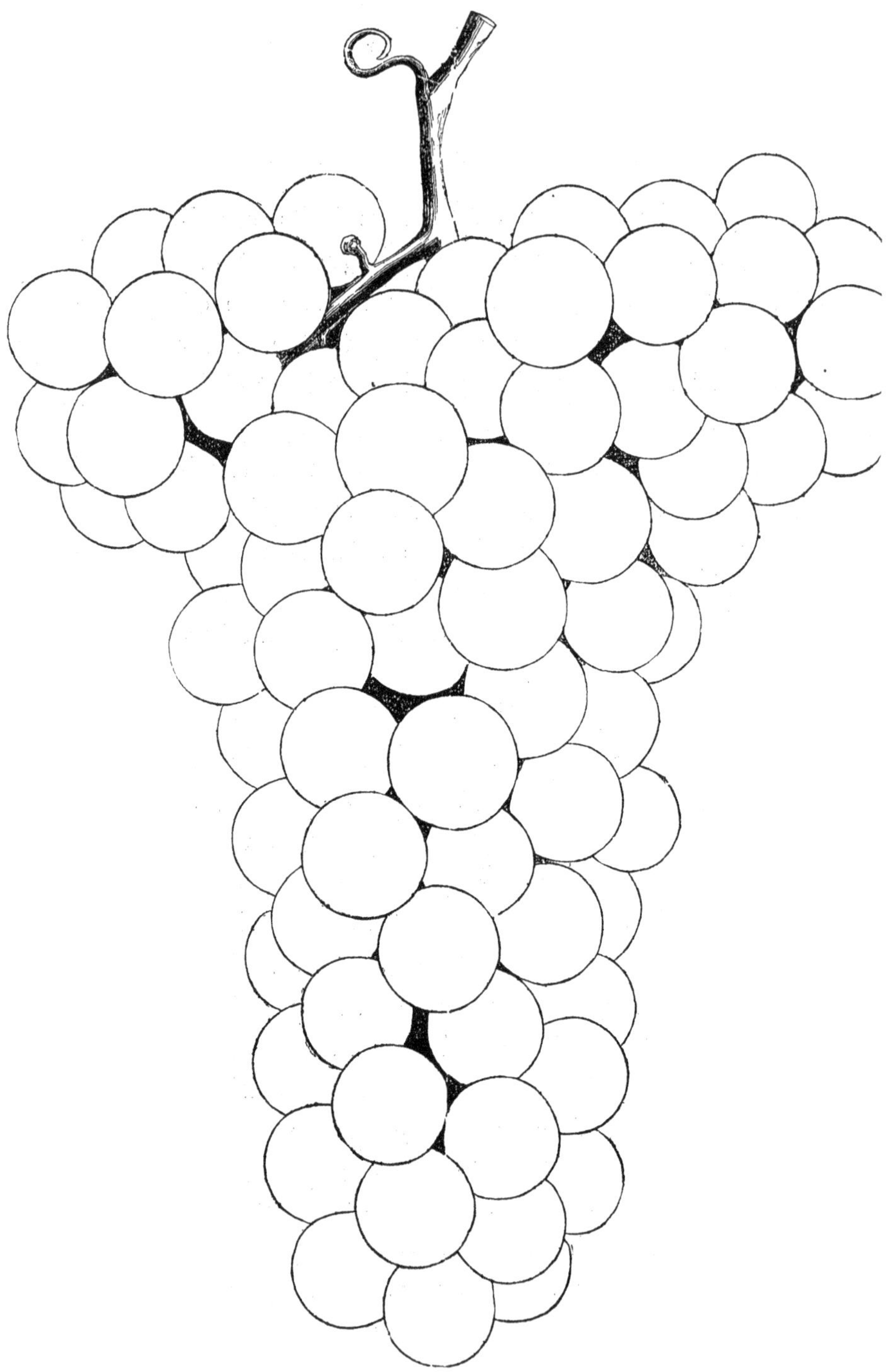

Fig. 103—Iona.

It is a long keeper, and dries into an excellent raisin. The hardiness of the vine and the early ripening of the fruit adapt it to general culti-

Fig. 104—Iona.

vation. It is the best of American grapes, both for the table and wine.

When the excellence of the Delaware had become fully recognized and appreciated, the wish was very generally expressed, that we might be so fortunate as to have a grape as good as the Delaware, but twice as large. The thought seemed to be, that nothing more could be desired. This wish was soon more than realized by the appearance of the Iona, which, in many respects, may be regarded as a Delaware greatly enlarged. There are some defects in the Delaware, however, which disappear in the Iona. Some of these may here be noted. For example, the small fibrous center of the Delaware is replaced by thorough ripeness in the Iona; all the flesh becomes equally ripe and tender, so that a berry, pressed between the tongue and roof of the mouth, melts entirely away, leaving nothing but the seeds and skin. There can be no perfection in the grape till this point is reached. Both are exceedingly delicate and refined; but the Iona has superadded a pure and delicate muscat aroma, generally wanting in the Delaware. The skin of both is thin; but that of the Iona is so finely woven together, that none of the goodness within can escape: the berries never burst, even when fully ripe, though the bunches be piled thickly upon each other. A thin but firm skin is necessary to all wine and raisin grapes. The flesh of the Delaware, except the small fibrous center, ripens into pure, sweet juice, and thus it remains as long as the berry retains its integrity; but when a change takes place, as in time it must, the animating spirit soon passes away; the small center finally breaks down by decay, which vitiates the whole mass. It is true that this does not take place till some time after the berries are ripe; but ultimately it does. Hence the Delaware is not a very long keeper. The flesh of the Iona, on the contrary, ripens evenly and thoroughly in all its parts; its uniform consistency is remarkable. It ripens into juice, it is true, from center to circumference; but this juice is held together, as it were, in little sacs, and has such a peculiar meaty consistence, that, instead of decaying, it is slowly converted into a rich sugary mass equal to the best Malaga raisins; hence it is a long keeper. It makes a good raisin without the help of artificial means; the Delaware will not, even with their aid. This property of gradually resolving itself into sugar without evaporating all its juice gives the Iona great value as a wine grape. The juice of the Delaware is rich in the peculiar sugar and acid of the grape, and hence it makes a fine wine; its defect is the small fibrous center, which affects the wine just in proportion as it is more or less ripe: its presence contributes an element which interferes with vinous fermentation, and prevents the wine from attaining perfection and maturity. The juice of the Iona is even richer than the Delaware in the peculiar sugar and acid of the grape; but, unlike the Delaware, it has no fiber or unripeness to mingle with the must, and hence it makes a perfect and enduring wine. The must of the Delaware has been recorded at 105°; it will probably go a little higher than that. We have seen Iona register 130°, the must being from grapes that had begun to shrivel. The must, indeed, is so rich in vinous properties, that we and others have made good wine from it in pint bottles, in a warm room, without the least disposition to acetous or destructive fermentation.

We present this brief but somewhat analytical comparison of our two best wine grapes, for the purpose of giving the beginner some useful ideas in regard to those nice shades of difference in the qualities of grapes, which not only impress a distinctive character upon them, but graduate their value for wine or the table. It is the only way in which we can acquire a real knowledge of the comparative excellences and defects of grapes, and form a true estimate of their value; and we have often wondered that it has been so entirely overlooked, more especially since it is a chief element in those questions already of general interest, the solution of which is so vitally important to all who contemplate planting vineyards.

Comparison of Varieties.—We now propose to compare the Catawba group in reference to the following points: 1st. *Quality;* 2d. Value for the *Table;* 3d. *Market;* 4th. *Wine.*

1st. *Quality.*—In regard to *quality*, they at once arrange themselves as follows: *Iona, Delaware, Allen's Hybrid, Diana, Catawba,* In making this arrangement, we are governed strictly by the sum total of goodness possessed by each kind. There can be no difference of opinion in regard to it, except that there may be a few who will prefer the Allen to the Delaware. It is certainly one of the best of grapes, but it lacks the pure richness of the Delaware. We desire the reader to keep constantly in mind the goodness and defects of each particular kind. All his plans must have their origin and aim here, if he would attain to the largest measure of satisfaction and success.

2*d. For the Table.*—For *table* use, we must be governed by tenderness of flesh, high flavor, general good quality, and long keeping; hence we place the grapes of this group in the following order: *Iona*, *Delaware*, *Allen's Hybrid*, *Diana*, *Catawba*. We look upon the grape as a nourishing and refreshing *food;* all grapes, therefore, that are not tender and digestible, should be excluded from the table. It is only the first three that fully meet these conditions.

3*d*. *For Market*.—We have already stated the conditions which should obtain in growing grapes for market. The following, then, will be the order of this group: *Iona*, *Delaware*, *Catawba*, *Diana*, *Allen's Hybrid*. The Allen is placed last because of our inability to produce it in quantity. It will always command a higher price than the Catawba. If the treatment of the Diana should ever be mastered, so as to insure its more general cultivation, it will be found more profitable than the Catawba: it is a better grape, and a better keeper. We imagine, however, that it will be chiefly grown for wine. In regard to the others, enough is known to place their relative market value beyond a doubt. It is by no means the most productive grape that is best for market; that clearly is best which will net the most profit. Up to a recent period the market was monopolized by the Isabella and Catawba, and other kinds could scarcely be sold, chiefly because the people had become familiar with the former, and knew nothing better; but all this is changing now; the people are breaking away from the bondage of names, and are rapidly learning to appreciate a fruit for its goodness and not for its name. Shrewd men are beginning to perceive this, and are wisely preparing themselves for the change. Have we not chased the "fox" long enough? and is it not time that he were finally "holed?" We have no doubt that a time will come when the merits of the last new fruit will be as eagerly discussed around the stands of the public market as they now are by pomologists in "learned assembly met," and possibly with nearly as much intelligence and good taste.

4th. *Wine.* — For *wine*, the arrangement will not vary much from that for the table. It is as follows: *Iona, Delaware, Diana, Allen's Hybrid, Catawba.* Our placing of the Allen is altogether guess-work, for we have never made wine from it, and do not know of any body who has; yet there can be no doubt that it will make a purer and much richer wine than the Catawba. It is not at all probable, however, that it will ever be grown in quantity to make wine from, and it therefore becomes a matter of small moment where it is placed in this list. There may be some, however, who would like to make wine from it in small quantity for their own use, and it is just as well that they should know that the wine is in the grape.

We have included in this group all that could be justly considered as having any claims as true wine grapes; if the list were still further reduced, there would be much gain to American wine making. In all that we have written, we have taken decided ground for *pure* wine; we have warred against adulterations in all their multifarious forms, and we shall do so to the end. Sugar, brandy, and alcohol are adulterations, and we are only grieved when we see well-meaning men propose and defend them. We do not mean to countenance any thing but the pure juice of the grape. No kind, the pure juice of which can not be made into an enduring wine, should be admitted into the list of wine grapes; otherwise we open the door, not only for sirups and confections, rhubarb and elderberries, but also for Gallizing, and other slow poisonings and absurdities. If drinks will be made from such things, give them their right names, but do not call them wine. We may talk as learnedly as we please about cane and grape sugar, and the chemistry of fermentation; we can only make real wine from the pure juice of the grape. We hope American wine makers will accept this truth, and not tamper with the public health and credulity. Our list, therefore, necessarily excludes all grapes that have large, unripe, acid centers, as well as those that are deficient in the acids and sugar peculiar to the grape, or in which these and other vinous elements are not properly combined. American wine making is beginning to assume such importance and proportions, that a candid treatment of the subject could not be passed over, even in an elementary treatise on grape culture. There is another, but small class of wine grapes, which will be noticed elsewhere.

We head the list with the Iona, not alone because we have tried it, but because it possesses in an eminent degree the qualities of the best known wine grapes, in this respect surpassing all other American grapes. This is not a matter of opinion; it is a verified fact. On a small scale we have made excellent wine from it; better than any that we have seen made from the Delaware, and that is great praise; but we have seen wine made from it by others in larger quantity, that was equal to the very best German wines. It has the richness, body, bouquet, and fullness of flavor that belong to the highest class of wines. If the fruit is good, so is the plant. This has now been sufficiently tried, and the testimony is pretty uniform in regard to its hardiness, health, and vigor. It is easily trained, and bears abundant crops of very beautiful fruit. The bunch is just sufficiently open to permit of the ripening of every berry. The skin, too, though thin, has such firmness of texture as to prevent even the ripest berries from bursting and wasting the juice. The fruit may, in consequence, be kept without loss till the berries begin to shrivel, when the expressed juice will be found to be exceedingly rich. In young vines, the bunches are sometimes a little loose, especially if the vine is growing with great vigor. We have given a fair description of the vine and its fruit, from which the reader can form an opinion as to its claim to occupy the position we have given it at the head of American wine grapes.

We place the *Delaware* second, because it possesses wine qualities in a greater degree than any other native grape, except the Iona; besides, such wine has been made from it in quantity by Mr. Mottier and others as to leave no doubt in regard to its proper place. To our taste, Catawba is a flat wine compared with the Delaware; besides, it is not half as enduring. We find in the Delaware many of the same wine qualities possessed by the Iona, but some of them less strongly marked. Just that little fibrous center, and still more the compactness of the bunch, sometimes make the wine slightly imperfect. In good seasons, however, and whenever the fruit ripens perfectly, these imperfections disappear, and we have a wine of great excellence. The vine is admirably adapted to vineyard culture, being so easily trained. A word of caution, however, may here be added: the vine is strongly disposed to overbear, and generally sets more fruit than should be allowed to remain. In all good seasons the bunches must be thinned out as soon as they set.

The *Diana* we have placed third. It makes a wine but little inferior to the Delaware when the fruit is fully ripe; it is not, however, so pure and refined in its flavor. The peculiar odor of the fruit of the Diana is objected to by many who have not seen it when fully ripe and in its best condition. This aroma is not, it must be admitted, very pleasant; the ripening process, however, works it mostly off, and the matured fruit becomes an excellent vinous grape, but still slightly objectionable on account of its odor. The Diana does not occupy its proper place, and perhaps never will till its treatment is better understood, and we are content to wait for its best fruit till the vine acquires age. It is, notwithstanding, a good wine grape.

The *Allen's Hybrid* was placed in this group because is to a good degree a vinous grape. It is not, however, sufficiently hardy for general cultivation. Its tenderness shrinks from the open exposure of the vineyard, where it soon dwindles and dies. It is really to be regretted that such an excellent grape can not be made more useful.

The *Catawba* is placed last, because its vinous qualities are the least of all the grapes in this group. The fibrous, acid center must always more or less impair the quality and durability of the wine. Its wine is good; but, compared with Diana, Delaware, or Iona, is wanting in purity, refinement, and life. It is not a wine of high flavor in any true sense, although it be strongly marked; it impresses the mouth and lips, but passes the palate with but little pleasurable sensation. Thus we have found it always when purest and best; and even then it has not richness enough to cover its rather decided acidity. The crops of 1854 and 1859 ripened uncommonly well, and hence the vintages of those years gave the best Catawba wine that has yet been put in the market. It was very good. The truth is, a grape may be vinous in its character; may contain in itself the chief elements of wine; yet, if these are not duly combined, and the fruit does not ripen fully and uniformly in all its parts, it can not make a perfect wine. The imperfections in the grape will appear in the wine, and not only impair its goodness, but hasten the period of decay in proportion as these imperfections may exist in a greater or less degree.

We have omitted from the wine list the Isabella and Concord, and all grapes of the Isabella class. We always have a reason for what we do; in this case it consists in the fact that they are not wine grapes, if we know what wine is. The elements which make real and durable wine are not combined in any one of them in such degree and proportion as to render the manufacture of true and durable wine possible. Sparkling wines are made from them, and also from cider; but this does not prove much. The majority of them have tough, fibrous centers, that never ripen, and supply an element incompatible with the manufacture of good wine, the presence of which prevents the perfection of the process. Others only become tender at the center by the breaking down of the mass by incipient decay, and not by ripening; and maturity acquired in this way is not calculated to enhance the goodness of any wine. The very few that do ripen make a feeble, flat wine, and all of them soon run to vinegar. These serious defects are in many cases met and overcome by the addition of sugar, alcohol, and other adulterations, which at once place the resulting liquor outside of our conception and definition of wine. All attempts to make wine from such grapes must necessarily end in failure. We would here make a suggestion. There is always a good market for vinegar: a fine article will command as high a price as poor wine. These grapes, when not too "foxy," will make fine vinegar. Let them therefore be devoted to a purpose more consistent with their character. It will pay very much better than to waste capital and labor in efforts to make wine where there is none.

But it is claimed that the Concord is an exception. Let us briefly examine this claim. It is said that the Concord at the West is a much better grape than it is at the East. We have been at much pains to procure the fruit from the West, and we are compelled to say that we can see no difference between a Concord of the West and a Concord of the East, both being equally ripe. This claim has no foundation in fact; an equally ripened Concord is the same in both places. It is doubtless true that it often ripens much better at the Southwest than it does at the Northeast; and that has probably given rise to the impression that it is quite a different fruit at the West. It is also claimed that the Concord at the West can and does make real and excellent wine. We have tasted it doctored and mixed, and know what it is in that state. We have taken much trouble to have procured for us samples of Concord wine from the cellars of some of the best known makers at the West, with the solemn assurance that it was pure, unadulterated Concord; and we have no doubt of it. A recently procured bottle of the pure Concord is before us as we write. We shall not undertake the impossible task of describing it, further than saying, that this, at least, resembles any thing but wine. We can not drink it; neither can our friends. It is certainly very peculiar. If the leopard never changes his spots, neither does the "fox" his odor. We wish to be good-natured about it; but the fact is, we are positively ashamed of our own face when we taste it. As the result of our investigations, we are forced back to the conclusion, that the Concord is not a wine grape, even at the West.

In addition to the leading varieties already described, there are other kinds more or less prominently before the public, which may be briefly noticed here.

UNION VILLAGE.

The *Union Village* originated with the Shakers of Union Village, Ohio, whence its name. The vine is pretty hardy, and perhaps the rankest grower of all our native kinds, the wood, leaves, and fruit being of extraordinary size. The bunch is extra large, compact, and shouldered. The color is dark purple, with a light bloom. The berry is extra large, (often an inch in diameter,) round, and has a moderately thick skin. The flesh has a fibrous center, small in proportion to the size of the berry, but is tender and juicy near the skin. The juice is sweet, and a little sprightly, but not vinous or high flavored. It resembles the Isabella in quality, and is no doubt a seedling from it. For a fruit of only moderate quality, its large size becomes a positive fault. Such a mass of flesh, of only negative goodness, when taken into the mouth, becomes really distasteful from its quantity. The bunch, however, is magnificent, resembling a well-grown Black Hamburgh. The vine is somewhat tender when young, and should always be covered. The fruit ripens about a week before the Isabella. The *Ontario* is identical with the Union Village.

REBECCA.

The *Rebecca* originated with Mrs. Peake, of Hudson, N. Y., after whom it was named.

The vine is not very hardy, but a fair grower, though the wood is not large. It is easily trained. The bunch is of medium size, very compact, and usually shouldered, except on young vines. The color is green, tinged with amber, which becomes quite deep on the sunny side, and has a fine white bloom. The berry is of good medium size, roundish oval, with a thin skin. The flesh is tender and juicy, with very little fiber. The juice is sweet and a little vinous, with a very pleasant flavor. There is a slight trace of the native odor in the unripe fruit. The Rebecca ripens quite to the center, and has consequently been much esteemed as a table grape. In some localities, generally where the soil is clayey, it has done well; but it is not recommended for vineyard culture, and often fails in the garden. It ripens nearly two weeks before the Isabella.

YORK MADEIRA.

The *York Madeira* is an old variety, and originated at York, Pa. It may be remarked here that there are two grapes known by this name, a large and a small one, the latter being the true York Madeira. The vine is not very hardy, often losing its leaves, and consequently failing to ripen its crop. The bunch is of medium size, compact, and generally has a small shoulder. The color is dark purple, with a light bloom. The berry is of medium size, roundish oval, with a tolerably thin skin. The flesh has a fibrous, acid center. The juice is very sweet, somewhat sprightly, and pleasant flavored. In quality it is better than the Isabella, and ripens a week before it. *Canby's August* is the same.

ELSINGBURGH.

The *Elsingburgh* came from a village of this name in New-Jersey, beyond which nothing seems to be known of its origin. It is hardy, and a good grower. The bunch is large, rather loose, and shouldered. The color is a dark, purplish black, covered with a bluish white bloom. The berry is very small and round, with a very thin skin. The flesh adheres slightly to the skin, and is tender and melting, with no fibrous center. The juice is pure and sweet, with a rich vinous flavor. Its excellent quality makes it desirable where variety is wanted for the garden. It ripens about a week before the Isabella.

CLINTON.

The *Clinton* is supposed to have originated in Monroe Co., N. Y. It is hardy, an exceedingly vigorous grower, has long joints, and is very impatient of restraint. Color, dark purple, covered with a light bloom. The bunch is medium, very compact, and shouldered. The berry is small, round, with a thick, very acrid skin. The flesh has a tough acid center. The juice remains sharply acid till after frost, when it becomes sweet, with some vinous spirit. It is not a table grape, and will only make a poor wine, by the aid of sugar. It becomes black early, but is not edible till touched by frost. The *Golden Clinton* is a sub-variety, differing in color, and producing a poorer fruit.

TO KALON.

The *To Kalon* originated with Dr. Spofford, of Lansingburgh, N. Y. It is hardy, and a vigorous grower. The bunch is large, moderately compact, and shouldered. The color is a dark bluish purple, thickly covered with bloom. The berry is large, varying in form, but is mostly oblate. The flesh becomes tender almost to the center, with but little unripe toughness. The juice is sugary and sweet, with a delicate and very pleasant flavor. When grown under favorable conditions, the vine is productive and the fruit excellent; but the crop is often lost from mildew and rot. It ripens about a week before the Isabella.

TAYLOR OR BULLITT.

The *Taylor* or *Bullitt* originated near Louisville, Ky., and was introduced by Dr. Taylor. It is hardy, and a vigorous grower. The bunch is small, compact, and sets unevenly. The color is green, tinged with amber. The berry is small, round, with a moderately thick skin. The flesh has but little fiber or unripeness at the center. The juice is sweet, spicy, and spirited, but a little rough or harsh. The vine is not very productive.

MILES.

The *Miles* originated in Pennsylvania, and was introduced by Mr. Hoopes, of Chester. It is hardy, and a good grower. The bunch is under medium size, compact, and shouldered. The color is a dark bluish purple, with a light bloom. The berry is under medium size and round. The flesh is tender, with but little unripe fiber. The juice is pleasant, but rather sub-acid than sweet, with very little if any of the "foxy" odor. It is about ten days earlier than the Isabella.

ANNA.

The *Anna* originated with Mr. Eli Hasbrouck, of Newburgh. It is a seedling of the Catawba. It is hardy, and a good grower The bunch is large, moderately compact, and shouldered. The color is green in the shade, covered with a thick pearly bloom, and dotted with claret; but in the light it becomes bright amber. The berry is large, round, with a moderately thick skin. The flesh is somewhat meaty, and has a fibrous center, which is very tough and acid when only partially ripe; but when fully mature, the juice is sweet and vinous with a pure and spicy muscat flavor. It begins to ripen early, but does not reach maturity till the end of the season. Like its parent, it is disposed to rot in unfavorable seasons, and is not adapted to general cultivation.

ROGERS'S HYBRIDS.

Rogers's Hybrids originated with Mr. Rogers of Salem, Mass. Much interest attaches to these seedlings, though we can not accept the idea of their being hybrids as fully established by the character of the fruit or the habits of the vine. They are all a great improvement on the wild native vine, and many of them are better than the Concord; but they all have the native characteristics strongly marked, while none of them possess the peculiar characteristics of the foreign grape. We may instance Allen's Hybrid as being strikingly different, in these respects, from any of Mr. Rogers's seedlings. It is to be regretted that Mr. Rogers did not test them all, and make a selection of three or four of the best, instead of putting that office upon the public; and yet we can not blame him for not having done this, well knowing the expenditure of time and money it involves. Our knowledge of these seedlings, acquired by six years' experience, leads us to divide them into three classes, according to color, making No. 4 the type of all the dark ones, No. 15 the type of the red ones, and No. 1 of the light ones. No. 19 so strongly resembles No. 4, and No. 3 so strongly resembles No. 15, that those who have the former would find their collection but little enriched by additional numbers. There is such a strong general resemblance among these seedlings, that we should not be much surprised to learn that one parent had produced them all. While in vinous spirit, freedom from foxiness, and ability to ripen to the center, none of them rise to the rank of first quality, all of the four named may, in these respects, be placed considerably above the Concord. If they could be advanced another step beyond that they have already taken from the original, they would be very good indeed; and we think this may be done by a proper observance of the well-known laws of thorough breeding, though not, perhaps, in one generation. We will now describe the three that have been selected as types of color. We may say that all of them are hardy, and good growers.

No. 1 is large, of a light amber green color, often with a shade of light crimson, and sometimes mottled with dark crimson. The flesh is disposed to tenderness, and has but a moderate amount of impurity in its flavor; but it is wanting in richness and spirit, in these respects falling below Nos. 4 and 15. There are several light colored ones, (commonly called white,) but none equal, on the whole, to the best dark colored.

ROGERS'S NO. 4.

No. 4 has large bunches, generally shouldered. Color purple, with a light bloom. Berry large, nearly round, with a rather tender but somewhat acrid skin, with considerable "foxy" odor. The flesh is buttery, with a fibrous, acid center, which the ripening process never reaches. The juice is sweet, somewhat sprightly, and moderately vinous, but with that deficiency in animation that characterizes all of what we have designated as the Isabella family. It ripens about ten days before the Isabella.

ROGERS'S NO. 15.

No. 15, rather large bunch, moderately compact. Color, reddish copper. Berry large, nearly round, with a rather tender skin. In other respects, the same as No. 4.

We notice next the group of small wine grapes, alluded to on a former page. They are of Southern origin, and are not extensively grown, though they are true wine grapes.

HERBEMONT.

The *Herbemont* is of Southern origin. It is a very handsome vine, and not very hardy, especially when young, but a very strong grower. The bunch is very large, very compact, and

Fig. 104½.—Herbemont.

shouldered. The color is a dark bluish purple, thickly covered with a light bloom. The berry is very small, round, with a thin skin. The flesh is tender and melting. The juice is sweet, pure, and refined, with a rich, sprightly vinous flavor. The Herbemont is an excellent table and wine grape, but is not sufficiently hardy for the vineyard at the North. It does very well in gardens in the vicinity of New-York, but young vines especially should always be covered in winter. It is an abundant bearer, and requires a longer season than the Isabella for the full maturity of its fruit.

LINCOLN.

The *Lincoln* is also a Southern grape. For a time it was thought to be identical with the Lenoir. The vine is a vigorous grower, more hardy than the Herbemont, and ripens its fruit earlier. The bunch is of moderate size, compact, and shouldered. The color is a dark purple, covered with a light bloom. The berry is small, round, with a thin skin. The flesh is tender, and ripens quite to the center. The juice is sweet and sugary, with a rich vinous flavor. The Lincoln is an excellent table and wine grape. The bunches are not proportionate to the size of the wood and leaf, and the vine is consequently only moderately productive. It ripens about a week before the Isabella.

LENOIR.

The *Lenoir* takes its name from Lenoir Co., North-Carolina, of which it is said to be a native. It bears a close resemblance to the preceding in the fruit and vine, but is readily distinguished by the leaves. The bunch is of medium size, compact, and shouldered. The color is a dark bluish purple, thickly covered with a light bloom. The berry is small and round. The flesh is tender, and ripens uniformly. The juice is sweet and sugary, with a pure, rich vinous flavor. It is an excellent table and wine grape. It ripens nearly two weeks before the Isabella.

NORTON'S VIRGINIA.

The *Norton's Virginia* is likewise of Southern origin. It is not very hardy, but a vigorous grower. The bunch is large, quite compact, and often double shouldered or winged. The color is a very dark purple, thickly covered with a light bloom. The berry is very small, round, with a thin skin. The flesh is tender and melting quite to the center. The juice is sweet, vinous, spirited, and rich in extractive matter, somewhat like that which distinguishes Port wine. The Norton is grown chiefly for wine, making a rather heavy, rough claret, free from all "foxy" aroma. The must is rich, and is often added to the juice of the Concord to improve it and make it durable.

The following may be simply noted:

Bland, (Southern,) long, loose bunch, good

medium sized, round, berry, pale red color, acid center, pleasant flavor; ripens late.

Brincklé, (Philadelphia,) large bunch, large, round berry, purple color, tender flesh, somewhat vinous flavor; ripens late; is essentially foreign, and mildews.

Alexander, (York, Pa.,) large, compact bunch, large, roundish oval berry, purple color, tough, fibrous center, sweet; ripens in mid-season.

Canby's August, same as *York Madeira.*

Cassady, (Philadelphia,) medium compact bunch, small, round berry, amber green color, tough, acid center; ripens late.

Montgomery, foreign; possibly a seedling.

Child's Superb, foreign seedling.

Clara, (Philadelphia,) medium loose bunch, medium round berry, amber green color, pleasant flavor; ripens mid-season; claimed as a foreign seedling by Mr. Raabe.

Emily, (Philadelphia,) also claimed as a foreign seedling by Mr. Raabe, by whom two varieties were sent out bearing this name; one proved to be foreign, and the other the Mountain Grape of Virginia.

Garrigues, (Philadelphia,) in all respects

like the Isabella, except that it ripens a few days before it.

Graham, (Philadelphia,) medium loose bunch, large, round berry, purple color, tough center, feeble flavor ; ripens late.

Hyde's Eliza, (Catskill, N. Y.,) strongly resembles the Isabella, but scarcely equal to it.

Louisa, (Calmdale, Pa.,) ripens about a week before Isabella, and much like it.

Mammoth Catawba, a large Catawba, but much inferior in flavor.

Marion, large compact bunch, large, roundish oval berry, purple color, tough center, austere flavor ; colors early, but ripens late.

Meade's Seedling is nearly or quite identical with the Catawba.

McNeil, medium compact bunch, medium oval berry, purple color, tough center, brisk and pungent ; ripens late.

McCowan, bunch and berry small, flesh tough, acid, and harsh ; has no value.

Albino, medium compact bunch, small oval berry, amber green color, tough center, low flavor ; ripens late.

Mary Ann, long compact bunch, large oval berry, purple color, tough fibrous center, feeble flavor ; ripens early.

Wright's Isabella resembles Clinton, but has larger berries.

Alvey, if not Lenoir, is so like it as to be scarcely distinguishable.

Logan, large compact bunch, large oval berry, purple color, tough center, low foxy flavor; quite early, beginning to ripen about ten days before the Isabella. It was first known as Urbana, and re-named by Mr. Campbell. It has also been confounded with Rulander, a foreign grape.

Wilmington, (Delaware,) large compact bunch, large round berry, whitish or amber green color, unripe center, rich vinous flavor: ripens very late.

Flora, (Philadelphia,) small, very compact bunch, rather small round berry, purple color, unripe acid center, sweet and pleasant flavor: ripens a few days before the Isabella.

Honey Grape, (Philadelphia,) small compact bunch, small round berry, small unripe center, very sweet and sugary: ripens with Isabella.

Mottled Catawba, (Carpenter of Kelley's Island, Ohio,) is like Catawba, except that the berries are mottled.

Lydia, (Carpenter of Kelley's Island, Ohio,) large compact bunch, large roundish oval berry, pale amber green color, unripe center, pleasant flavor: ripens late.

Elizabeth, (Western New-York,) large compact bunch, large oval berry, dull green color, unripe center, feeble flavor: ripens late.

Coleman's White, medium compact bunch, oval berry, pale amber green color, unripe center, pretty good quality, but late and unproductive.

Cuyahoga is *Coleman's White* revived under another name.

Maxatawny, (Pennsylvania,) compact bunch, round berry, tough center, rich vinous flavor, but ripens very late.

The *Scuppernong* is a Southern grape, with a very small bunch, and large round berry, tough, fibrous center, thick skin, sweet juice, and a strong, unpleasant aroma. It is the Southern "fox." The berries drop as soon as ripe. There are two kinds, a light and a dark-colored one.

The *Kansas July* is a very early grape, from Kansas, bearing small bunches of very small berries, quite meaty and very sweet. The vine is very handsome.

The *Eureka* is identical with *Diana*.

Manhattan, (New-York City,) small, compact bunch, medium-sized berry, amber green color, tough center, good flavor; unproductive, and ripens late.

Aiken, an Isabella producing large fruit under peculiarly favorable conditions.

Cunningham, a grape of the Southern family, scarcely distinguishable from the Lenoir.

Rentz, (Cincinnati,) large, loose bunch, purple color, large, round berry, with the flesh and odor of the wild grape.

Yeddo, from Japan, and altogether too tender for our climate.

Cynthiana, a purple grape, said to be from Arkansas. It has the flesh and odor characteristic of the wild grape.

The *Charter Oak*, *North America*, *Corail*, *Northern Muscadine*, *Dracut* (so-called) *Amber*, *Underhill's Seedling*, *Perkins*, *Sage*, *Massachusetts White*, *Miner's Seedling*, *et id omne genus*, may be disposed of in a few words as unmitigated "foxes" from the woods.

There are several seedling grapes that have either just been given to the public, or probably will be, in regard to most of which but little is known.

It is much to be regretted that we have not some means by which seedlings could be thoroughly tested in various parts of the country before they are sent out to the public. If three or four unprofessional men, living in different sections, could, by common consent, be selected for the purpose of testing seedlings and newly introduced fruits, much disappointment and expense would be saved to fruit growers generally. It would perhaps be difficult to find competent and disinterested men who could give the necessary time to the task, or who would be willing to undertake the labor; yet it would be a profound satisfaction to know that the fruit we are planting is precisely what it is represented to be. We shall probably, however, have to go on for some time yet, and take our chance. Some seedlings stand for years so exposed as to leave no doubt of their hardiness and period of ripening under similar conditions elsewhere; but others are so covered and walled in as to prevent us from gaining any real knowledge on these points till it has lost most of its value to the public. If those who raise seedling fruits could be protected in their rights by law, as authors and inventors now are, the way would be opened for fully testing fruits, and the public spared the mortification and loss not only of planting inferior fruits, but old kinds under new names, and the production of seedlings would be encouraged, and the number of good grapes thereby more speedily increased. A man who, through fraud or otherwise, plants an inferior fruit, supposing it to be a good one, loses so much of his life as is wasted in proving it: a loss which can never be repaired. There is room for wise legislation here.

The new grapes alluded to above are as follows:

BRACKETT'S SEEDLING.

Brackett's Seedling, large in bunch and berry, and bearing a close resemblance to the Union Village. It originated near Boston.

DIANA HAMBURGH.

The *Diana Hamburgh* was raised by Messrs. Moore and Charlton, Rochester, N. Y., who say it is a hybrid between the Diana and Black Hamburgh. It resembles the Diana very closely in quality, the flesh, however, being more meaty in its consistence, and the skin thinner and darker. It is supposed to ripen late. Of the hardiness and general character of the vine we know nothing.

FANCHER.

The *Fancher* is in possession of Mr. F. B.

Fancher, of Troy, N. Y. Having examined the vine and the fruit on his grounds, we were led to the conviction that it is identical with the Catawba. We could perceive no difference in the wood, foliage, fruit, and general habit of the plant. It is affected by mildew and black rot precisely as the Catawba is. The vine is so situated as to favor its early ripening; other vines, similarly located, showed as much maturity as the Fancher. It is either the Catawba, or a pretty exact reproduction of it, an opinion which half a dozen or more examinations of the fruit has only tended to confirm.

SARATOGA.

The *Saratoga* is also in possession of Mr. Fancher. His published account says he got it of Dr. James, of Waterford, N. Y., who received it twenty years ago from New-Orleans, under the name of *Scaberan.* This account leaves no doubt whatever that the *Saratoga* and the *Fancher* are one and the same grape.

WALTER.

The *Walter* originated with Mr. A. J. Caywood, at Modena, N. Y. It is said to be a cross between the Diana and the Delaware. It bears a very close resemblance to the Diana, of which we think it is a seedling. It has the same sweetness, the same flavor, and the same consistency of flesh; and the form, size, and color of the bunch and berry are the same. Its value will depend upon its hardiness, vigor, and early ripening, of which we have no knowledge, the vine having fruited only in the garden of the proprietor.

MARTHA.

The *Martha* was raised by Mr. Samuel Miller, of Calmdale, Pa. It is said to be a seedling of the Concord. It is hardy, and a strong grower. The bunch is of good size, and the berry large, of a pale green, a little warmed with chocolate or copper color. It has a buttery flesh, an unripe acid center, and a sweet juice, with some sprightliness, but no vinous flavor. Like its parent, it has a pretty strong "foxy" odor.

DANA'S SEEDLINGS.

Of *Dana's Seedlings* we know nothing, except that some of them are said to be promising, and bear a general resemblance to the Rogers's Hybrids.

EUMELAN.

The *Eumelan* sprang up, some twenty years ago, in the yard of Mr. Thorne, at the end of the Long Dock at Fishkill Landing, where we should little expect to find a grape. Mr. Thorne died; and his brother, perceiving its excellence, determined to transplant it to his own grounds; but it died in consequence of having its roots badly broken off among the rocks. A few cuttings, however, had been taken off, and from these the present vines were grown. We know but little of the habit of the vine, except that it is hardy, ripens early, and bears good crops. The fruit, however, is excellent, and entirely distinct, resembling none of the Isabella family, except in color, and is free from "foxy" odor. The bunch is of good size and compact, and the berry nearly round, of a deep purple or bluish black color, and thickly covered with a light bloom. The flesh is thoroughly tender and melting, ripening uniformly to the center, and the juice sweet, sprightly, and decidedly vinous. It is a pleasure to meet a grape sometimes that is in no danger of being confounded with something else. It is now in the possession of Dr. C. W. Grant.

Of most of the following new kinds we have

little or no personal knowledge beyond their names:

Eva, *Black Hawk*, *Young America*, and *Macedonia*, seedlings of the Concord, raised by Mr. Samuel Miller, of Calmdale, Pa.

Modena, a seedling of the Concord, raised at Modena by Mr. A. J. Caywood. It is said to resemble the Concord in quality, but is smaller.

Pœschel's Mammoth, represented to be a large fruit, ripening a week or so after the Catawba.

Lorain, a seedling raised at Sandusky, of which we know nothing reliable.

Hattus, (perhaps the same as *Hattie*,) a claret-colored grape, said to be a seedling of the Catawba, but of smaller size and quite acid.

Laura, raised by Mr. H. B. Lum, of Sandusky, Ohio, said to be sweet, but "foxy."

Framingham, (Boston,) a purple grape, resembling the Hartford Prolific, but having stronger native characteristics.

Dorr's Seedling, said to have been raised from the Delaware, which, except that the berries are larger, it resembles in form, color, and bunch; but it has the coarse flesh and strong "foxy" odor of the wild grape, and if really a seedling of the Delaware, possesses some interest; but we would suggest to the originator not only not to name it after Mr. Downing, as proposed, but also not to disseminate it.

Canadian Hybrid, raised by Mr. Arnold, C. W. It is said to be a hybrid, but the fruit shows it to be a native of the Isabella family.

Arnold's No. 1, recently figured in the *Gardener's Monthly*, and said to be a seedling of the Clinton. The bunch and berry are large. No mention is made of its quality.

Charlotte, said to resemble the Diana, and ripen as early as the Delaware.

Telegraph or *Christine*, represented as vigorous and productive, having a large bunch and berry, and ripening before the Concord.

Neff, sometimes also called the *Keuka*, medium sized bunch and berry, copper color, with the flesh and "foxy" odor of the native: ripens rather early.

Salem, (No. 53 of Rogers's Hybrids,) is said by Mr. Rogers to be the best of his seedlings. It is described as being hardy, vigorous, and productive, having a large bunch and berry, sweet and sprightly, and ripening as early as the Hartford Prolific or the Delaware.

Carpenter, raised by Mr. Thompson, of Green

Island, near Troy. It resembles the Black Hamburgh, of which it is a seedling. Having seen it, we are prepared to say that it is in all respects inferior to its parent. It is totally unfitted for vineyard culture, in common with all the kinds that we have designated as foreign. Mr. Thompson has a number of other seedlings, both foreign and native, and of these the Catawba seedling is the only one that approaches its parent in excellence.

Just here is a proper place for a few remarks that will be of much benefit to the beginner. The foreign grape has been so often and so thoroughly tried, and so uniformly failed, that we should regret to see the experiment repeated under the supposition that it is still an open one. There is scarcely a single variety of the foreign grape that has not been tried in every conceivable variety of soil and locality, and under every kind of treatment; they have been tried, not by dozens or hundreds, but by thousands, over and over again. Skill and money without stint have been lavished upon these experiments, and they have been persisted in for years, but always with the same results, and there can, therefore, be no doubt of the unfitness of the foreign grape for vineyard culture here. This is the rule; but, like many other rules, it has its exceptions. Here and there in cities, and in a few sheltered positions possessing peculiarly favorable conditions for growing the grape, a few vines of the Early Black, Miller's Burgundy, the Chasselas, or even the Black Hamburgh, have been grown with tolerable success, the fruit, however, falling much short of its characteristic excellence, being, in fact, quite inferior to several of our best native varieties. We know, indeed, of several instances where the Chasselas, under such conditions, has for a number of years produced moderate crops of inferior fruit; but such sporadic instances do not in the least invalidate the fact, that the foreign grape is wholly unfitted for vineyard culture here. That fact will remain intact until we can command a much more uniform temperature than we now possess, and the hygrometric conditions of our atmosphere have been considerably modified. But even if the foreign grape were fitted for the vineyard, wherein consists the wisdom of introducing seedlings inferior to their parents?

CHAPTER XIII.

TASTE, AS APPLIED TO FRUITS.

We must add here some remarks on the subject of *taste*, in its application to fruits; a subject that can only be fully treated in an extended essay. We wish, however, to present some facts that may lead the general public to do what is as yet done only by comparatively few, to regard grape culture from a higher stand-point than they have heretofore done; and to point out to them the source whence they can draw the greatest enjoyment in the use of the products of the vine. And as an inseparable part of the subject, we wish to indicate, also, some of the reasons why good grapes only should be planted in the future.

The grape, in its best varieties, is truly a nourishing and delicate *food*, possessing valuable hygienic properties, and the public will not be satisfied with those that are indigestible and ill flavored, when they can just as well have those that are tender and good. While we had only the Isabella and Catawba, a necessity was laid upon us, and we were constrained to be content with them; but we now have those which are far better, upon which we can really feast. We have only to come prepared for their full and proper enjoyment: the table is set, and all who will may come and eat of the best.

The public taste, so far from having been cultivated, has been depraved by the use of ill-flavored and indigestible grapes. The force of circumstances has compelled it to remain so for a time; but there is no longer any reason why this should continue. It has ceased to be a matter of necessity, and has now become one of choice. Each one, therefore, in his own interest, should seek to free his taste from the bondage in which it has been held, and rise to the liberty of a purer enjoyment. Some have not been slow to do this; and the number has been much increased by those accustomed to the use of the foreign grape. Experience, gained by comparing the different kinds, will soon show the public the broad distinction between the good and the bad, and they will not be slow to choose the one and reject the other. We have only to show them that, while the good yields both nourishment and enjoyment, the bad yields but little of either, and they will be at no loss which to select. We have no more faith in pandering to a depraved taste in matters of food and drink, than we have in pandering to a depraved taste in morals, literature, or the arts. All are essentially bad, and equally to be condemned.

It is a fallacy to suppose that poor kinds of grapes can be grown cheaper than good ones, and that we must therefore grow the poor kinds for the "million." No sensible man should try to deceive himself with that specious kind of reasoning. Good grapes, in this happy land at least, are not to be a luxury for one class alone. They can, and must, be placed within the reach of all, rich and poor alike. Taste is the common inheritance of man, and not, as is often supposed, something which follows in the wake of wealth. It is sometimes found as keen and appreciative in the cottage as in the palace. It is doubtless preserved in greater purity by some classes of society than others, and always will be; but that should not content us; it should rather stimulate us, seeing how altogether beautiful it is, to induce a healthy tone in the taste of all classes of society. We must dismiss the illusion that a poor man, simply because he *is* poor, can not appreciate the enjoyments of taste; and we must no longer do him the injustice of growing for his special use an inferior class of food. The "millions" must have as good grapes and as good grain as the "tens." It is their right, and they are beginning to comprehend it. There is a power at work which will at no distant day sweep from the market every grape inferior to the Diana. No greater service could be performed for both grape growers and grape consumers.

We can already see the beginning of the end. Many intelligent vineyardists, perceiving the impolicy of spending their capital and labor in the cultivation of inferior varieties of grapes, are replacing them by better kinds. Causes are at work which will in time, and that no very distant time, effect a complete revolution in our estimate of the value of grapes for the vineyard. The change, indeed, is now going on pretty fast, and it would be at least wise to accept what must and ought to be, rather than to fight against it. It is better to accept the situation while we can do it without loss, than to wait till it is forced upon us, with its consequences. It would, notwithstanding, in many cases, be a hard, and in some perhaps an impossible task, to convince those who already have vineyards of poor kinds, that they would in the end be gainers by immediately, or even gradually, replacing them by better ones; and yet we believe this to be strictly true. The change, notwithstanding, will not be delayed; having been begun, it will go on just as rapidly as the material for effecting it can be produced.

It is for those, however, who are now planting vineyards to choose wisely as to the part they will take in carrying forward this reform movement in grape culture. Happily, they are aiding it to an extent that could hardly have been hoped for, so largely are they planting the good kinds; and thus the movement goes on. There will be a strong opposition to it, no doubt, on the part of some who have vineyards of poor kinds, since they will think that it involves a sacrifice of their invested interests; but herein they will most certainly be wrong, as a little calm reflection can not fail to convince them. Their trouble will consist in preparing the way for calm reflection by first casting aside their prejudices. Others will continue to insist that poor grapes are the grapes for the "million," and not deceive even themselves; but the "million" will insist that they are not, by eating only the good; and thus the good, in the end, will prevail over the evil.

For many years the conviction was strong, that American grape culture occupied much too low a position; and that an intelligent application of the means within our reach would greatly improve both its modes and material, lift it to a much higher level, and give it an important place among the chief industrial interests of the country. Under this conviction a movement was begun, and both in public and private, we have not ceased to urge it on. The movement was slow at first, but it has gathered numbers, and is now becoming imposing in its proportions. We propose to go on, and "fight it out on this line, if it takes all the summer" of life. Nothing but the best of grapes, and an improved public taste to enjoy them, will satisfy us.

In partaking of food and drink, our enjoyment is mainly a matter of taste. If the taste be paralyzed to such a degree that the food passes the palate as it were without a sensation, eating has ceased to be a pleasure, and fails, in a measure, to perform its function of supporting the body. Eating and drinking are necessary to sustain life; but both were intended to be a pleasure as well as a necessity. The taste may become so depraved as at last to yield us no appreciable enjoyment in the act of doing either; and thus we may sink to the level of mere animals in all that pertains to what was intended to be one of the purest pleasures of life. On the other hand, the taste may become so vitiated and artificial as to receive but little pleasure from natural flavors; it then depends for excitement upon stimulating and pungent compounds. We say excitement; for the capacity to receive pleasure from the normal exercise of the sense of taste is so greatly impaired, that the nerves must be sharply excited to produce a response, which comes quickly and as quickly passes away. These two extremes are by no means uncommon. There are persons to whom all flavors are nearly alike; and there are others who have no perception of flavor except in its intensest form. The last are insensible to delicate and refined flavors, which are usually the most delightful of all; their nerves can be excited by the flavor of our rankest "fox," but remain insensible to the delicate and pure flavor of a Frontignan. All this results from abuse. The nerves of taste, when in their natural and healthy condition, not only vibrate to the most delicate touch, but the vibrations linger like those of a musical chord, passing away by such delicate gradations, that we scarcely know when they cease. Our pleasure is just in that degree prolonged.

If so much enjoyment may be found in the natural use of the taste, it becomes a matter of much moment to preserve its healthy tone. We should do nothing that may deprave or vitiate it; but, on the contrary, do every thing to give a healthful vigor to its tone. Still further, we should, as it were, so educate it as to discriminate promptly and nicely between the good and the bad in flavors, and thus increase not only the amount but the degree of our enjoyment. In all matters of taste, whether relating to the intellect or the sensibilities, our enjoyment must be more or less enhanced by our ability to perceive even the nicest shades of difference in any object. There is a degree of pleasure in the very consciousness of possessing the power to do so. The want of this perceptive power reduces all flavors, good and bad alike, to one common level, and that level a low one.

We have the evidence of this before us every day, and marvel that it is so common. What we wish to do here is to impress the reader with the fact that, on the integrity and preservation of his taste, will depend a large measure of his enjoyment. As grape eaters and wine drinkers, the great mass have this important lesson to learn. They have yet to learn that there are simple, natural pleasures, arising from the proper use of taste, which are far more satisfying and enduring than any derived from artificial forms. Such knowledge would exercise a beneficent influence on intemperance in both eating and drinking.

But we must not be content with the power simply to know what is sweet or what is sour, or what is essentially good or essentially bad; we must not stop short of the power to perceive all the gradations which connect these together. We must know not only wherein one thing resembles another, but wherein they differ, and in what the difference consists. We must be able not only to recognize the excellence of both, but to know wherein one is better than the other, and why it is better. We must be able not only to appreciate all the goodness of the Delaware and the Iona, but also to know wherein and why the Iona excels the Delaware; what, in fact, are the real excellences which place the Iona above all other American grapes. When we can do this, we shall be the possessors of real knowledge, and know what its pleasures are. All may not attain to this immediately, or by intuition, but all may and should strive to reach it quickly by prompt and thorough training of the taste. In all that pertains to taste, no less than to knowledge, we should seek for the substance, and not the shadow: we should do our own tasting as well as our own thinking, always happy in having the intelligent in sympathy with us.

Our taste, at present, is at a very low standard; too many of us are content with the positively coarse and bad, to the neglect of the delicate and good. Forced by circumstances to begin low, we are too easily beguiled into remaining so. There is no longer any excuse for this; for we have now within our reach the means of gratifying the most refined perceptions. Our taste for grapes really began in the woods, and it is surprising how many still seek its gratification there, unsatisfying as it must be, while the good is so plainly in sight. But a movement has already begun; the masses are turning their faces to the light; numbers have already reached the outskirts of the woods, and some may be seen wending their way up the fair hill of culture, rosy with the excitement of their new-found pleasure. This must go on till the great body of the people are able, not only to distinguish between a good grape or a good wine and a poor one, but also to appreciate in good grapes and wine those nice shades and degrees of flavor which give a distinctive character to our best grapes and wines, and from which is derived the chief zest of our enjoyment. Then, and not till then, shall we be able to put a just value upon grapes as a nourishing food, and wine as a refreshing drink.

CHAPTER XIV.

WHEN GRAPES ARE RIPE.

ONE of the most important parts of an elementary work on the grape is that which relates to the ripening of the fruit, more especially when that work regards the subject from the stand-point of *food*. The novice should be furnished with so much knowledge as will enable him to know when his grapes are ripe, and in what ripeness consists; indeed, it is equally important to the grape grower and the grape consumer. Such knowledge is important to the grape grower, whether he purposes using the fruit for his own table, sending it to market, or making it into wine. For all these purposes, it is essential that the fruit should be *ripe;* and we hope that all who read these pages will be too conscientious to use grapes for food until they have at least acquired a tolerably good degree of ripeness, and in time we hope we may add, full maturity. Those who are careful to send to market only ripe fruit, nicely put up, always obtain good prices, and find fruit growing profitable: grapes ought not much longer to form an exception to the rule of ripe fruit.

In every city that has a market, there ought to be a Board of Health, composed of conscientious and honest men, like that instituted in New-York last summer; and it should be their duty to see that no unripe fruit is offered for sale; for of all complaints that affect the public health, there are none that run their course more rapidly, or prove more fatal, than those that have their origin in the use of unripe fruit. Grapes are no exception: eminently healthy when ripe, they are just the reverse when unripe. Each one, therefore, should gravely ask himself, how far he can conscientiously become *particeps criminis* in destroying public health and life.

It becomes important, then, that those who plant vineyards should have some means of judging when the fruit is ripe. In the apple, pear, etc., mellowness is a good external indication of maturity; but we have no such guide in grapes, for mere appearance and touch are no criteria. In our ordinary native kinds we must accept an approximation to ripeness, and not look for full maturity. If we judge by what we see in market, the conclusion is inevitable, that there are a great many vineyardists who do not know when grapes have attained even this degree of ripeness. This is the most charitable construction we can put upon the fact that meets us every where. Some lots are so positively bad that the best arts and *finesse* of the agents can not "work" them off upon the public, and they are sold at a low figure to the "doctors" for making so-called wine! and not only so, but these "wine doctors" go about among the vineyards, and buy up the worthless refuse for the same purpose. We hope that a practice so utterly disgraceful is not known out of New-York. Grapes that are not fit to eat are good enough to make wine of, forsooth! Let those who buy wine bear this fact in mind.

We have found two opinions quite prevalent in regard to the ripeness of grapes: one, that they are ripe when they are colored; the other, that they are ripe when they are sweet. But being simply colored or sweet is not of itself a safe guide. For example, the Isabella and Concord are *colored* two weeks or more before they are ripe, while the Diana and Iona are *sweet*, but only a little colored, a couple of weeks before they are ripe. Color and sweetness are both important elements of ripeness; but there are degrees of sweetness and color, and these must attain their full degree of force and depth before they can be regarded as indicating ripeness.

It will assist us much in understanding what ripeness is if we first have some knowledge of what the flesh of the grape is composed, and what changes take place in it. The flesh is composed chiefly of grape sugar, tartaric, tannic, carbonic, and other acids, potash, etc. These elements are contained in the juice; the juice is held in little sacs or cells composed of cellular tissue, and the mass of cells are inclosed in the skin, and we thus have the berry. The berry is increased in size by the multiplication of the cells. The changes that take place as the berry proceeds to maturity are vito-chemical. The fruit will be good or bad as these changes are more or less perfect, and it will depend chiefly for its flavor and spirit upon the presence and due commingling of the sugar and acid of the grape. Some varieties of the grape are constitutionally incapable of carrying the ripening process to maturity.

From what has been said we may derive the following brief rule for ripeness in the grape: The berry is ripe when it is tender and melting in all its parts, without loss of its characteristic spirit and flavor. If the spirit and flavor are gone, we may conclude that the tenderness proceeds from incipient decay, and not from natural maturity. The berry is then in the condition of an overripe apple or pear. Ripening does not destroy the goodness of the fruit; it only carries it forward to a perfect condition. And just here is presented the line of demarkation between a good and a bad grape. In the latter, the ripening process, owing chiefly to constitutional causes, never performs its office fully, and the berry fails to mature; a portion of the flesh remains tough, and the acids unchanged; the sugar in the juice is imperfectly elaborated, and there is a marked deficiency of spirit and flavor, or they are so poorly developed as to be scarcely appreciable. In the good grape, on the contrary, ripening proceeds uninterruptedly to full maturity, and reaches all parts of the berry in consequence of the more delicate texture of the cellular tissue; the flesh becomes tender, melting, or juicy, and thoroughly digestible. The flavor will be more or less vinous and spirited, according as the sugar and acids may be more or less perfectly elaborated, and as the aromatic principle may be present in a greater or less degree.

But the reader may ask if there are no outward signs by which the ripeness of the grape may be determined. There certainly are such signs, and they have some value. The color of the skin constitutes one of these signs; but there are others which can be recognized by the practiced eye alone. In purple grapes, like Isabella, the color should be uniformly deep. If, on holding the bunch up to the light, the skin shows a tinge of red, the berries are not ripe; but if the color be uniformly deep and dark, with a thick bloom, it is a pretty sure sign of ripeness. In dark claret-colored grapes, like Catawba, the color should be pure and deep, and covered with a thick bloom. In light clarets, like Iona, the color should be bright and pure, and well covered with bloom. Claret-colored grapes are sometimes described as amber colored, but there is not a particle of amber about them. In light or green-colored grapes, like Allen's Hybrid, the green should have a tinge of amber, which should be quite deep on the sunny side, and the berry covered with a bright, pearly bloom. In unfavorable seasons and conditions the color will be imperfect in all these cases, and so will the ripening.

Though the condition of color above described indicates ripeness, the grapes should not be cut for a week at least after this deep color is established, if they are wanted fully ripe. In purple grapes the color is deceptive; it will seem to be dark and pure to ordinary observation, but on holding the bunch up to the light a reddish tinge will be seen, which shows that the berry is not ripe. The longer some kinds of purple grapes are left on, the better, for they never get fully ripe. In some of the light claret and green-colored grapes, ripeness is also accompanied with a certain degree of transparency; the Iona, however, begins to be transparent just after stoning.

But tasting is the surest and safest of all means for determining ripeness in the grape. The touch is of no use to us here. We can not feel the ripeness of the grape as we can that of the apple, the pear, or the peach, and we must therefore have recourse to taste. If, on tasting a grape, we find the flesh tender or melting throughout, with a sweet and sprightly juice, accompanied with the characteristic flavor of the kind, it is ripe, and we may place it on the table, send it to market, or make it into wine, if it is a wine grape. If it is not in this condition, it should remain on the vine till it is, or be given to the pigs, (if they will eat it,) or made into vinegar, but it should not be eaten or made into wine.

There are only a few of our native grapes that ripen their skins, so that they may be eaten. They are not only generally sour, but often acrid and pungent to a degree that can not be tolerated by tender mouths. A few only of our best grapes are free from this fault. It is only when the skin ripens in common with the rest of tho berry, that it may be eaten like the skin of the foreign grape. In certain conditions of the body, the astringent principle that resides in the skin of the grape is a valuable medicine, and the edible condition of the skin therefore adds to the value of the grape.

We shall get a better idea of ripeness if we take the foreign grape as an illustration. This, as a class, ripens uniformly, and hence its great excellence. Its chief characteristic, that which gives it its greatest value, is the perfection of the ripening process, which reaches every part of the berry. This is fully recognized, and every advantage taken of it by the skillful gardener. He not only places the vine under the most favorable conditions for growth, and carefully removes every cause which may interfere with the full development of the fruit, but he applies his art in such a way as to facilitate the development of the highest condition of excellence that the vine is capable of attaining to. In a true sense, he becomes a co-worker with nature.

Let us take an example, say the Chasselas Musqué or the Grizzly Frontignan, and see how the fruit is developed into this excellent condition. The vine, when started, is bent down, to equalize the action of the plant, and secure a good "set" of fruit along the whole length of the stock or cane; for the gardener dislikes to see the bottom of his vine naked of fruit. When the fruit sets, he finds he has too many bunches, and the bunches are too compactly set. His object is handsome, well-colored, and high-flavored fruit; quality, not quantity; but still, all the fruit his vine will carry from year to year without injury. He judges how much the vine will mature *thoroughly*, and removes the rest at once. But the bunches left are too compact to have the berries all ripen at the same time, or to admit of their being eaten conveniently; he therefore removes a half or more of the berries while they are very small, and as the result he has a bunch quite as heavy as it would have been without the thinning; but the thinning has admitted light and air to all parts of the bunch, and the vital force having a fewer number of berries to act upon, they are made much larger, and the ripening process is more thoroughly performed.

He wants the vine now to work principally upon the fruit, and he therefore pinches out the end of the cane a few leaves above the last bunch, athallizes promptly, and thus concentrates the action of the vine on the fruit and the development of the buds for next year's canes. The fruit swells rapidly, and recourse is had to various means for securing handsome bunches of fully-ripened and high-flavored grapes; and to this end, among others things, water is applied in due quantity and at proper intervals, and ventilation so regulated as to furnish fresh air without having a current blowing directly on the vines, or causing a sudden change of temperature. When "stoning" takes place, it is accompanied by a beautiful translucency; the berries "clear," and the ripening process has fairly begun. It is not confined to any particular part of the berry, but involves the whole mass at one and the same time, like ferment in a lump of dough. Air and water now more than ever influence the goodness and flavor of the fruit: the first is carefully regulated, and the last gradually withheld. Not a bunch is disturbed till the ripening is complete, and then he has grapes of such excellence as to reward him for all his labor, beautiful to look upon, and exceedingly good to eat: the flesh is tender and melting, the juice pure, sweet, and vinous, with a delightful muscat aroma, the skin quite edible, and there is no waste except the small seeds. He eats his grapes with great enjoyment, and both body and mind are refreshed. Here skill, working on proper subjects, produces its legitimate results in a high degree of excellence.

Thus we see, in the best foreign varieties, that all the elements of a good grape have been brought together, as it were, in *equilibrio*, and so nicely adjusted under the most favorable conditions, that when motion begins in one, it is immediately communicated to all the rest: all move, and each performs its allotted task in producing a perfect fruit. There are no woody, fibrous barriers to impede or shut off access to the interior, and which the ripening process can not overcome, but it finds, as it were, open doors and ready passages to lead it to the remotest parts of the berry, and it thus takes possession of the whole, converting it into a uniform mass of goodness.

It is these elements, under precisely the same conditions and operating in the same manner, that have heretofore been wanting in the native grape; and they had been so long and so earnestly hoped for, that most people had begun to think it impossible that they ever would be found there; but the supposed impossibility having been proved possible, we may confidently look forward to the time when truly good grapes will be as common in our markets as poor ones now are. The structure of our native grape is radically faulty: woody, fibrous walls meet the ripening process at every step; it finds no open doors or ready passages, but must perforce knock a hole through the inosculated cells, the obstructions becoming more formidable as the interior is approached, till at last it is fairly turned back by the impenetrable center, so weakened by its fruitless efforts to overcome the obstacles opposed to it, that it is incapable of completing its allotted office. This is the general fault of the native, and a complete remedy can only be found in a new structure of the flesh, such as we find begun in the Diana, greatly improved in the Delaware and Allen, and completed in the Iona.

CHAPTER XV.

PROPAGATION.

WE propose here to give a description of the several modes in which the vine is propagated. There are perhaps few of our readers who will propagate their own vines; still, it is just as well that they should know how it is done; if for no other reason, because it is an important link in the circle of knowledge pertaining to the vine. Nurserymen, who make propagation a specialty, surround themselves with the necessary appliances in their most approved forms, and can therefore not only make better plants, but make them at a much less cost, than those who have nothing of the kind.

The grape vine is propagated from *single eyes* or buds, *cuttings*, and *layers*, and also by *grafting*. New varieties are raised from seed. We shall take them up in the order in which they are named.

Single Eyes.—The most perfect mode of propagating any plant is that furnished by nature, which is the seed. The seed contains the perfect plant in embryo or miniature. The nearest approach to seed is the bud, which may also be said to contain the plant in embryo, with perhaps the single exception of the radicle; the germ of which, however, may be said to exist, at least in some buds; for if the bud of a grape vine, and the buds of some other kinds of plants, be carefully dissected or detached from the parent plant, and placed under favorable conditions, they will develop into perfect plants of their kind. We have conducted a series of experiments with a view of establishing a general rule for all buds, but we are not prepared quite yet to state it. The analogy, however, between a seed and a bud, is a recognized fact. In the seed, the cotyledons support the plant while the mouths or rootlets are being formed on the radicle. Now if, in the grape vine, for example, we take a small portion of the cane (or mother plant) on each side of the bud, to support the infant plant while it is forming mouths of its own, we have something that answers to the cotyledons in the seed, and the analogy between the two becomes almost perfect. If the beginner will bear these things in mind, he will the better understand the process of propagation, and it will become invested with a new interest. The reader will infer, correctly, that we esteem a grape vine made from a single eye or bud the best that can be produced by any artificial means.

Vines from eyes are propagated under glass. In order that the reader's mind may not be diverted from the main subject as we go along, we will here notice an objection made to this mode of propagation, and which, to many, seems to have considerable force. It is objected that propagating plants under glass is an artificial process, and makes plants weak and tender. The sufficient answer to this is, that all modes of propagating plants from cuttings are strictly artificial, and that is clearly the best which places the cutting under the most favorable conditions for its full development into a perfect plant. This is so self-evident that it should need no argument. Now, it is found, as the result of repeated and careful experiment, that shelter, shade, moisture, etc., are indispensable to the production of the best plants from eyes or cuttings; and it is further found that these, and all other requisites needed, are best furnished by glass houses constructed for the purpose. In short, better vines can be grown under glass in one year than can be grown in the open air in the old way in three years. Poor vines in abundance, however, are grown in both ways. We want chiefly a porous, moist, warm soil, and a moderately cool but uniform and moist atmosphere. These conditions are needed with almost unvarying constancy, and are admirably supplied by a glass house; but in the open air we have them only "by fits and turns." The infant plant must be nursed into a vigorous childhood before it is exposed to the rigors of a changing climate, and not stunted and dwarfed by exposure before it is scarcely born. In breeding, this principle is now fully recognized. Exposure and hardiness were so intimately associated at one time, that it was thought necessary to rear young animals exposed to all the inclemencies of the weather, no shelter being afforded against even the rigors of winter; but it is now found that the shelter of a good barn gives a degree of vigor, health, and general development, and consequent hardiness, never attained in the old way. We must make an animal healthy to make him hardy.

Single eyes are prepared in several ways, but

they are substantially alike. Some are cut with an inch or so of wood above the bud; some

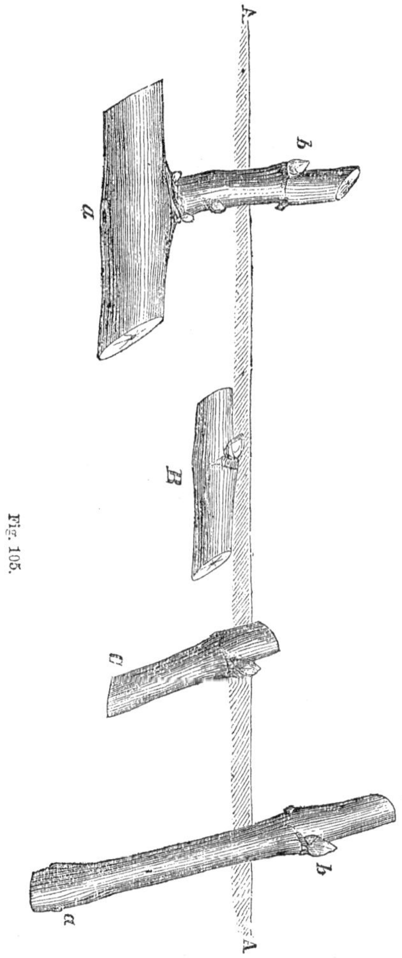

Fig. 105.

with the wood below the bud; and others,

again, with the wood equally divided on each side of the bud. Some place them in the soil upright; some at an angle; and others horizontally. Various forms and modes are shown in *Fig.* 105. When the cane on which the bud is growing is large, it is usual to split it lengthwise through the middle. It is well to prepare the buds a week or two before they are used, and pack them in moist sand or moss. The cut will then have become dry, and be ready to "callus;" the eyes, indeed, by cutting early, may be callused before they are placed in the propagating bed, and a little time thus gained. The eyes will root a little more readily if the bark is removed; but this is so troublesome, and the gain so small, that it can not be thought of on a large scale.

At the proper time, say from the middle of February to the middle of March, the eyes are to be placed in the propagating bed. Two or three modes obtain here: some place a single eye in a very small pot, and plunge the pots in the beds; others place the eyes about an inch apart in large pots; and still others place the eyes from one to two inches apart in the propagating beds. The eyes will root most readily in pots.

Just here we must stop a moment, and ascertain what are the conditions needed to convert these eyes into strong and healthy vines. We want a clean, sharp sand for the sake of its porousness; one of the largest and most successful propagators that we know is so particular as to wash his sand thoroughly clean. We want a suitable bed in which to place this sand. This may be made of planed or rough boards, so put together as to form an open box from three to five feet wide, and about one foot deep, the joints in the bottom being covered with thin slips or laths to prevent the sand from running through. This bed should run along the sides of the house, and also through the middle, when the house is wide enough. The top of the bed should come nearly up to the sill of the house, and be supported by posts and cross ties. The height of the bed, however, in reference to the sill, must be regulated by the form of the house. The pipes or tanks for supplying heat must run under the bed. If pipes are used, then all the space under the beds must be boarded in for a hot-air chamber, with doors at short intervals for regulating the heat. If a hot water tank is used, no boarding in will be needed, for the beds will rest immediately on the tank. Next, sashes must be provided for covering the beds. With a proper glass structure covering these appurtenances, we have all that is needed for propagating the best class of vines, except the knowledge, skill, and care of the propagator, which are brought into almost unceasing requisition.

All things being ready, the sand is put in the bed from three to six inches deep, and in this the eyes are put from one to two inches apart, the sand pressed firmly about them, and gently watered. If the eyes are put in pots, the pots must be plunged in the sand. The sashes are then placed over the beds, and the boiler fired up. The sashes should be used chiefly for shade, and should therefore, during most of the time, be kept partly raised. On clear days the sashes should be shaded during the middle part of the day, by laying paper on them, which should be removed as the sun declines, and kept off entirely during cloudy weather, the object being to admit as much light as possible to the infant plants, but not the direct rays of the sun till they have become able to bear them. If the sashes are kept shut down, the plants are apt to damp off. This matter will need constant attention.

The next condition to be provided is a warm bed for the eyes to root in, and a cooler, but moist and uniform atmosphere for the tops to grow in. The heat for the bottom is obtained by closing all the doors of the hot-air chamber, which prevents the heat from the pipes from escaping into the house. A good thermometer must be used here, and strict attention paid to the fires, so that the heat may not at any time become too great. The bottom heat may go as high as 70° or 80° with safety, but from 60° to 70° should be observed as nearly as may be. The temperature of the house should be kept about ten degrees below the bottom heat. This is done by regulating the heat from the pipes, and opening the ventilators of the house. As the season advances, this matter will need a good deal of attention. Changes in the weather must be watched for and provided against, and every precaution taken to secure and maintain great uniformity in all the conditions named as necessary to success.

Now, let us see what takes place in the bed. In a few days the buds will begin to swell, and then growth will begin; but no roots have yet been formed. After the first start, the motion for a while is scarcely apparent: the cuts are "callusing," and the infant plant is being nourished by the small amount of matter previously laid up. In from eight to twelve days the process of "callusing" will be pretty well completed, and soon thereafter the roots will begin to appear. When these are about an inch long, the eyes are taken from the propagating bed, and put in small pots in a good fine soil, prepared for the purpose. They have heretofore been shaded, and for a little while the shading must be continued, when the plants should be exposed to the light just as fast as they are able to bear and profit by it, and no more. They must now for a while be watched constantly, and not allowed to want for any thing. Water must be given just at the moment it is wanted, and then in sufficient quantity to go through the pot. Special care must be taken not to check root action. In two or three weeks the small pots will be well filled with roots, and the plants must be put in larger pots, and staked. When these pots get filled with roots, the plants must be changed to others still larger, and so re-potted from time to time as they need it, until at last they occupy pots holding gallons. The pots must at no time be allowed to get so full of roots as to check the growth of the plants: there must be an uninterrupted growth of top and bottom. In the mean time, the plants must be carefully watered, tied up, athallized, and gradually hardened by exposure and the admission of more air daily.

In the best arranged places the plants, when sufficiently advanced, are moved to unheated houses, with movable top sashes, which are more or less opened or entirely removed, as may best secure the health and ripening of the cane and roots. Sometimes the plants are turned out of the pots and planted in the borders of this house. At other times they are planted in the open air. There are a great many advantages gained by the use of the "hardening off" house, as it may be called, chief among which are these: the plants can at any moment be secured against sudden and unfavorable changes of weather, and the ill consequences that always follow such changes; and if the season proves short, with early frosts, the sashes can be put on, and two or three weeks gained in this way for the perfect ripening of the plant. These advantages can scarcely be overestimated by those who buy plants. It is very seldom that they are secured by open air propagation of any kind. *Fig.*

106 is a good example of plants made from single eyes.

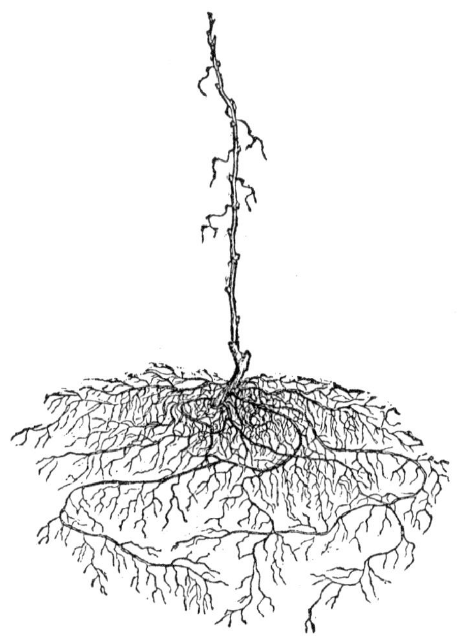

Fig. 106.

Single Eyes in Hot Beds.—Very good plants may be made by placing single eyes and two-eyed cuttings in a common hot bed frame.

The frame of the bed must be made to accommodate the size of the sash, which may be of any convenient size. A sash four feet wide and four and a half long we have found to be the most convenient of all that we have used. It is usual to make them long and narrow, and such can generally be bought ready made. The front of the frame should be about a foot high, and the back from four to six inches higher than the front, according to the width of the frame; in other words, there should be just slope enough to shed water. It is a very common mistake to make the slope quite steep. The frame may be made of common rough boards, or it may be made of worked boards, and painted, and put together with screws and hooks, so as to be taken apart: there are vari-

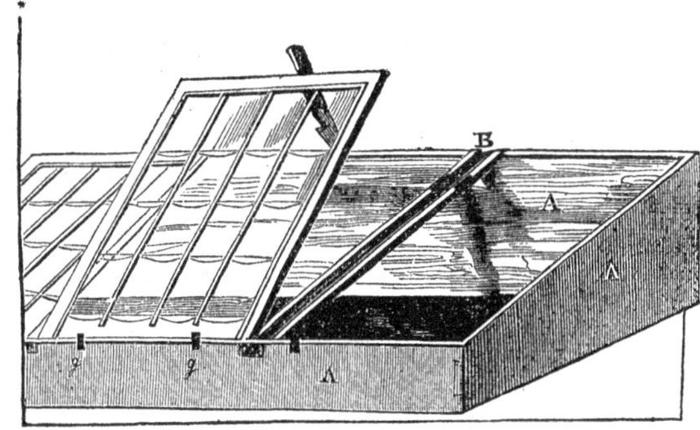

Fig. 107.

ous ways of making them. A good idea of the frame and sash, with its fastenings, etc., may be got from *Fig.* 107.

A covering of some kind must now be provided to protect the plants at night, and prevent the loss of heat. For this purpose, straw mats are commonly used, as they are convenient and easily made; boards, blankets, carpets, etc., are also used; but the best thing we have tried is a light frame made of laths and filled with straw, and fixed to the back of the bed with a bolt hinge, so that it may not only lie flat on the sash, but be moved to any angle. When placed upright, it forms a good protection from northerly winds. It is in common use among the French, who generally weave the straw together in mats, which are stiffened by wooden slips on the edges, and at intervals through the middle, if necessary.

Hot beds are commonly made by using long and coarse manure for the heating material; but we must alter and vary the material in this case, in order to produce uniform and good results. For our purpose, dead leaves are the best material. Manure alone makes too strong a heat. Equal parts of leaves and horse manure make a very good and durable heating material; but leaves alone make the "sweetest," most even, as well as most durable bed, one five feet thick sometimes retaining its heat for a year. If leaves alone are used, they should be gathered in the fall or early winter, and placed loosely together, and under cover, if convenient; or boards may be laid over them to keep off snow and rain. It matters but little what kind of leaves are used; they may be gathered indiscriminately in the woods.

About two weeks before making the bed the leaves should be prepared as follows: make a layer of leaves about two feet thick, of any convenient size, and just moisten them with water from a watering pot, if they are dry; they must then be beaten down pretty firmly, and another layer added, and treated in the same way. The layers are repeated till the heap is finished, when boards should be so laid on the top as to shed rain. In from six to ten days the heap will begin to warm.

Having the materials all ready, the bed should be started somewhere from the first to the middle of March, or even as late as the first of April. Select a dry spot, where surface water will flow off readily. Cart the leaves to the spot, and proceed as follows: mark out the size of the bed, which should run lengthwise east and west, and be two or three feet wider than the frame; then spread a layer of leaves about a foot thick, and beat them down firmly; if they are dry, moisten them with warm water before beating them down. Repeat layer after layer in the same way, beating each one down firmly, till the bed is raised three or four feet high. Unless the mass of leaves are put firmly together, it will not only require considerable time for them to heat, but the heat will be low and not uniform; and they will not heat at all unless they are moist. These two particulars must therefore be attended to carefully. If leaves and manure are used together, they must be well mixed. The operation should be performed quickly, in order that the small amount of heat already in the mass may not be lost.

Having laid up the bed of leaves, the frame is put on so as to set level. For raising vegetables, etc., the frame is placed with its front to the south; but for our purpose we shall place the front to the north. Leaves must then be packed around the outside of the frame up to the top. Next, clean sand must be put in to the depth of about six inches, leveled off neatly, and the sashes put on. All these things must be done as rapidly as possible, in order that there may be no unnecessary loss of heat.

The sashes must be left on for a few days before the eyes are put in, in order that the sand may become uniformly warmed. In consequence of the sashes facing the north, the sun will have comparatively little effect upon the heat of the bed; still it will be necessary to raise the sashes a little on warm days when the sun is out; they must not be raised too high nor kept up too long just now. In ventilating a hot bed, always raise the top or side opposite the point whence the wind comes. In this way the wind will never blow directly into the frame. As the sun goes down the sashes must be well covered, and the covering removed when the sun is well up in the morning. This is a general rule to be observed every day.

When the sand becomes warm, single eyes or two-eyed cuttings may be put in precisely as was directed for the propagating bed; there is much advantage, however, in hot-beds, in putting the eyes in pots, and plunging the pots in the sand. *Cold* water must never be used.

The frame will now need considerable care and watching. The same conditions, as nearly as possible, should obtain here as in the propagating house. Ventilation must be so adjusted as to preserve a rather low, moist atmosphere above the plants, without wasting the heat of the bed. The sashes must therefore be raised from a mere crack to several inches, according to the state of the weather, and the advanced condition of the plants; but the sashes must be raised at the top, bottom, or either of the sides, according as it may be opposite the point whence the wind comes. Water, also, must be faithfully applied, but only when it is wanted, and no more than is wanted. The wants of the plants in these two particulars must be carefully and constantly watched and ministered to.

No very precise rules can be given for shading and ventilation. We have several times stated the importance of having a uniform moist atmosphere for the young plants to grow in, and it seems hardly necessary to repeat it here; yet it is a point that must be constantly borne in mind. The importance of a strong light without the direct rays of the sun has also been alluded to: it is the colorific and not calorific rays that are wanted. Ventilation and shading must have reference to these two points. If the sashes face the south, as is almost universally the case, the sun heats the frame early, and by mid-day it becomes almost seething. The plants would speedily die if left to such conditions, and it therefore becomes necessary not only to ventilate and shade early, but to exercise the utmost vigilance all through the day to regulate the ventilation so as not to reduce either the heat or the moisture below what is necessary for the wants of the plant. Each of these must be nicely adjusted to meet the changes that are constantly occurring. Painting with white lead, sanding, etc., are usually resorted to; but a better plan is given below.

By our arrangement of making the sashes face the north, the necessary conditions are obtained with much less labor, and with a much greater degree of uniformity; and this latter point is of the utmost importance. Not having to battle constantly with the direct heating rays of the sun, less ventilation is needed, and the proper degree of heat and moisture is more easily and uniformly maintained. We have found the labor to be reduced fully one half, and the success increased much beyond that amount; besides which, the plants are of a better character. A good plan for shading is to make a light frame, of the size of the sash, and cover it with thin brown muslin. By resting one end of the frame on the sash, it may be adjusted at different inclinations, so as to afford more or less shade to the plants without obstructing the light entirely. If a frame of this kind is not used, newspapers may be spread on the sash at the times needed, and secured there by laying strips of board on them. They should be kept on no longer than is necessary. If the reader bears in mind that a constantly uniform moisture is necessary for the young plants, he will by this time be able to secure it by a proper adjustment of shading and ventilation, being careful not to carry the latter too far.

The strong light in which the plants have been growing will make "hardening off" an easy process. This should be begun as soon as the plants are well rooted, by admitting a little more air from time to time, thus preparing them for full exposure to the sun and air. When rooted, the plants should be separated and put in small pots, in soil prepared for the purpose, and the pots placed in the frame. For a few days after this they must be shaded from the mid-day sun, and the sashes kept a little closer shut; at the end of which time the admission of air must be daily increased, and the sashes finally removed, as the weather, by this time, will be sufficiently warm to continue the growth without the aid of a frame. The plants may be shifted from time to time into larger pots, and thus grown during the season; but they will become stunted in pots unless protected in some way. A better plan, therefore, is to plant them in nursery rows, in well prepared soil, or to plant them where they are to remain. These directions, in connection with what has heretofore been said, will enable one to grow good plants in hot-bed frames, from single eyes; very much better, indeed, than any that can be grown in the open air.

By beginning later in the season, eyes may be started in a cold frame, which is simply a frame and sash without any heating material. The plants, however, will not be so good, since they will not make as good roots, nor have as long a season to grow in. The cold frame is made as follows: a dry spot is selected as before, and the ground spaded up and leveled off. The frame is then set on the ground, four or five inches of sand put in, and it is ready for use. The treatment of the plants is substantially the same as for a hot bed.

We have said that vines can be made better and cheaper in regular propagating houses than in the ordinary way in the open air; but there are certain adaptations or arrangements, by means of which those who have time, and delight in such employment, (and there are many such,) may grow tolerably good vines; better than can be grown without their aid. A description of one such has been furnished us by a friend, and we give it in his own words. It afforded him much pleasure in times past, and we have no doubt will yield a similar pleasure to any one who may try it. It is as follows:

"*Domestic Propagation.*—Good vines may be produced with very little outlay, except that of constancy of attention, by any one who will unfailingly observe the following very simple directions. We will suppose the ground already well prepared, and so thoroughly mixed together as to be strictly one homogeneous mass suitable for inviting and entertaining the roots of young plants. Have in readiness three pine box boards about one foot wide and thirteen feet long, or of any other convenient length. Nail three battens, about two inches wide and eighteen inches long, across one of them, placing one near each end, and the other near the middle, leaving the ends to project equally on each side.

"Dig a little trench, three inches deep, with neat perpendicular sides. Set one of the boards on edge in the trench, at its southerly or front side, and drive three little stakes into the ground on the trench side to keep it there. Have the tops of the stakes a little lower than the upper edge of the board, through which drive one nail into each of the stakes. Drive three stakes in a row close to the back of the trench, placing them like those already driven in front; but these are to be set close against the back, to keep the rear board at the surface. Set the other board on edge, the lower edge resting on the surface of the ground, and nail as before. Shut up the ends, and place the board with the battens upon the top, and the house is made. Two pieces with notches taken out to form the slots for the end battens should be nailed upon the upper edge of each of the side boards. (See *Fig.* 108.)

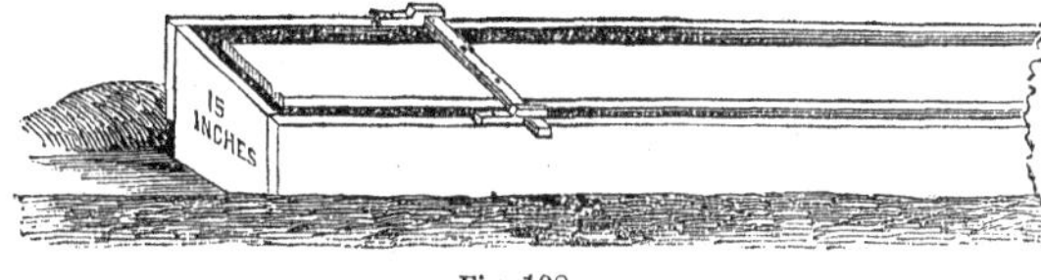

Fig. 108.

"The room inside is fourteen inches wide, to be divided for three rows of cuttings, the first to be set two inches from the front board, the next two inches from the back of the trench, and the third in the middle. The cuttings may be six inches apart in the rows. Good two-eyed cuttings of the free rooting kinds will grow with a great degree of certainty in this simple arrangement, and make good plants for the nursery in one season, and very good plants for the garden or vineyard the next, under the following management:

"Plant as just directed. As early in the morning as the atmosphere begins to be warmed, take off the cover, placing it bottom side up back of the 'house,' to let the under side dry. At about eight o'clock put on the cover, to remain till four or five, if the day should be very hot and dry, or windy. The state of the weather must also regulate the time of taking it off in the morning. A little before sunset it is to be put on for the night. The cover should be placed so that the opening on each side of it will be equal; that is, about an inch and a half each, if the board is one foot wide, which is about the

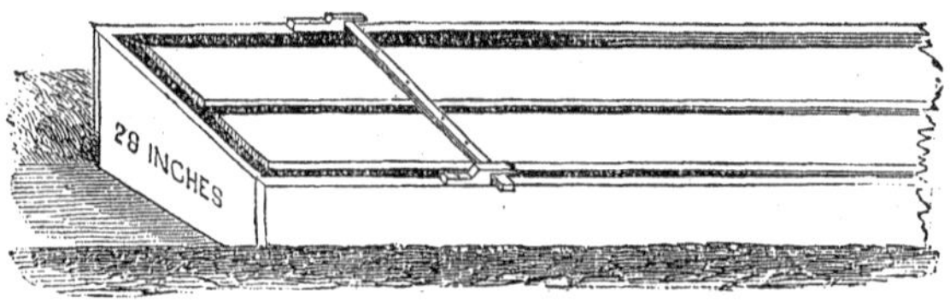

Fig. 109.

right proportion. Notches in the battens may regulate this with certainty.

"This arrangement may be continued to any length desired, or may be multiplied indefinitely. It may also be made larger for the production of stronger plants, as represented in the illustration. (See *Fig.* 109.) In this the number will not be increased in proportion to the size, but the plants may be made much better. Every length of thirteen feet in the former will receive about seventy-five cuttings at the distances named, and about one hundred in the latter. In the last, good vines for vineyard planting may be made in one season. The first of April, in the latitude of New-York, is generally about the time for setting the cuttings.

"The conditions of success in management are, ground always moist, and never wet; water not permitted to remain on the leaves for want of ventilation, and no exposure to strong drying winds, but careful increase of light and sun as the plants are able to bear it. The space of an inch and a half at each side of the cover will afford sufficient light to maintain healthiness of the leaves during the early stage, if the most advantage that can be had with safety is taken of the early morning and evening sun, without letting in enough sunshine to injure. After the plants have become pretty well rooted, the covers may be put on with the battens under, which will nearly double the light. One hour of sunshine that can be borne without injury is worth several hours of shade for giving increase and strength to the plants.

"The careful propagator meets with no accidents, but one act of negligence may be fatal to the season's hopes. One of the first conditions to success is good, well-ripened wood, and that from strong vines, well grown in houses, is much the best. One good cutting is worth more than several poor ones. It is only very good ones that are fit to use for this purpose, and these are much less abundant than those that are tolerably good or poor. The watering should be done from a watering pot with a fine rose; large streams act unfavorably upon the soil. It is most properly done in the morning, in the early part of theseason, and in the evening, after hot weather is established. The quantity should be sufficient to keep the soil *always* moist through its whole depth, but it should never be applied when not needed. In very drying weather, if the plants begin to droop during the day, and water seems to be called for, do not hesitate to apply it from fear of injury in consequence of the sun shining.

"This arrangement is commended to all of both sexes, who feel themselves willing to give the requisite attention for three or four months, and who find enjoyment in observing and co-working with nature in her most interesting operations. Such will find the interest and delight constantly increasing with increase of knowledge and experience, and those who desire it may reap a handsome pecuniary reward for their leisure hours."

Single Eyes in the Open Air.—It is sometimes asked whether the vine can not be propagated from single eyes in the open air; and the fact that the French have within a few years succeeded in doing so, seems to have given some interest to the question. About fifteen years ago we tried the experiment in a very thorough manner. A bed four by ten was prepared, and eyes from about a dozen different kinds of the native grape were put in, but the result was far from satisfactory. The experiment was repeated several times more carefully, and recourse had to watering, mulching, partial shading, etc., with much more gratifying results. Some kinds rooted much better than others. The constant care and labor necessary to success were ten-fold greater than are demanded in growing eyes under glass, and the results so greatly inferior, that we have not repeated the experiment since. An enterprising nurseryman, however, at our request, tried the experiment three years afterward, but his success was far less than our own. It is safe to conclude, therefore, that the native vine can not be successfully, or at least profitably, grown from eyes in the open air. Because it has been done in France, it does not follow that it can be done here. The climate of the two countries is entirely different.

CHAPTER XVI.

PROPAGATION—CONTINUED.

Cuttings.—If we succeeded in giving the reader a clear idea of how plants are made from single eyes, he will readily understand how they are made from cuttings. These consist of pieces of cane having from two to five eyes or buds. A cutting of two eyes is seen at the right, *Fig.* 105. Cuttings are prepared by making a clean cut close under the lowest bud, which is removed, as is also the one above it when there are three. The cane is cut half an inch above the top bud, the slope of the cut being on the side opposite the bud. Only thoroughly ripe canes should be used for cuttings, and those of medium size are best. Cuttings of two eyes are sometimes grown under glass. They are placed in the propagating bed, with the upper bud an inch or so above the surface, as shown on the right in *Fig.* 105. Their management is then the same as for single eyes. In small, short-jointed wood, the bud should be just above the surface.

Cuttings, however, are generally grown in the open air, and some kind of preparation is necessary to secure a good degree of success. The best soil is one that is light and porous, and at all times free from standing water. If not porous, it can be made so by the addition of sand. It should be worked deep, to insure against the ill effects of drought. It can hardly be made too mellow and fine. The cuttings having been prepared as above, are to be planted as follows: stretch a line, and along this line put in the cuttings about one foot apart; they are often put in much closer, but this is close enough. As they are put in, the soil must be pressed against them firmly. This is particularly necessary with two-eyed cuttings, to prevent them from being displaced; but, aside from this, it is necessary to insure ready rooting. If the soil is not quite mellow, a dibble should be used for making the holes. The top eye of the cutting should be about an inch above the surface of the soil. Having completed one row, stretch the line two feet from it, and plant another, and so continue till all are planted. These distances are greater than are sometimes observed, but none too great where good plants and much success are expected. Indeed, if they are not to be transplanted, they should be three or four feet apart. No weeds must be allowed to grow; the hoe should be used before the weeds are fairly out of the seed leaf.

The cuttings should be put in as soon as the ground can be thoroughly worked. When warm weather fully sets in, but not before, the ground may be mulched with straw, having first been well weeded. In case of drought, mulching will be found a great benefit. If the ground is not mulched, it should be repeatedly hoed to keep the weeds down, and make it mellow. With watchful care, you may expect a fair proportion of tolerably good plants. We have seen acres of cuttings that did not produce a plant fit to sell at the end of the year. It often becomes necessary to transplant them, and grow them a second, and even a third year, to make salable plants of them.

Layers.—Though this is the easiest and most certain method of propagating the vine, it requires some knowledge, if not skill, to perform it in such a manner as to produce really good plants: poor ones are very common. The mother plant requires some kind of preparation, and should have age, before being tasked to produce plants in this way. No vine should be expected to produce good fruit and layers at the same time; we may go further, and say that no vine can produce good fruit and layers for any length of time together. We say this for the benefit of those who think they can persist in layering their vineyards without injury to the fruit or the plant.

A layer consists of a portion of cane laid in the ground while still attached to the mother plant, where it remains while taking root, and until the end of the season, when it is detached. The vine from which the layers are to be taken should be at least three or four years old, and the canes should have been well ripened the preceding year. The canes layered on the same plant should always bear a small proportion to those not layered; for example, a plant of three canes should not have more than one layered. A layered plant is shown in *Fig.* 110 The soil around the mother plant should be made fine and mellow. A trench is to be made some ten or twelve inches wide, and six inches deep, but it must not approach nearer than two feet to the mother plant, to avoid damaging the roots, or having them interfere with the layer. The cane to be layered should be cut some four or five feet long. When the buds have broken, the cane should be laid carefully in the trench, secured there by pegs, and all the lower buds rubbed off. Of the remaining upper buds, from two to four may be selected for making the young plants, the interval between the selected buds being as great as possible. When the young canes have grown about six inches, a couple of inches of soil must be heaped about each of them in such a way as to leave six or eight inches of the layered cane uncovered between each of the growing canes, which must remain uncovered for a week or so; the object being to cause the roots to grow about the young canes, while the uncovered portion has none. The root action, in this case, is concentrated upon given points, and produces better results; and in the fall there is a naked portion of cane that may be cut off without destroying any roots. An inch or so of soil must be added as the young canes progress in growth, till the trench is finally filled. Stakes should be put in at the beginning to tie the canes to as they grow, as shown in Fig. 110. *a*, *a*, show where layers have been taken from the plant in former

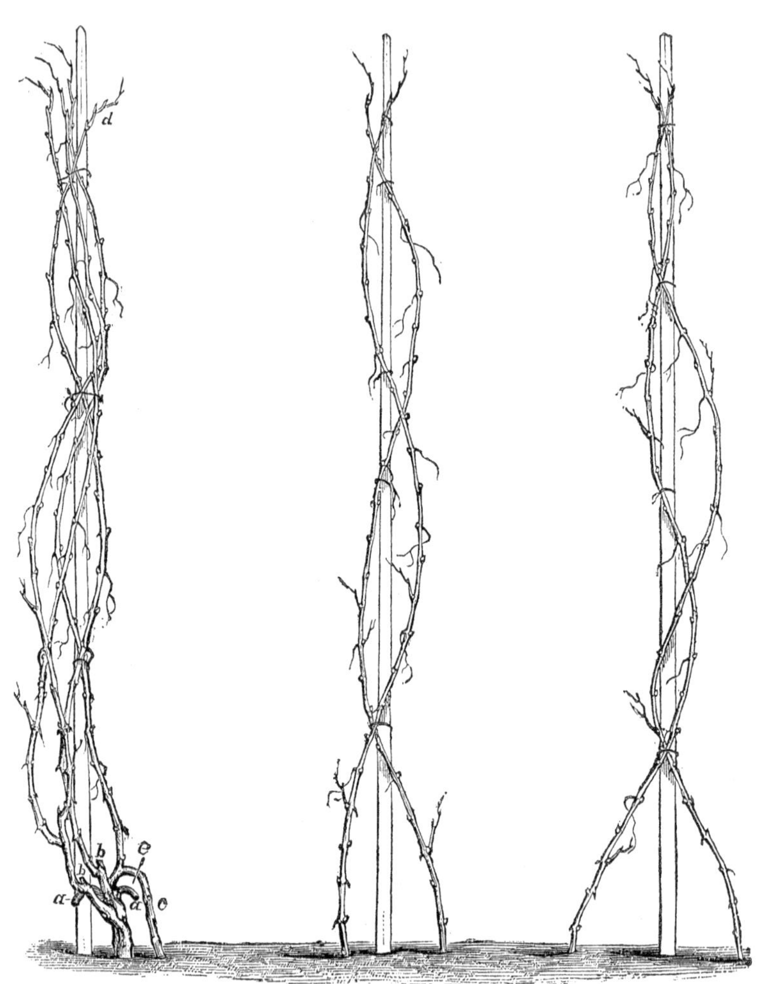

Fig. 110.

years. *e* shows where the present layer is to be detached. The thallons should be athallized in the usual manner.

This is quite a different thing from laying a cane in the ground, and letting all the buds grow that will; but it is the way to make good layers. Not more than four plants should ever be taken from one layer, and two or three will generally be much better. This number can not be exceeded with any hope of making good, well-rooted plants. The plants must be taken up in the fall, and divided by cutting off the unrooted portion of the old cane.

Grafting.—The native vine is sometimes, though not often, propagated by grafting. This process for the vine possesses very few of the advantages it has for the apple, pear, and some other fruits. There is seldom any need for it, for we can get fruit quite as soon by planting. In the green-house or grapery, vine grafting succeeds very well; but in the vineyard the cases of failure greatly exceed those of success. The union between the stock and graft is always imperfect; hence it is best to perform the operation under ground, where the graft will take root, and become an independent plant

There are several modes of grafting the vine,

two of the best of which we shall illustrate and describe. They are both performed under ground. The earth is removed from around the stock of the plant, so as to lay it bare some six or eight inches, as shown at A in *Fig.* 111. The

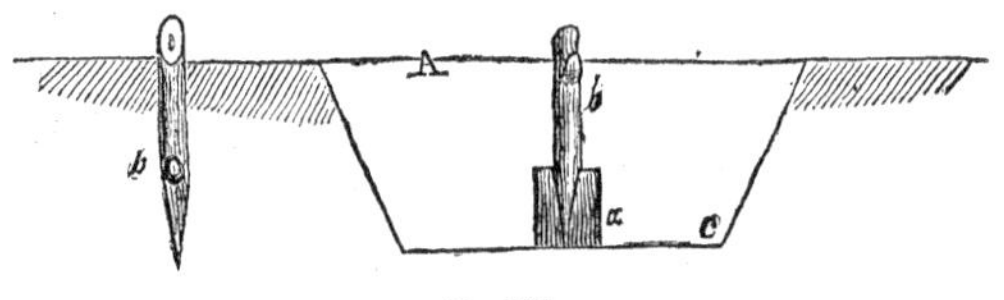

Fig. 111.

stock is cut square off four or five inches beneath the surface. The graft is then prepared by cutting it wedge-shaped at the bottom. It should have two buds, one of which should be between the wedge, as shown at *b* on the left of the figure: the other bud being on the opposite side, is not seen. The split through the middle of the stock should be made with a thin-bladed knife, and held open with a thin-pointed stick while the graft is inserted in its place, so that the bark of the stock and graft meet on the outside edges. The operation completed is shown in the engraving. A strip of bast should be bound around the stock sufficiently firm to keep the graft in its place.

The success of the operation depends very much upon keeping the graft in its place; great care, therefore, should be used to prevent it from being displaced. The hole should be filled up very carefully, and without pressing the soil against the graft. It should be well protected from disturbance of any kind. About a foot from the plant put in sticks at such an angle that their ends will meet over the plant, and about a foot above it; tie the ends together, and over the sticks put a piece of oiled paper, muslin, or matting. If done right, it will look like a miniature tent, and protect the young plant from sunshine and weather as well as animals. It should be removed when the plant has got fairly started. If the graft is inserted in the fall, it will be well protected by heaping sand over it in addition to the above.

In the next method the grafting is also done under the surface. The cut, however, is less simple, but may be understood by examining *Fig.* 112. The graft is first cut square off at the

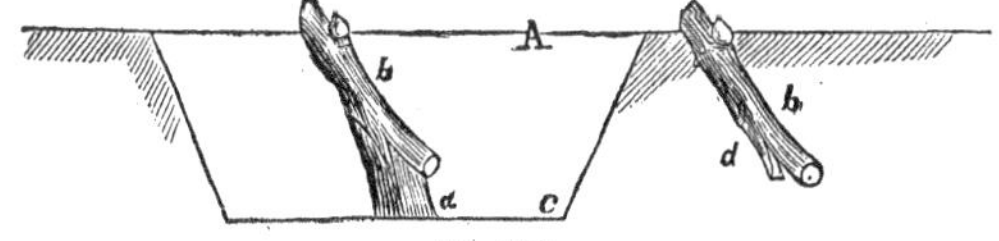

Fig 112.

bottom. A thin chip is then pared from one side to the bottom, *d*, and the knife next entered at the edge of the bottom, and drawn up, so as to cut a thin tongue where the chip was taken off, as seen at *d* on the right of the figure. The stock is cut nearly at an angle of forty-five degrees, and split through the center at right angles with the sloping cut, and the upper edge of the slit rounded off. The tongue is then inserted in the split, so as to cover the surface of the angular cut on both sides of the split. The engraving shows the manner of doing this very plainly. The graft should be tied in its place with strips of bast or cotton twine. The operation completed, the hole is to be filled up, and the plant protected in the manner above described. The portion of the graft projecting beyond the stock allows the graft to take root more readily than the first plan, and in this respect it is better; but not being so simple, is less likely to be well done, and its advantages, in consequence, mostly lost.

There are several other methods of grafting the vine, some of which answer the purpose of amusement; but there are none better than those given above, and few as good.

Something may be said in regard to the best time for grafting. It may be done in the fall, early in the spring, or after the vines have begun growing. It has been successfully done at all these times, and so it has failed at all of them. There can be no doubt that success is affected to a considerable degree by the weather, climate, and condition of the vine. In the grapery success is quite common; in the vineyard it is quite the contrary. This, and other circumstances, would seem to indicate certain hygrometric conditions as influencing success. At one time it will be highly gratifying; at others quite discouraging. All that is certain is, that grafting the grape in the vineyard is an uncertain thing. Far north, fall grafting is not advisable; where the climate is mild, however, it may be practiced with tolerable success. Dr. Massie's published experiments, conducted about six years ago, went to show that the success of fall grafting depended measurably upon the kind of winter that followed, notwithstanding all the care that was taken to protect the grafts by various appliances. That is precisely our own experience. To conclude, graft in the fall in mild latitudes, or in early spring, as may be most convenient, and do not expect any large measure of success in either case; but if you fail, do not mourn over it, for your loss has been small. Grafting the native grape is at best but an amusement, and should be so regarded. In our climate, it will probably never be reduced to a certainty; and this is the less to be regretted in a plant that produces its fruit so soon from an eye or a cutting.

Seeds—Hybridizing.—It seems hardly necessary to remark that new varieties are produced from seed alone. It has been thought by some that we should look chiefly to hybrids between the native and foreign grape for any marked improvement in the quality of the former, while others have doubted the possibility of getting a hybrid between them. We believe it is possible, though quite difficult; but we are by no means convinced that it is desirable, or that we shall gain what we wish. The Allen may be taken as an example. This presents good evidence of being a true hybrid. The fruit is excellent, but the vine is tender and susceptible, and withers away when exposed to the force of our trying climate: in this respect yielding to the fate that has always overtaken one of its parents. No fact in grape culture is better demonstrated than that the foreign grape is not adapted to our climate. It has cost us many thousands of dollars to prove the fact, and that ought to satisfy us. Is it wise, then, to seek an infusion of blood from a source that has been proved to be constitutionally unfitted to our wants? Can we produce a hybrid that will not possess this constitutional failing? We think not. It must appear, more or less, in the whole race produced in this way. If we get enough of the goodness of the foreign grape to make itself apparent in the seedling, we shall just as certainly get enough of the evil to make the goodness of little or no use to us. The characteristics of one parent or the other will, as a rule, predominate in any hybrids that may be raised in this way, though we are not unmindful that crosses, where both parents possess the requisite hardiness, may, in time, be produced that shall unite the most desirable qualities of both; but, aside from the remoteness of the possibility, it may well be doubted whether such crosses will, after all, be so well suited to our climate as to possess any great value for general cultivation.

But we may be pointed to Rogers's Hybrids as militating against this view of the subject. We think they fail to reach it; or, if it be admitted that they do, they are only examples of the native parent predominating in a very remarkable manner, and thus support our view. But there are good grounds for questioning the hybrid character of these grapes. A very critical examination of the wood, leaves, and fruit, fails to detect the foreign element in either. They possess, on the contrary, all the peculiar characteristics of the native grape in wood, leaves, and fruit. The flesh of all of them is more or less "buttery," like the Concord, though in several the fibrous center ripens much better than in the Concord, and, it may be added, they are much better grapes. In a very few there is a little of the meaty consistency seen in the Diana, and these begin to be vinous in their flavor, and in quality are the best of these seedlings. But in all this we can not detect the mixture of any foreign element. The experiments of Mr. Rogers are exceedingly interesting, not because he has failed or succeeded in producing hybrid grapes, but because he has demonstrated that the wild grape, through its seedlings, is susceptible of a very high degree of improvement. That is the source to which we must look for any valuable results. We would not say one word to discourage him in his efforts to produce hybrids, but would suggest that he also use some of our best native grapes of a vinous character in his experiments. He will find less trouble in fertilizing, and produce far more valuable results.

To hybridize the grape is no easy matter; yet there are scores of people who think they have succeeded, and the country is likely to be flooded with their hybrids. There is one man, indeed, who claims to have discovered a simple way of hybridizing the grape, which makes the process *positively* certain: he has learned the "signs" by which we may know that hybridization has been really accomplished. This man sent to a friend for some Black Hamburgh pollen. This friend being somewhat of a wag, sent him instead some pollen of the spinach. On being written to for the result, the reply came that "It had taken beautifully!" "There was no mistake about it!" We mention this circumstance to show how easily one can deceive himself in supposing that he has hybridized the grape.

The theory of hybridizing is simple enough, and easily understood; but its practice in the case of the grape is not without its difficulties. There are two important parts of flowers, the male and female, the latter being the pistil, and the former the stamens; the last bear at their ends the anthers, which furnish the pollen. It is the pollen from the anthers, falling on the pistil, which effects fertilization, and the consequent production of seed or fruit. To produce hybrids and varieties, pollen is taken from the anthers of one species or variety, and applied to the pistil of another species or variety. But, in order to secure fertilization by the pollen used, the stamens must be removed from the flower fertilized before the anthers have shed their pollen. It becomes necessary, therefore, to cut off the anthers some time before the pollen is ripe. In some kinds of flowers it becomes difficult to do this, since fertilization takes place before the flower expands, and the difficulty is greatly increased when the flower is so small that it is almost impossible to handle it.

The flower of the grape, among others, is difficult to fertilize artificially in the open air. The first thing to be done is to remove the stamens from the flower to be fertilized, and this must be done some time before it expands, or sheds its envelope, or the flower will be fertilized in the natural way, and it is never fertilized a second time. It is next absolutely necessary to protect the flower, not only from the access of insects, but also from the air, or the pistil will be fertilized by the pollen that is always floating about the vineyard at this time. When the flower has opened on the vine that it is proposed to cross with, the pollen must be collected from it on a fine camel's hair pencil, and brushed over the pistil of the flower previously prepared. This is a critical moment; for just as you remove the covering from the prepared flower the pollen floating in the air may rush in and fertilize the pistil before you can touch it, and thus your purpose will be defeated. The fact is, there can be no certainty about hybridizing the grape unless the vine is shut up by itself, and all flowers removed from it except those to be fertilized. Hence it is that many think they have raised hybrids when they really have not, and it is nothing but the imagination that sees in them any thing of a hybrid character. The hybrid business is being rather overdone.

Carefully conducted experiments in raising seedlings and hybrids should be encouraged, even to the extent, as elsewhere remarked, of extending the protection of the law to all plants raised in this way. Proprietorship, in this respect, should be as absolute as it is in regard to any other kind of property. If this were so, it would make inoperative the excuse often given for "coddling" seedling plants to a degree that renders any real knowledge of their hardiness and period of ripening almost an impossibility.

It may be remarked, in conclusion, that seedlings from our cultivated varieties vary greatly in their character. The great majority of them will be inferior to the parent, showing a marked tendency to go back to the woods; some will resemble the parent so closely as to be scarcely, if at all, distinguishable from it, being, in fact, simply reproductions; and very rarely one may be found superior to the parent. Seedlings just like their parents are getting to be quite common; but we can not perceive any good reason for multiplying kinds in this way. A seedling ought not only to be better than its parent, or than other kinds, but also have some distinctive characteristic. Seedlings, again, will often differ broadly from their parents in color. Those from the Isabella, for example, are not unfrequently green in color instead of purple. It is characteristic of varieties to vary in this way.

CHAPTER XVII.

ADDITIONAL REMARKS ON PLANTING.

Additional Remarks on Planting.—The directions already given are intended for general application, and will meet the requirements of all ordinary cases; but there are here and there peculiarities and extremes which are best treated by themselves; for we could not, in planting a single vine, stop to explain exceptions to the general rule, without greatly endangering the clearness of the subject. There are certain conditions of soil which call for exceptional treatment in regard to the depth at which the roots of the vine should be placed. A very heavy clay, under certain circumstances, may require the roots to be quite near the surface, while a gravelly, stony, shaly, or other light or very porous soil, may require them to be below the usual depth.

There are two quite common and fatal mistakes: one consists in planting too deep, and the other too shallow, and it would be difficult to say which has destroyed most vines and trees. If vines are planted too deep, they become enfeebled, and are winter killed; if they are planted too shallow, the frost heaves the crowns above the surface, and they are also winter killed. The vines are then said to be tender, and the variety, in consequence, suffers in reputation; whereas the cause of winter killing often lies, not in the tenderness of the vine, but in the want of knowledge or judgment in the planter. There are other causes of winter killing, it is true, not related to planting, but which, as we have remarked elsewhere, are, to a good degree, within the control of the vineyardist.

A very common fault in planting consists in not placing the *crown* of the plant at the necessary depth. We have seen many hundreds of vines with the middle and ends of the roots six inches below the surface, while the crown was scarcely two. The winter often kills the roots of such vines, but it first strikes the crown. Now, it should be borne in mind, that when the roots (in this book at least) are directed to be covered four or six inches deep, it is the roots proceeding immediately from the crown that are to be covered four or six inches, and not the ends of the roots; the last, when the work is well done, will be a couple of inches deeper than the crown. The crown of the plant, if the hand is taken from it before the soil is worked firmly about it to the depth of two or three inches, will commonly spring up, often two or three inches; and when the ground becomes settled, the crown of the plant will be found within two or three inches of the surface. We have found this to be very common, especially where vines are planted in large numbers, and consequently in much haste. Thus it is often the case that those who think they have planted ten or twelve inches deep, have really not planted more than six or eight, while those who think they have planted five or six inches, have not planted more than three or four. It seems to be very little understood, also, that the soil will settle without carrying the plant down with it; and this constitutes another element of deception, for which allowance is seldom made.

These grave errors may be easily avoided by observing the following practice: when the hole or trench is dug, press the soil down firmly, but without packing it; this may be done with the feet; then make a nice bed of fine soil for the roots to rest on. The plant having been put in its place, and the roots spread out, it must be held there until two or three inches of soil are worked in among the roots firmly; but if, in the act of removing the hand, the plant shows any signs of springing up, the hold must be retained, and more soil worked in. It takes but an instant to ascertain whether the plant will retain its place. When made secure, the hole may be filled up rapidly; but as the soil is thrown in, it should be made just firm, and no more. The technical term for this is "firming." When planted in this way, about an inch may be allowed for settling; in the common way, three or four inches must generally be allowed; that is to say, where the roots are wanted about four inches from the surface, they must be placed three or four inches deeper than this. For example: when we say, in planting, that the roots must be covered about four inches, they must be placed three or four inches deeper than this to allow for settling, if the common method of planting is pursued; but if the bottom of the trench or hole is "firmed," as well as the soil as it is put in, not even an inch need be allowed for settling; for the word covering, as we use it, means the distance between the roots and the surface when every thing has settled to its place. It must be remarked, that some soils sink or settle much more than others, and this condition must also be taken into consideration.

In planting on hillsides, if they are steep, we make a considerable departure from ordinary conditions. It is often supposed that the roots here are a foot or more deep, when they are really not more than six inches. We surprised a large planter recently by convincing him that his roots were six inches deep, and not a foot. Care must be used, in planting here, to have the roots deep enough on the face of the hill: the hole would be better if dug a little sloping. If the reader will exercise a little good judgment in these and similar matters, he will have little or nothing to fear from the winter killing of his roots, provided there is no standing water about the roots or the collar of the plant. Where much planting is done, it is a good plan to divide the men into sets, selecting two good men to put the plant in its place, with enough soil worked around it to hold it there, while others follow and fill up.

In this way both skill and labor will be economized.

The opposite or extreme conditions alluded to above will be best illustrated if we select, as examples, an account of two well known vineyards.

At Kelley's Island the soil is generally clay, with just enough limestone, sand, and gravel to make it the most adhesive and compact possible, so that the labor of first breaking it up is very great, and not to be accomplished by the usual means. The underlying rock is often not much more than a foot below the surface, and prevents the escape of water in times of wetness. Here the vines can not be set or covered deeply, nor can the ground be deeply worked. If this shallow soil should be worked and enriched down to the point where water lodges, the roots formed there in time of drought would suffer in time of wetness, and the health of the vines and the quality of the fruit would, in consequence, be greatly impaired. Here the indications are, to plant as near the surface as will permit of shallow cultivation, and be consistent with winter endurance under the very favorable modifying influences of the lake, without which the locality would be very unsuitable for a vineyard.

In contrast to this, may be adduced the steep, gravelly hillside which generally prevails at Hammondsport, where the drift soil has no practical limit to its depth, and where water at the roots is never feared. Their enemy comes to young vines in the form of early drought, and the indications in this case are as deep planting as may consist with the avoidance of what is very indefinitely called "smothering" the plants. Four inches of depth at Kelley's Island would not be more than equaled by eight or ten inches at Pleasant Valley.

In that remarkable vine district occupying a great part of the shore region of Lake Erie, these two extreme conditions are often found in immediate contiguity, and present a geological study but little less interesting than the Valley of the Walkill. The tenacious clay and the deep gravelly drift meet in some places as if on a dividing line, while in others they run into each other by almost imperceptible gradations. These soils, under propitious circumstances, are so favorable to grape culture, that the fortunate possessor of any one of them, if we may judge from what is said, thinks his own the best. Under adverse circumstances, however, like those of last winter, which are always liable to occur, they will all suffer unless the treatment conforms to the principles we have laid down; and we may confidently add, as the result of long experience and widely extended observation, that when these natural principles are mastered and judiciously applied, no such deep discouragement as followed the effects of last winter will again occur, nor will young vines, soon after being brought to a bearing condition, begin to suffer from exhaustion. Success will always be best assured by working with nature rather than against her.

In planting large vines, such as are represented in *Figs.* 3 and 8, or any other, the roots of which, after proper pruning, remain long, large holes will be required. If the plants are to be set as near as two or three feet in the rows, it will be better to make a continuous trench, as represented in *Fig.* 113. Preparatory to planting in this case, a trench is made fourteen inches deep, and in the bottom of it is placed a little more than two inches in depth of good surface soil, leaving it twelve inches deep for beginning to plant. At the place for each vine a little mound is raised about two inches high, on which set the vines, and the planting proceeds as we have already described, until the trench is filled to within six inches of the surface. During the early part of the season, and until the last of July, the trench is not permitted to fill up. *Fig.* 114, at D, D, D,

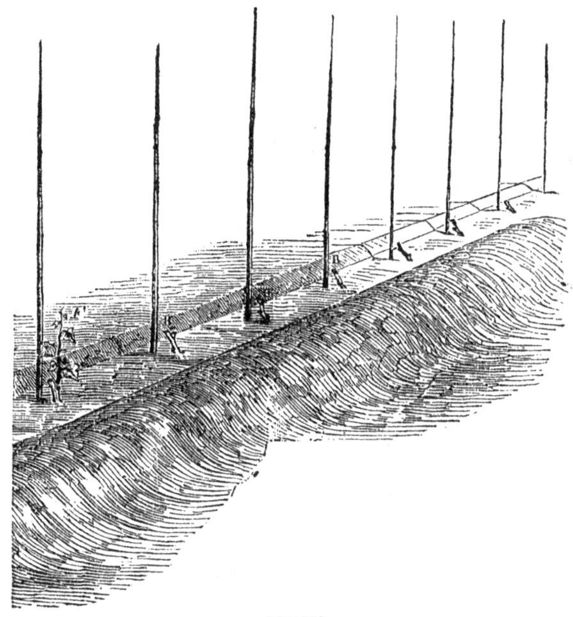

Fig. 113.

represents the appearance of the vines about the first of August, after having had all the summer operations properly done. F (*Fig.* 113) shows one of the vines as it appears when ready for the first tying, which should not confine it closely to the stake, but only be sufficient to secure it from being broken by the wind. When large plants are used, it is well to take the canes from the second or third buds, so that the subterraneous portion may consist entirely of old wood.

In compact, clayey soils the vines may be set two inches less in depth, and the basin left open

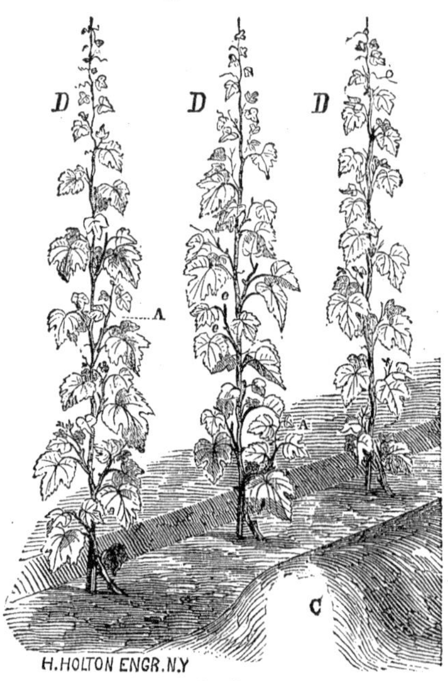

Fig. 114.

one inch less in depth. In November, if it has not been done before, the trench may be entirely filled, and made a little rounding over the vines, so that the water will run off. The work of filling may be chiefly done with a plow, (pruning having been done as already directed,) leaving a small dead furrow midway between the rows.

CHAPTER XVIII.

REPLACING AND RENEWING SPURS AND ARMS—OPPOSITE ARMS—LENGTH OF ARMS—THEIR GENERAL MANAGEMENT—OVERCROPPING.

Replacing Spurs.—When detailing the manner in which arms and spurs are formed, the reader's attention was kept fixed directly on the object before him, so that he might obtain a clear idea of the principles applied, leaving exceptions and accidents to be treated of separately. We therefore propose now to speak of such of these accidents as the novice would not be likely to remedy, with the limited knowledge which he is supposed to possess.

When giving the details for the formation of *spurs*, it was taken for granted that every bud set apart for the purpose would grow and make a spur; but a bud will sometimes get accidentally rubbed off, or the young cane will get broken, or some accident will leave a vacancy just where a spur ought to be. There are several ways in which such a vacancy may be filled, one of the simplest of which is shown in

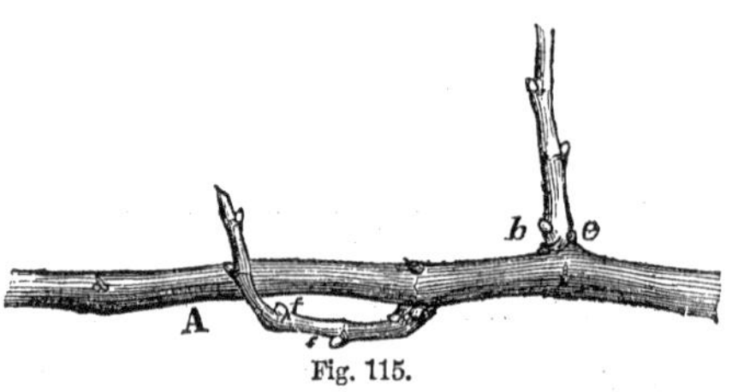

Fig. 115.

Fig. 115. A is a portion of an arm from which a bud is missing. Its place is supplied by taking a cane from the nearest adjoining bud on the under side of the arm, and bringing it up to the place of the missing bud in the manner shown. The buds *f*, *f*, are rubbed off, and a double spur formed from the two upper buds.

In case there should be no lower buds from which to grow a cane, as may be the case when

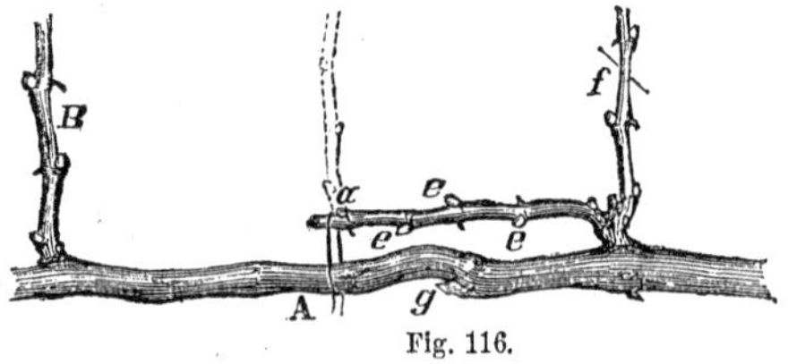

Fig. 116.

they are rubbed off, then the next simplest method is shown in *Fig.* 116, in which A is a portion of an arm. Cut an adjoining cane down to the two lowest buds, and grow two canes from it; if the cane next the missing bud be from a base bud, so much the better. At the next pruning, bend this cane down parallel with the arm, and, selecting a bud over the missing one, cut the cane at that point, as shown at *a*, and tie it there securely with bast or twine. The buds *e*, *e*, *e*, must be rubbed off. A cane will grow from *a*, as shown by the dotted line, and this is converted into a spur. The cane *f* will make a spur in its proper place. This arm was extended from the point *g*, and the bud there "missed," and this method was taken to replace it.

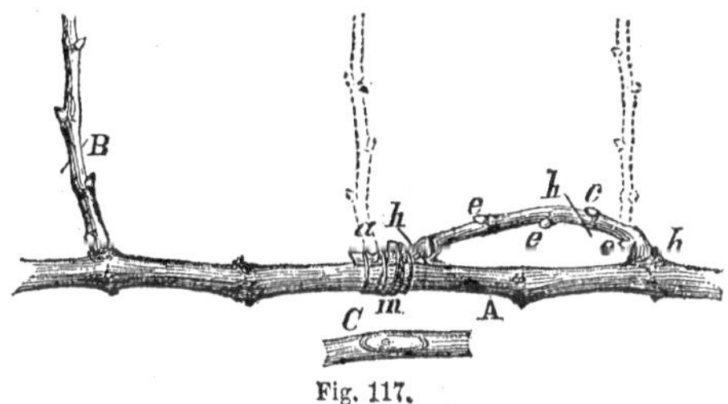

Fig. 117.

Another plan is seen in *Fig.* 117. In this case, a chip is cut from the arm, as shown at C. The adjoining cane is then bent down, and cut off at the proper length. About one third of the thickness of the cane is then shaved off, so as to fit nicely the cut in the arm. It must then be bound firmly with bast, but so as not to interfere with the bud *a*. All the buds marked *e* must be rubbed off. If the base bud, *b*, has not been injured, it will break strongly, in which case grow a cane from it for a spur; otherwise grow a cane from the lowest bud *e*, as shown by the dotted lines. In many cases the union will become so perfect by this method that the connecting cane, at the next pruning, may be cut off at *h*, *h*. If it does not become thus perfect, the cane may remain as it is. A cane will grow from *a*, as shown by the dotted lines, which is to be converted into a spur.

Still another method, but not very different from the last, is shown in *Fig.* 118, A, as be-

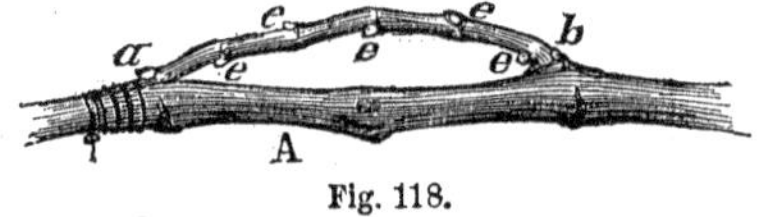

Fig. 118.

fore, being a portion of an arm. In this case, bend down an adjoining cane, and cut it off at the proper length. Next cut the end at an acute angle, and from the extreme end cut a piece so as to leave an angular face about one third the thickness of the cane. Now cut from the arm an angular piece that will admit the end of the cane exactly and evenly, as shown in the engraving. It must then be bound in its place firmly, and the cane also tied to the arm in the middle, to prevent it from springing. The buds *e* are to be rubbed off. A cane must be grown from the bud *b* for a spur, and another from *a* for the same purpose.

By one or other of these methods a spur may be readily replaced at any time, and the arm kept in full bearing. The union of arm and spur is not essential; the spur will do well without it, as in the example first given. In the examples above, the arms are young and only just ready to spur; but the spurs may be replaced on an old arm just as easily by taking the lowest cane from an adjoining spur. On an old arm, however, there is seldom a necessity for replacing spurs in this way, if the vine has been well used; for dormant buds seem to collect in proportion to the age of the vine; they would seem, indeed, to be a "provision against old age."

Renewing Spurs.—It sometimes, however, becomes necessary or desirable to *renew* old spurs. In time some of them may get to be inconveniently long or ill-shaped; and if for this, or any other reason, it should be wished to renew them, the reader should know that he can generally do so. We present some examples, all of them taken from life. It will give the reader a clearer idea of the subject if we describe what was actually done in each case. *Fig.* 119 is from an arm that had been laid

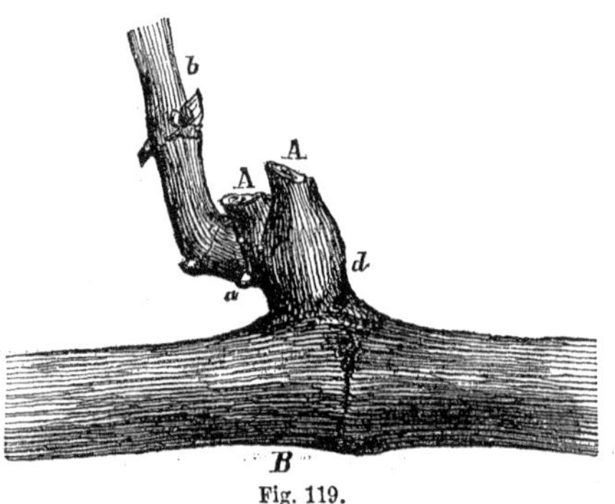

Fig. 119.

down one year. The A on the right shows where the cane had been pruned. It was cut low to start two base buds, but only one grew, and the cane from this got so broken during the winter that it became necessary to start again. It was cut at the left A, and made a fine cane for a spur. It is ill-shaped, to be sure, but in two or three years, or as soon as elaborated matter has accumulated at the junction of the arm and the spur, it may be cut off at the point *d*, *a*, and renewed. We have had several cases presenting this general appearance, but not all arising in the same way. All we wish to do here is to make the reader familiar with the principle and its application.

We may remark here, that as the spur increases in age elaborated matter collects at the junction of the arm and spur, and is concerned in the formation of many dormant buds. It is no doubt also concerned in producing the increased flavor which we always find in fruit on

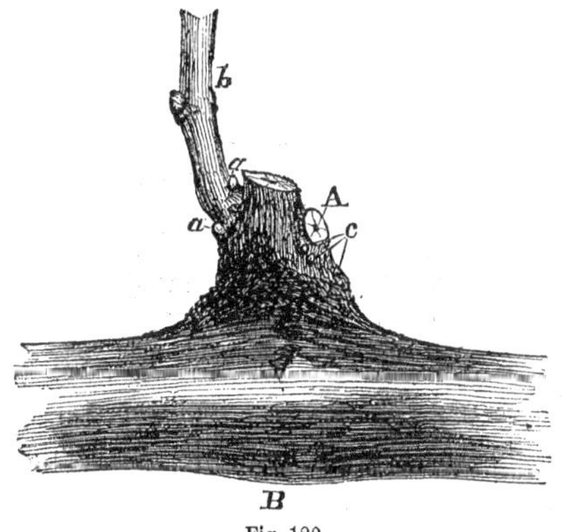

Fig. 120.

old arms and spurs. It presents the granular appearance shown in *Fig.* 120. The little globules at *c* are all dormant buds. The reader will now understand how it is that we get new canes when old spurs are cut down. The spur in this example was cut down, and two canes selected, the one seen and another at A. Two canes having been allowed to grow, they were both rather less in size than was desired. The cane A was therefore cut off to strengthen the one left. By pruning this cane just above *b*, and retaining the upper base bud *a*, a good double spur was formed. It might have been pruned below *b*, as there were two very nice base buds, *a*, *a*.

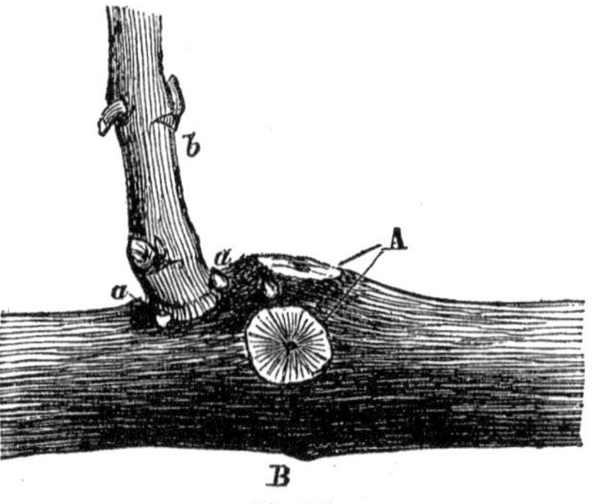

Fig. 121.

In the next example, *Fig.* 121, the spur had become rather long, and was narrow at the base, (not filled out like *Fig.* 120,) and not satisfactory in several particulars. The base being examined, and the appearance of dormant buds proving satisfactory, it was determined to cut the spur entirely away, and this was accordingly done, as shown by the scar on the top of the arm. Two or three little shoots in due time made their appearance, but none of them well placed; the best, however, was selected, and grew finely. The next season a bud broke in a very good position, and the new cane grown last season, after some hesitation, was cut off, as shown by the scar on the side. The newly selected shoot made a fine cane, as the reader may see. The progress of such a case would naturally be watched with a great deal of interest.

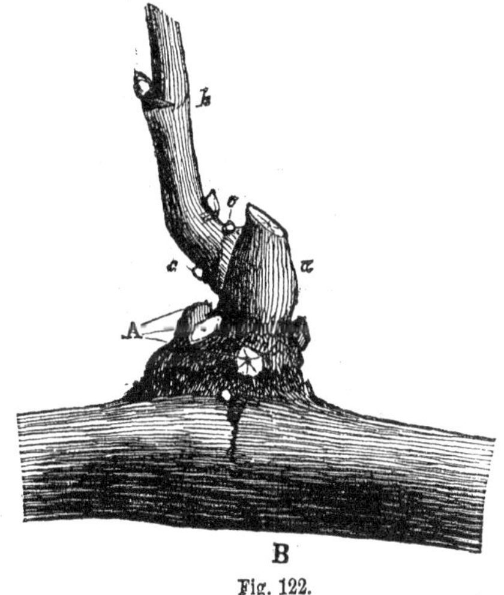

Fig. 122.

In the last example, *Fig.* 122, the spur was cut off nearly half an inch above the arm, and the cane *a* selected and grown. This cane was cut to its lowest bud, with the intention of using a base bud for a second cane; but the case was neglected for some time, and several small canes grew from the remains of the old spur, and spoiled the intention; these little canes, however, were at once removed, as shown by A, and the cane from the renewed spur made a very good growth. If it had not been for this neglect, the little stump seen just below *a* would have made a good cane, and, being well placed, it would have been taken for this purpose.

We have now given the student a sufficient number of examples to make him familiar with the principle, and its application to a variety of cases. In renewing spurs, the chief thing to be looked after, in the first instance, is the appearance of the wood at the base of the spur. The condition of the little protuberances or dormant buds will be a good index of success. It is very seldom the case in old spurs, however, that there are not dormant buds present. In the second place, the young shoot must be selected early, and all the others rubbed off, so as to concentrate the action of the plant on this one, and not have it uselessly wasted on many.

Renewing Arms. — It sometimes becomes necessary to renew or replace an arm from accidental causes, and our work would be very imperfect if we failed to explain how it is to be done. In the Guyot plan, with a permanent arm, the renewal is comparatively easy. The reader will remember that in this system we have two or three long canes or safety-valves, and these furnish the ready means for making a new arm. Let us suppose the arm in *Fig.* 48, p. 102, is to be renewed. If it has a spur or two that will bear fruit, it need not be cut off yet; but unless a few bunches of good fruit can be got from it, it should be cut entirely away at once. Now proceed as follows: Take the lowest-placed cane, *d*, cut it one third the length of the arm, and lay it down horizontally. From this point extend the arm in the usual manner. If the old arm, or any portion of it, was left on for growing fruit, it should be cut away at the end of the first season. One of the advantages of this system consists in the facility with which an arm may be renewed.

Double Horizontal Arms. — As a general thing, the best way to renew the arms is to cut each arm off at the spur nearest to the stock, and grow a single cane from the lowest bud on the spur. This cane must next be bent to a horizontal position, and the arm formed by degrees in the usual way. This severe cutting back will cause a number of dormant buds to break around the stock, all of which must be rubbed off. They have been called "water shoots," and are fruitless. If the spurs next the stock are poor, then the arms must be cut pretty close to the stock, leaving no spurs whatever. There need be no apprehension in regard to getting canes in this case; there will be an abundance of them, and the trouble will consist in making a choice and keeping the others from growing. The canes grown under such circumstances should early be bent to an angle, and the end pinched out when the cane is about five feet long. When the bud at the end breaks, let the cane extend a couple of feet before it is pinched again. The pinching should be repeated three or four times. Unless these precautions are taken, the lower buds will be very small. More than the usual means will be necessary to equalize the action of the plant, as it will be exceedingly vigorous. In other respects, the new arm will be formed in the usual manner.

When only a portion of an arm is to be renewed, the cane for the renewed part must be taken from the lowest bud on the spur situated at the point from which the arm is to be renewed. It will make the arm just a little crooked there; but this, aside from its being a little unsightly, will in no respect be an injury to the vine.

If, in double horizontal arms, each arm, as we suggested some years ago, was provided with a safety-valve, or upright cane, at some point below the bend in the arm, the arms in this system could be renewed just as easily as in the plan of Guyot. Besides this, they have considerable value, when understood, in equalizing action throughout the arm. We consider them an important feature in the horizontal arm system.

Upright Stocks.—The way to renew these is to cut within a foot of the ground, select one from among the many canes that will make their appearance, and treat it in the manner in which the stock was first formed. It seems not to be generally understood that an old stock is full of dormant buds, and that they will start into growth just as soon as the vital force of the plant is concentrated upon them by cutting away the parts above.

Opposite Arms.—The French, with characteristic ingenuity and love of system, have a fondness for growing vines with the arms and spurs opposite each other: they have utilized the method beyond all other people. In the case of arms, they proceed from the same level; and in the case of spurs, they are directly opposite each other on upright stocks. It involves some time and trouble, but will, no doubt, interest the novice, and we therefore propose to explain and illustrate the method by which it is done, leaving the reader to apply it according to his convenience and taste.

Let us, for an example, take a cane at the end of the first year, such as is shown in *Fig.* 23, p. 65, and cut it down to two buds. Select the strongest cane, and rub the other off. When the new cane has grown from twelve to eighteen inches above the point where it is desired to have the arms, cut the cane off at this point. Action, in this case, has been arrested; the vital principle has been checked in its upward course. For a moment, as it were, it seems quiet, but it is only to gather at all points with renewed energy.

The thallons make a vigorous appearance, and would soon take the place of the cane that has been stopped. But this we do not want. We are aiming now to develop and burst the buds which, if left to themselves, would not grow till next year. The thallons are, therefore, in our way, and we remove them entirely. This concentrates the action upon the buds; they soon begin to swell, and in no very long time break into leaf, and our chief purpose is accomplished. As soon as growth is fairly established in the young shoots, we select the top one, and pinch all the others entirely out, for we not only have

Fig. 123.

no use for them, but they would be in our way. When the new cane has grown about eighteen inches long, it will have the appearance shown in *Fig.* 123 which also shows where the cane was cut off. When the young cane has grown three or four feet, the end should be pinched, and the operation repeated as often as the new growth has three good-sized leaves. The thallons must be athallized the same as any other cane.

At the end of the season it will be found that the base of the new cane is larger than the cane that was stopped, and has come round on the top of it, so as to be very nearly in a straight line with it. At the base, too, will be found several well-developed buds, on opposite sides, and also some smaller ones, all on the same level. It is from these base buds that the arms and spurs are taken.

If we wish to grow an upright stock with

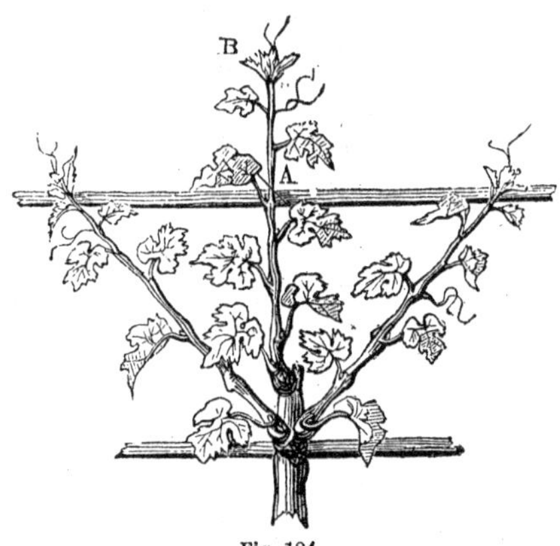

Fig. 124.

opposite *spurs*, the cane is pruned to the first bud above the base buds. This bud, and two base buds opposite each other, are selected to continue the system. When they get fairly started, they will look like *Fig.* 124. About a foot above the opposite canes two more are formed by cutting at A, and proceeding as before. In this way the stock can be extended as far as wanted with opposite spurs, which are formed in the usual way after the canes are established.

If we want opposite *arms*, the new cane is cut

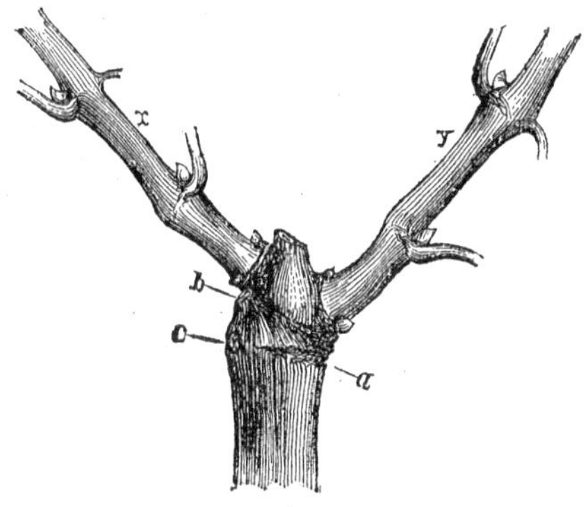

Fig. 125.

about an inch above the base buds, two of which are selected for canes, as shown in *Fig.* 125, which is an exact representation from life. Having thus explained the principle, we leave the reader to work it out fully on the vine.

Length of Arms.—In this connection we reiterate that arms can not be made much more than four feet long, without greatly weakening the spurs near the stock. The reader should, indeed, determine his mode of training before planting, so as to provide for the proper length of the arms. The horizontal arm, whether double or single, is undoubtedly the best system. The plan of making *double tiers* of both is a good one. Four feet is the proper distance to plant for single arms, whether of one or two tiers. Four feet is also the proper distance for double arms of two tiers, the rows in both cases being six feet apart; but for double arms of one tier, six feet is the proper distance, the rows in this case being from four to six feet apart. With two tiers, the upper one is a little more trouble to cover. It is done as follows: lay down the first tier, and cover by applowing, as elsewhere explained; before turning the second furrow slice, lay the arms of the second tier in the furrow just made, and finish the plowing as usual.

General Management of Arms.—The reader should be quick to perceive that he can only attain a full measure of success, in respect to both pleasure and profit, by first acquiring a knowledge of the wants and capacity of the vine, and then ministering to them with constant good faith. A watchful supervision is needed at all times, and a few suggestions here will give a proper direction to this supervision.

In the spring, in particular, when the vines are beginning to grow, the vineyard should be gone over frequently and carefully, to see that every thing is going on as it should. It may be that a cane has made its appearance by the side of a spur, which it would be desirable to retain to take its place; or it may be that several little shoots are growing around the spur, which would prove hurtful if not speedily removed. It will sometimes be the case, also, in double spurs, that the lower cane, for spurring next season, may be trained into a better position, if attended to in time. Sometimes, too, there may, at first, be a want of action in the spurs nearest the stock, which may be supplied by lowering the end of the arm until the equilibrium is restored. If some canes are growing stronger than others, pinching the strong, if done early, will strengthen the weak. If you want two canes on a stock to grow of about the same length, and see one *beginning* to take the lead of the other, bend it immediately toward a horizontal position, and place the weak one upright. If done at the right moment, success is quite certain; if long neglected, the case is somewhat difficult to manage.

We may state here that buds are sometimes *double*, or even *treble;* that is to say, two and three shoots will sometimes grow from the same bud. As a general rule, one of these shoots must be rubbed off when about an inch long, leaving only one to grow. Sometimes double buds can be advantageously used in forming spurs, or even in extending the arms. In the latter case, if both the end buds break double, one shoot can be used for the upright cane, and the other for the extension of the arm. On the whole, however, it is best to follow the usual course.

Tying up must not be neglected. The young canes should have their first tying early, to prevent their accidental loss. Till the young canes get to be about a foot long, they are easily broken at the base, some kinds more easily than others. If, therefore, a young shoot is growing angularly, and needs to be straightened, or is growing straight, and requires to be bent to an angle, it should be done by degrees, or there is much danger of its breaking. In tying, the string should be loose, or only just tight enough to keep the cane in its place. Various things are used for tying, but, on the whole, we have found nothing better than cotton twine.

The fruit, too, must receive attention. Resolve at the beginning to become one of our students, and grow only *good* fruit, *ripe* fruit. As a general rule, no cane, in any arm or spur system, should carry more than two bunches. If all that set are left, the vine is overtasked, and the ripening process imperfectly performed; but if part are removed *early*, the ripening process is strengthened rather than weakened, and the goodness and ripeness which would have been diffused and imperfect in four bunches, is concentrated and made perfect in two. Here and there a strong cane will be an exception to the rule, and may carry three bunches; here and there, also, a weak one will form another exception, and should carry only one, or even none. The canes must all be examined, and the fruit adjusted to its capacity.

The evil of *overcropping*, especially young vines, is very great and very common, and is sometimes indulged in by persons who should know better. The vine, no matter how healthy it may be naturally, is enfeebled and made sickly by it. The vital force is weakened, and is unable to perfect the ripening process; the fruit is consequently imperfect, and the vine itself becomes a prey to mildew. When, therefore, a person who has enfeebled vines a couple of years old by letting them carry twenty or more bunches of fruit, says to you that such kinds "won't do well with him," you will understand that the fault lies in his treatment, and not in the vine. He has overdone the thing, and the work of his own hands condemns him. The ill effects of overcropping are not confined to the grape; they are more or less seen in all kinds of fruits. Let nothing, therefore, tempt you into overcropping your vines; justice to yourself, to others, and to the vines, demands this.

We may as well correct here a common misapprehension, that the largest wood is the best for fruit. This is not so; the best grapes are produced on medium-sized wood, round, short-jointed, and having full, plump buds; and the second bud from the base will produce larger bunches than the first; hence the advantage of the double spur, in which we use the first bud for wood, and the second for fruit.

A word or two in regard to the *safety valves*. If there is one to each arm in the double arm system, and there never should be more than one, their management is easy. Many years ago, in making some experiments, we found that a cane left to grow *below* the bend in the arm exercised considerable influence in equalizing action in the arm; in other words, we discovered a less disposition to extreme growth at the end of the arm, the spurs near the stock being about as strong as those near the end, and in some cases even stronger. This, with us, was the origin of the safety valve. We were not then as familiar with the effects of pinching as we have learned to be in later years, and used to bend the safety valve down to a greater or less angle, as we wished to modify action in the arm. Pinching or bending the safety valve, or both, will give us a very considerable control over action in the arm, if recourse is had to them at the right time. This is the general principle which governs the safety valve, and the reader will be able to apply it for himself.

The upright canes in the Guyot plan should be used in the same way, though we used the safety valve years before we heard of Guyot. We may remark here, that to obtain the full benefit of the upright canes, the spur from which they are grown should be *below* the bend in the arm, and not, as in the Guyot proper, above it. This is readily done by making the arm from the upper cane. In this system, we have found that two canes are as many as should be used. If more are used, the action is diverted too strongly from the arm. A friend, who grows a part of his vineyard on the Guyot plan, meeting with the same difficulty, we advised him to lay down one of the canes at right angles with the permanent arm, and let it carry a little more fruit. This he has done for four years past with satisfactory results, thus combining the renewal and the permanent arm. This would be a good plan to follow in some cases, while the vines are young. The rule should be, not to have more than two safety valves. If more action is needed in the arm, the uprights must be pinched; and if this is not sufficient, they must be bent to an angle, but restored again if action becomes too great at the end of the arm.

In conclusion, a general supervision should be exercised, to see that every thing is done at the right time and in the right manner. Such supervision should never be intrusted to negligent or incompetent hands.

CHAPTER XIX.

STAKES AND TRELLISES.

Trellises.—This is a subject of no little importance, not alone because it is a necessity, but also because of its considerable cost, whatever form it may take. Various forms have been proposed and used, few of which need be noticed here, since they are mostly wanting in either durability or convenience. Something "cheap" seems to have been the leading idea in most of the contrivances that have been suggested; that is very desirable in itself, but it is not all. What is wanted is, not something that is cheap as a part, but something that is cheap as a whole. We have seen some contrivances in this way that "ate themselves up" in less than ten years, and a good trellis besides.

Where stakes alone are used, there is nothing so good and durable as red cedar and yellow locust. The chestnut is next in value; the oak, also, is tolerably lasting. The bark should in all cases be removed from the portion put in the ground, since, in decaying, it produces various forms of fungi, some at least of which are hurtful to the vine.

One of the simplest forms of trellis is that shown in *Fig.* 126. If made entirely of cedar,

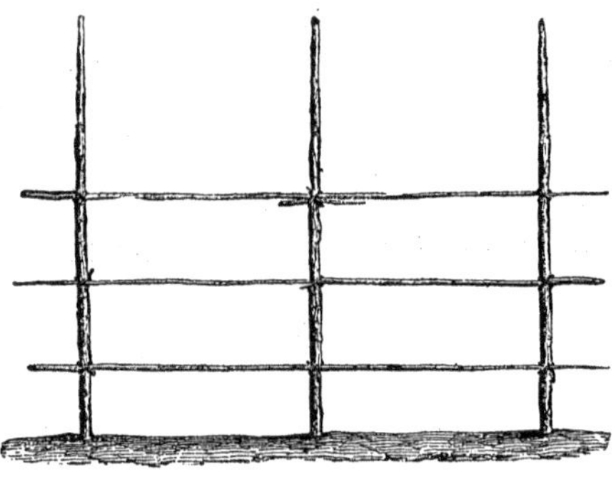

Fig. 126.

it will be quite durable; and by putting it carefully and neatly together, it can be made to assume a considerable degree of rustic beauty. If cedar is not plenty, common "hoop poles" may be used for the horizontal pieces. If cedar or locust is not used for the posts, it soon goes to pieces. When made altogether of cedar, it is one of the best forms of wooden trellis that can be used. If the system of training should make it desirable, the poles can be placed vertically instead of horizontally; in which case none but the top and bottom horizontal poles will be needed. This trellis can

Fig. 127.

be made of any height desired. The ends of the posts should be cut off about three inches above the top piece.

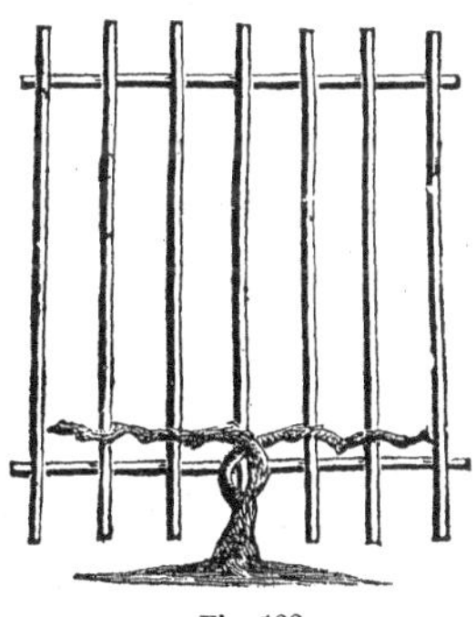

Fig. 128.

Another kind of wooden trellis is shown in

Fig. 127. In this the strips are upright, and the posts quite stout. The construction is so simple as to be easily understood from the engraving. This kind of trellis will suit the "fan" form of training, (*Fig.* 88, p. 153,) or any other in which the canes cross the uprights angularly. If used for horizontal arms, like *Fig.* 128, (which is an example of *reversed*

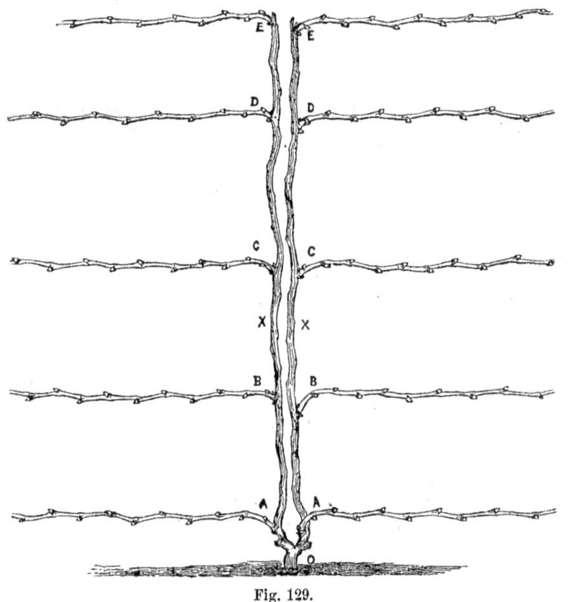

Fig. 129.

arms,) it is exceedingly inconvenient, as the uprights seldom come where they are wanted. In this instance, however, the stock is to be carried higher, as shown in *Fig.* 129, which is a

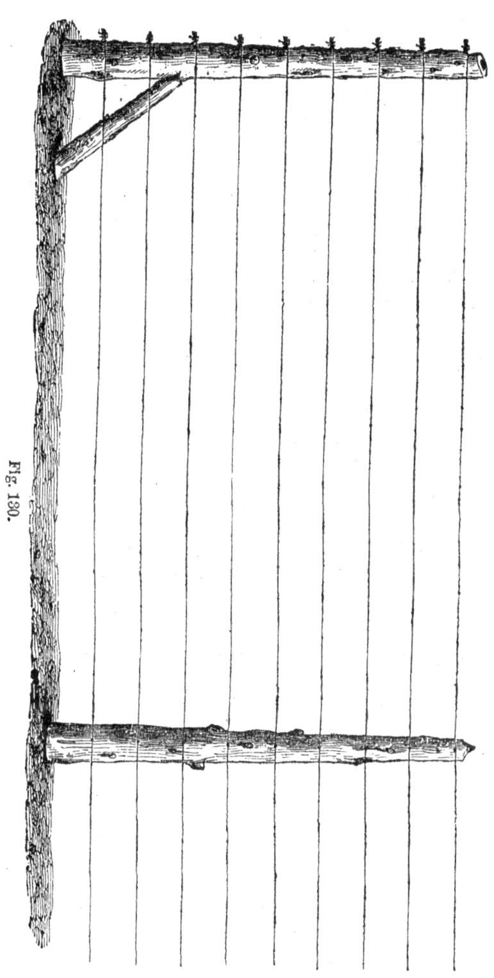

Fig. 130.

part of the very extended and complicated system of Bronner.

But the best of all trellises for the vineyard is that made of wire supported by cedar or locust posts. Its first cost is greater than most other kinds, but it is cheaper in the end. When well made, it is not only of great durability, but it is always in order and always ready for use. *Fig.* 130 is a trellis of this kind. It was made for growing several tiers of arms on, like the Thomery, and is consequently much higher than is needed for vineyard use.

A trellis should be firm, the posts securely set in the ground, the wires made so tight as not to sway in the wind, and with the means of being loosened in winter. We will explain how this may be done. A hole should be dug about four feet deep, and in connection with it, and in a line with the trellis, a trench of the same depth, and eight or ten feet long. A cedar of this length, and of considerable stoutness, should have a hole or socket at one end for the end of the post to rest in securely, and the other end notched for a brace, which should also be of cedar or locust. The manner of fixing the post in the ground will be made plain enough by an examination of *Fig.* 131, in which the fine line denotes the ground level. It will be seen that this arrangement fixes the post immovably in its place. All the end posts are to be fixed in this way. If the trellis is long, smaller posts must be put in at intervals, but

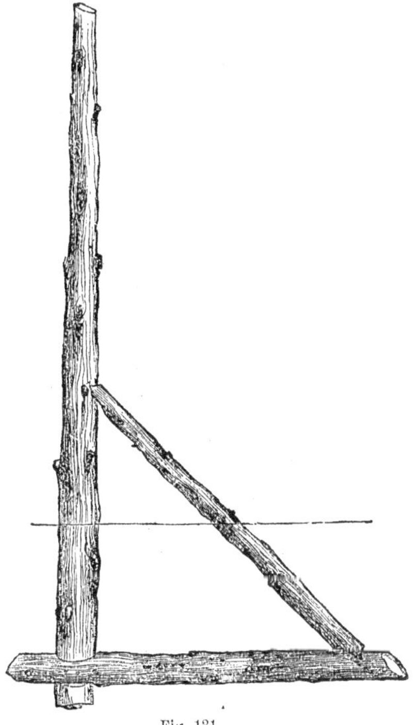

Fig. 131.

sufficiently close to give proper support to the wire, which will be twelve, fifteen, or twenty feet apart, according to circumstances and the weight of the wire.

Some good mode of tightening the wires has always been a desideratum; indeed, the trouble and vexation of doing this has deterred some from using a wire trellis. There are two or three plans that will accomplish the purpose; but we are enabled to present one so simple and effectual that it will be unnecessary to describe any other. It consists only of an iron pin with a square head, as shown at A in *Fig.* 132. It

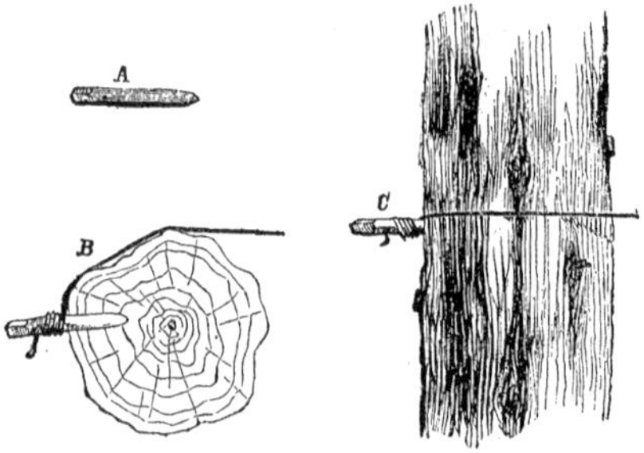

Fig. 132.

should be about six inches long and half an inch in diameter, or about the size of a common bed screw. About two inches from the end it should have a small hole pierced through it for holding the end of the wire. It can be readily and cheaply made by any blacksmith. The pin is driven into the post about half its length, as shown at B, which is a section of the post. The pin being driven into the post, the wire must be drawn as tight as it can be by hand, the end passed through the small hole, and the pin twined a few times around. If a bed wrench, or any of the wrenches in common use, be put on the square head of the pin and turned, the wire can be made literally as "tight as a fiddle string." This is a simple and effective contrivance within the reach of all. If the end posts are not pretty stout, the top wires should be tightened first, and it would be better to do so in all cases. Turning the pin in reversed order will loosen the wire as much as may be desired in winter.

Fig. 133 is the form of trellis which should be used for the Guyot plan of training. The small posts that extend above the wires are for tying the long canes or safety valves to, a vine being planted at each post.

Fig. 134 is the proper form of trellis for double horizontal arms. If two tiers of arms are grown, it is only necessary to make the trellis higher.

There are other forms of trellis, but they are so much less desirable than those just given, that it seems hardly worth while to illustrate them.

In regard to wire, it is now used of much less

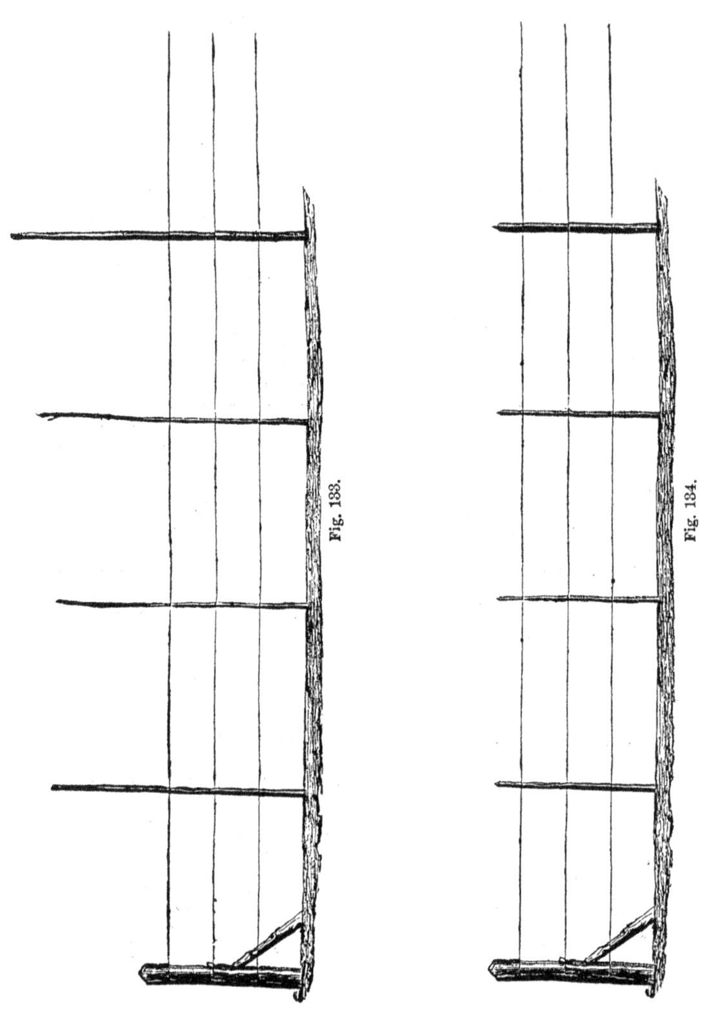

Fig. 133.

Fig. 134.

size than was common some years ago. The numbers most frequently used now are from ten to fourteen. It should either be annealed or galvanized, the last being the best, but costing about double. There are two kinds of wire, hard coal and charcoal. The former is very brittle, and wears away pretty fast by oxydation, and is therefore not the best for the vineyard. Charcoal wire is tough, pliant, and durable, and is the kind that should be used. We have found No. 14 of this wire abundantly strong.

If posts other than cedar or yellow locust are used, the portion put in the ground should be covered with coal tar, or, better still, plastic slate. Both should be applied when the posts are dry, and the coal tar will be more effectual if warmed before it is put on. The plastic slate is mixed with coal tar, and applied with a whitewash brush.

CHAPTER XX.

CULTIVATION — WINTER MANAGEMENT — MARKETING—GROWING PLANTS BETWEEN THE ROWS—HOW TO KEEP GRAPES IN WINTER — SHELTER FOR PROTECTION AND RIPENING—MANURES—NON-MANURING.

Cultivation.—The object of cultivation may be considered as two-fold: the intermingling and ameliorating of the soil in such a thorough manner as to make it a fit "house of entertainment" for plant food; and keeping the surface mellow and clean, so as to maintain a healthy root action; the two comprehending tillage, which has in view the health of the vine, and the ripening and excellence of the fruit. The first point is best accomplished by fall plowing, which may be repeated in a very stiff new soil, so as to more thoroughly break it up and intermingle it, and expose all its parts to the action of the air, and the ameliorating influence of winter. The second is accomplished by plowing again in the spring, and the proper use of weeders and cultivators during the growing season. The plowing should not at any time be so deep as to cut the large or primary roots. The small hairy or fibrous roots near the surface may be plowed at the end of the season without injury.

It will give the reader a clearer idea of this part of the subject if we repeat a part of what has elsewhere been said. We have noted the importance of having the primary roots proceed from the crown of the plant, and of having the crown at a suitable distance beneath the surface, according to the nature of the soil in which it is planted. If another system of primary roots is allowed to establish itself *above* the first, and take possession of the soil near the surface, it will, by degrees, if left to itself, appropriate the chief part of the root action, and to that extent weaken the lower system, if not ultimately destroy it; besides, cultivation is seriously interfered with, and the vine made liable to suffer from drought. Now, the young vine has a strong disposition to emit primary roots from the stock very near the surface. These, therefore, should be removed when they first appear, and not left to attain size. It is just here that a mistake is often made, in allowing the disposition to become established, and then a good deal of time and labor must be wasted in trying to correct it. It is an accepted rule, that it is best to break bad habits in childhood, since it is then easiest done. If, when weeding with the hoe, the soil be drawn from around the stock a few inches deep, it can readily be seen whether such roots have formed or are about forming, and it is a very easy matter to remove them. It takes but a moment, and is a very much better plan than to leave them till they get large and in the way. By persevering, for a while, in removing the roots as they appear, the disposition to make them will be overcome, and will be assisted by the increasing age of the plant. The object, then, should be to keep the stock free from roots for a few inches beneath the surface; thorough cultivation, indeed, up to the stock of the plant, would almost regulate this matter of itself.

Let the novice remember that the primary roots must not be cut and dragged to the surface, and we will proceed to describe two kinds of plowing, the application of which he will now readily understand. As plowing can not well be done till the vines are pruned, this should be done soon after the fall of the leaf. Of the two kinds of plowing alluded to, one consists in beginning next the vines and turning the furrow slice to the vines, which may be called *applowing*, or plowing *to* the vines; the other consists in beginning in the middle of the row, and turning the furrow slice from the vines, which may be called *deplowing*, or plowing *from* the vines. In deplowing, the dead furrow is left next the vines; in applowing, it is in the middle of the row. When this dead furrow is needed to carry off surface water, it should be finished by hand with the hoe. The reader will get a tolerably good idea of deplowing by examining *Fig.* 40, p. 93, in which, however, there are only two furrow slices, in consequence of the vines being planted close together. The number of slices will be in proportion to the width of the rows.

In plowing, much time and many steps will be saved by beginning and turning at the right place. It will assist the beginner if we give an illustration, by taking the space between two rows of vines running east and west, and dividing this space by an imaginary line through the middle, calling the space on the north the *upper* side, and the space on the south the *lower* side. We will describe the operation of *applowing*, or plowing *to* the vines, which will leave the dead furrow in the middle, or where the imaginary line is. Beginning on the *upper* side, enter the plow three or four inches deep, and throw a furrow slice *to* the vines. When the end of the row is reached, turn to the lower side, enter the plow as before, and turn a slice to the vines; after which, go to the upper side again, and turn a slice into the furrow first opened; then to the lower side, and turn a slice into the open furrow there; then again to the upper side, and so repeat till the space between the rows is all plowed. The dead furrow will be through the middle. *Deplowing*, or plowing *from* the vines, consists in beginning at the middle or the dead furrow, and reversing these furrow slices, which fills the dead furrow, and finishes by leaving the ground as it was at the beginning. Having explained and illustrated the meaning of ap-plowing and deplowing, we shall now be able to apply these terms without further circumlocution. We may remark here, that plowing should never be done when the soil is wet.

Soils that are new, heavy, or stiff are specially benefited by fall plowing, which mellows them, makes them easier to work, and better fitted for sustaining the vines. For such soils proceed as follows: Early in November, the vines having been first pruned, deplow, and harrow well with a coulter harrow or a cultivator. In from one to two weeks, applow and harrow. The vines are now to be laid down, and covered by applowing, and the dead furrow, where necessary to carry off water, cleaned out with a hoe, removing the "balk" or little ridge left by the plow. This may seem like a good deal of labor, but for new or stiff soils the advantages are sufficiently great to warrant the labor.

For ordinary mellow soils, the following is the proper course: The vines having been pruned as soon as the leaves fall, are laid down, covered by applowing, and the ground harrowed. The dead furrow through the middle of the row is then put in condition for carrying off water, and the vineyard is prepared for its winter rest; in some sense, it may be said to have been put to bed and blanketed. In the spring, deplowing will fill up the dead furrow and uncover the vines, which should at once be tied to the wires to prevent loss by accident. The ground should then be thoroughly harrowed. If the common harrow is used, the ground beneath the surface is packed; but with the coulter harrow or a cultivator it is not only broken up, but left porous. The cultivator or the coulter harrow should, therefore, be used in the vineyard instead of the spike harrow.

The operation that has just been described combines so admirably the advantages of winter covering and fall plowing, that it ought to be universally adopted. The primary roots are not cut and dragged to the surface, as they often are, even within a foot of the stock; on the contrary, they are not only not damaged in this way, but an additional covering is placed over them. The ground is mellowed and aerated, and when reversed in the spring by deplowing, is charged with ammonia and other gases, as well as the liquid manure absorbed from the top dressing, all of which are placed within reach of the mouths of the plant ready for appropriation, and the new growth starts with a healthy vigor which it will maintain throughout the season, unless checked by unusual atmospheric conditions. These are great and substantial advantages, which should not be lightly esteemed. Those, however, who plow in the fall very much as if the vine were not a thing of life, and sensitive to the mangling of its vital parts, should leave nature to take care of the roots during the winter. When the vine is young and lusty with vigor, it may not harm it much to check it in this way; but the practice can not be persisted in without damage.

When the plowing is done, there will be a narrow slip along the vines which has not been moved by the plow. This must be thoroughly broken up with either the pronged hoe (sometimes called a potato hook) or the pronged spade; and which is best we have found to depend a good deal upon the countryman that uses them. In stiff or stony soils, a stout double pronged hoe, like *Fig.* 135, is used. This

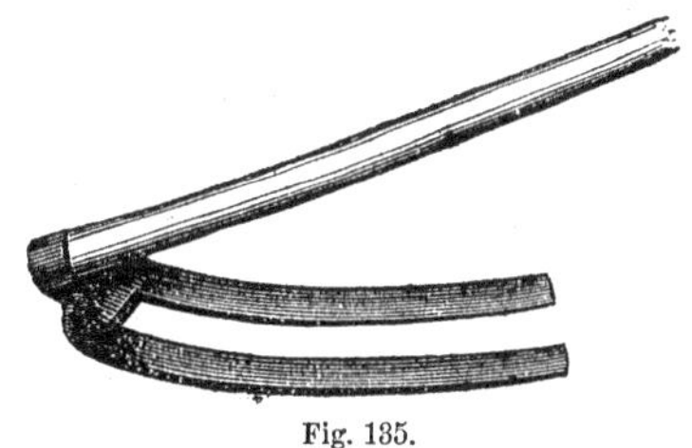

Fig. 135.

instrument is also used for working the soil on steep hill-sides, where the plow can not be run. It is in common use by nurserymen, and is a very good implement to have at hand for various purposes. In deplowing in the fall, the unmoved strip along the vines must be moved by hand at the time of plowing, so as to leave the stock of the vines in the open furrow.

After the ground is plowed and harrowed, there is one object which must be kept steadily in view, and that is, to keep the soil mellow and free from weeds. For weeding, we have used nothing so good as the improved horse-hoe, made of steel, and fitted with an adjustable wheel and clevis. It can be expanded from one to three feet wide, and has different sets of teeth, one for cutting weeds and stirring the soil, another for turning one or two light furrow slices, and so on. With a single horse it may be run from one to three inches deep. With this implement the soil may be easily kept clean and mellow. The reader, however, should try various implements as they come into use, and retain those which are best adapted to the purpose. Implements are not yet perfect. The time to weed is just as *soon* and as *often* as the weeds can be seen, or just as they are leaving the seed leaf. The labor is then comparatively light and easy, but it becomes very hard work when the weeds get large enough to dispute the ground with you. It is also desirable to stir the ground as soon after heavy rains as it becomes dry enough to work.

The slip along the vines not stirred by the horse hoe must be weeded by hand. When the soil is light and mellow, and not stony, the pushing hoe will be found more convenient than the draw hoe; but better than either, and combining the advantages of both, is a recently introduced triangular hoe with a double cutting edge, being an easy tool to handle, and very thorough in its work. It is one of the few horticultural implements in which the true principle of cutting is introduced; in other words, it makes an angular instead of a square cut. All square cutting weeders are imperfect, and inventors should bear this in mind. After mid

Fig. 136.

season, the skim teeth should be used on the horse hoe. In general terms, begin the season by running the hoe two or three inches deep, and gradually lessen the depth, till at last only the surface is stirred. The novice will soon learn to adapt his implements to the purpose.

We introduce *Figs.* 136, 137, 138, 139, as examples of implements in use among the French. We have never used them, but they have the appearance of being good of their kind. Some

Fig. 137.

reader may take a fancy to some of them, and have them made for trial. They bear a close resemblance to implements already in use among us, which can doubtless be improved. We have several times imported foreign imple-

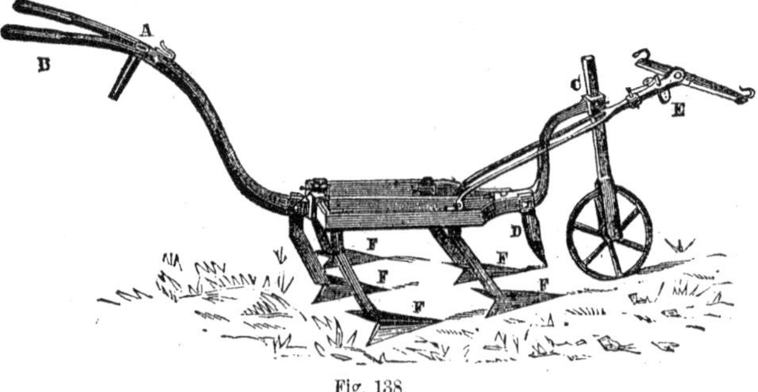

Fig. 138.

ments, but never found them to excel our own, except in clumsiness and weight; and it would, therefore, be better to have them made here rather than import them. *Fig.* 136 is a plow. *Fig.* 137 is used as a substitute for the plow, turning two small furrow slices. *Fig.* 138 is a cultivator, or weeder. *Fig.* 139 is a triangular hoe, used for the same purpose as *Fig.* 135, above.

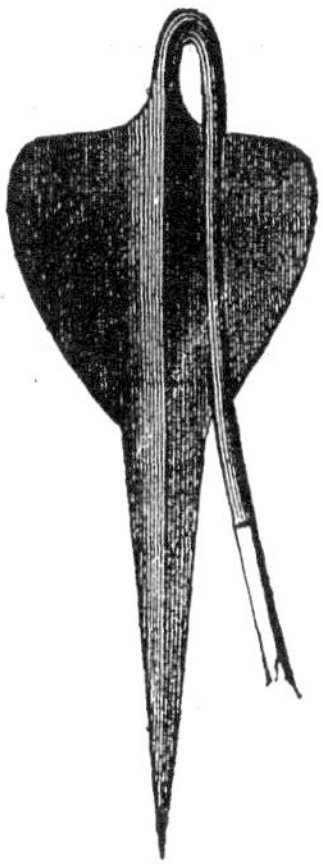

Fig. 139.

Winter Management.—There are some matters connected with the winter care of the vineyard which are too important to be overlooked, chief among which is *covering*. This, in some portions of the country, is a necessity, and in most others an advantage sufficiently great to warrant the trouble. Its object is to protect the buds and wood as well as the roots from being injured or killed by the severity or changes of the winter. It is supposed by some that covering the vines causes them to start earlier in the spring, and in that respect is an advantage; but early starting is no advantage, and covering has no such effect; on the contrary, it retards the spring growth, and that is a real advantage. Others suppose that covering "makes the crop finer;" but it can have no effect in *making* it finer: it can only preserve what is already there. Its effect is simply preservative, and in this respect it is very important.

There are several modes of covering the vine; some use the spade and others the plow for throwing earth over the vines, while still others cover with brush. There has been a supposed difficulty in bending the stock of the vine, and several methods are used for overcoming it.

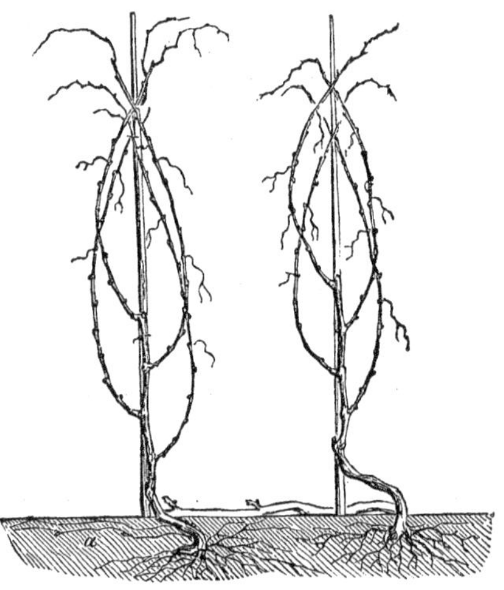

Fig. 140. Fig. 141.

One plan is to sėt the trellis from six inches to a foot in front of the vines, and bring the stock up to the wire at an angle. In this way the stock is very easily bent to the ground. Another method is to plant the vines as usual, start the arms near the surface, and carry them to the wire at about an angle of forty-five degrees before bending them horizontally. This is the plan of Dr. May, shown in *Fig.* 87, p. 152.

Where only a few vines are grown, they are pegged down and covered with the spade. Vines that are grown against walls and buildings receive from these generally as much protection as they need; but if more is thought to be necessary, as may sometimes be the case, they can be bent down and covered with earth or brush. For this purpose nothing is better than branches of hemlock or cedar. The vines are sometimes bedded in straw, which affords a good protection; but there is this objection to it, that it harbors mice, which often destroy the vines. Manure litter is objectionable for the same reason. If it should not be desirable or convenient to lay the vines down, they may be protected by laying straw mats against them on the trellis. Buildings and walls, however, present such favorable conditions for the growth of the vine, that the wood becomes thoroughly ripe and hardy, and hence, as a general rule, needs no further protection than these afford.

Figs. 140 and 141 show a good plan of preparing the vines for covering, in which each alternate vine is placed just beneath the surface, as seen at *a* in *Fig.* 140, and the others on the surface, as seen in *Fig.* 141. All modes of covering are defective which expose the roots, or leave the ground in such condition as to favor the accumulation of water in any degree whatever. After the vines are laid down, they should be covered by applowing, or plowing *to* the vines, as explained under "*Cultivation.*" In this way, the roots as well as the tops are covered and protected, and fall plowing thus becomes an advantage instead of an evil, as it is when done in the usual way. In the spring, the vines are uncovered by deplowing, or throwing the furrow slices *from* the vines, as also explained under "*Cultivation.*" In this way spring plowing and uncovering the vines become one and the same operation, and much time is saved.

In the common method the stock is bent down toward the middle of the row, covered with the plow, and the finishing done by hand with the hoe. When the vines are bent down, they must either be pegged, or enough earth thrown on the stock to keep it down. The covering of soil need not be more than two or three inches thick. Where cedar or hemlock is abundant, the vines may be pegged down and covered with brush. It is better to place the vines so as to be covered with snow than not to cover them at all.

In localities subject to late frosts, the vines should be left covered as long as possible, which generally has the effect of retarding the growth, and thus secures a degree of immunity from injury from this cause; besides, if not started till the weather becomes settled, an unchecked growth is made, which is in all respects a great benefit to the vine. Care must be taken, however, not to leave them down too long. When taken up, they should at once be tied to the stake or wire, as the case may be, taking every precaution not to injure the buds.

There is a prevalent cause of "winter killing," especially in young vines, which seems not to be generally understood. We refer to standing water. This should not be allowed in the vineyard at any time. The water that accumulates around the stock in little pools is a source of much injury, both in summer and winter. Where applowing is not done in the fall to cover the vines, or where brush is used as a covering, a man should go through the vineyard with a hoe before the ground freezes, and round the earth up against the stock of every vine that has a depression around it where water can settle.

The trellis wires should be moderately loosened in winter. The bark of the posts affords a convenient harbor for insects; this might, therefore, be stripped off in winter, and the cracks and crevices filled with soap or coal tar. A general supervision of the vineyard is almost as necessary in the winter as in the summer.

Marketing.—Those who grow grapes for profit as well as pleasure will appreciate this part of the subject. The object here is to get the fruit to market in such form and condition as to realize the highest price. Ripeness is the first consideration. It is unnecessary to repeat here what we have elsewhere said on this subject. The grapes should be well ripened before being gathered. Baskets and boxes are used for receiving the bunches as they are gathered, the ordinary bushel basket being in common use in some places, but a shallow basket is much better. The bunches should be cut with scissors, and handled so carefully as not to rub off the bloom. The best scissors for the purpose are those which hold the bunch when cut, called grape-gathering scissors

When gathered, they should be carried to the packing-house, or some other suitable place under cover, where they are to be prepared and assorted for market. There should be a smooth, clean table in the room, on which the bunches should be carefully laid as they are prepared. The packer can then assort them without unnecessary handling, which destroys the bloom. Having the bunches in full view, he is enabled to take up the best, or the second best, as may suit his purpose, and they are at once packed in boxes without handling again.

The preparation is done as follows: Being provided with a pair of sharp-pointed scissors, called grape scissors, each bunch is taken up carefully by the foot-stalk, and all the unripe, imperfect, and bruised berries cut out. As this is done, the bunches are laid on the table, and the packer takes charge of them. They should be assorted into at least two qualities, the first comprising the largest and finest bunches. Parties can always be found who will take such grapes at an advance that will pay handsomely for the additional labor. This is one of the chief secrets of success in fruit-growing. As soon as it becomes known that your best and ripest grapes are put up fairly and honestly, a demand will be created for them; they will be sought after, and not have to go begging for customers. It should be the aim of the novice to establish such a reputation from the start. It is only too common a practice to pack the bunches as they come, with a few good ones on the top as a decoy: a species of deception which is sure to be discovered sooner or later, and followed by its appropriate reward.

There will be some bunches too small and others too loose for market, besides "odds and ends." The small and loose bunches can be sold for a less price, or kept for home consumption, or, if the variety is a wine grape, those that are *thoroughly ripe* can be made into wine; otherwise they can be put with the "odds and ends," and made into vinegar, which always commands a good price. There need be nothing lost. We hope, however, that no reader of this book will attempt to make wine from unripe or imperfect grapes.

Boxes and *baskets* of various forms and sizes are used for marketing. If baskets are used, they should be strong, and have wooden covers, provided with lock and key. Wooden boxes are much to be preferred to baskets. There are several in use which answer the purpose well.

Small boxes packed in crates, however, are the most convenient for marketing grapes. The best that we have seen are those used by Mr. Wagener. The crate is eighteen and a half inches long, nine and a quarter wide, and eight and five eighths deep. The ends are made of inch board; the two sides are formed of three laths one inch and a half wide, one at the top and bottom, and one in the middle; and the top and bottom are formed of two laths, dividing each into three equal spaces. A narrow strip of half inch stuff is nailed on each end for handles or ears. The boxes are nine inches long, six inches wide, and four and a quarter deep, made of scale board an eighth of an inch thick. They are made by French & Co., of Pulteney, N. Y. The boxes hold five pounds, and the crate six boxes, making thirty pounds. These crates are of convenient size, carry well, and are easily handled. Their cost is trifling, and they are not generally expected to be returned. For small quantities of a few pounds, fancy and plain pasteboard boxes are sometimes used; but they should be packed in wooden crates, to prevent them from being crushed, and the fruit spoiled.

It requires some skill and experience to pack

grapes so that there shall be no space to permit of jarring in handling the boxes, and no crushed fruit. It is a kind of knowledge that can be acquired by practice alone. In handling, care should be taken at all times not to rub the bloom from the berries, and thus mar their beauty.

We may remark in conclusion, that while poorly ripened and ill-assorted grapes are often sold with difficulty at low rates, those that are ripe and selected with care are uniformly sought after at high prices.

And here we would add a concluding word to every fruit grower upon the advantage of earning a good reputation for growing the best kinds in their greatest excellence, and also for fairness in all the operations of preparing them for market, so that the "brand," when once introduced and known, shall be eagerly sought after by all consumers. Such reputation and superiority, it is true, can only be acquired by high culture and a strict regard of the moralities as respects both the man and the business; but it produces that fine, manly development of the faculties which should be the emulation of all pursuits, and for which grape culture affords such a generous scope. No one need fear that a time will ever come when the superiority that results from a high degree of skill in the management of the vine will fail to meet a correspondingly high pecuniary reward.

Tying.—It will do no harm to repeat the caution against tying too tight. Young canes are often tied so tight as to be cut nearly in two as they increase in size. The object of tying is simply to keep the cane in its place, and the string should be sufficiently loose to admit of a little play, which not only avoids cutting, but prevents the canes from being broken short off at the point of tying, an accident which often happens. Arms, in being laid down, sometimes require to be tied firmly; but in such cases the string must be loosened in good time. A small rope of straw may be used for tying the arms, and left to take care of itself.

Should Plants be Grown between the Rows?—This question has no little importance, and should not be overlooked. There seems to be a great reluctance to give up the whole ground to the grape, especially when it is young. There can be no question that the vines will be all the better for having the soil entirely to themselves, and the best advice we can give is, to grow nothing between the rows; not even a weed.

How to Keep Grapes in Winter. — Grapes have been supposed to be difficult to keep in winter; but they are about as easily kept as apples or pears. All kinds, however, will not keep any more than all kinds of apples or pears. The keeping qualities depend upon the character of the flesh, which must be meaty to keep well; the Diana and Iona are consequently good keepers; but one might as well try to keep a Jargonelle pear as a Concord grape. Some kinds will keep longer than others, the best at the last drying into good raisins, showing but little tendency to decay. The conditions are, a moderately cool, dry, still air. These may be found in a suitable room (not artificially heated) of a cool, uniform temperature.

Sulphite of lime has been successfully used for absorbing the moisture of fruit rooms, and this may be employed advantageously in any room where much fruit is kept. The lime may be placed in a trough standing on legs, and fitted with a faucet for drawing off the water absorbed. The lime may be dried and used again. A refuse product from the salt works is used on a large scale. The French sometimes make a rack, the cross pieces having circular holes on the sides for suspending bottles by the

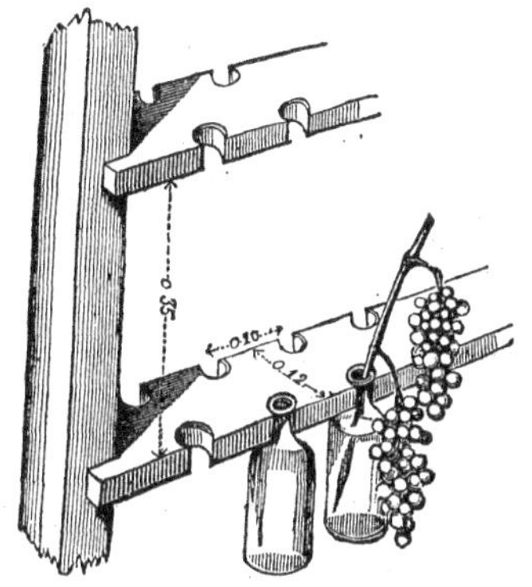

Fig. 142.

neck, as shown in *Fig.* 142. The bottles are filled with water, in which a portion of cane,

Fig. 143.

with the grapes attached, is placed. In this way they will keep good for some time. Another mode of keeping small quantities is to suspend them from hoops in the manner shown in *Fig.* 143. The hoops are provided with small wire hooks, from which the bunches are suspended with the stem end down. On a large scale, a frame is made resembling an arbor, from which the grapes are suspended as shown in *Fig.* 144. By multiplying the cross pieces, large quantities may be kept in this way.

Fig. 144.

In house rooms, under the conditions heretofore named, grapes may be kept in a closet, or in a bureau drawer. Clean white paper should be spread on the bottom, and the bunches placed on the paper singly, so that they do not touch each other. The drawer should be kept partly open till the weather gets cold, when it must be closed. But the best of all arrangements for keeping grapes in rooms is that shown in *Fig.* 145. It may be made of any convenient size, so as to hold from one to three hundred pounds of grapes. Its manner of con-

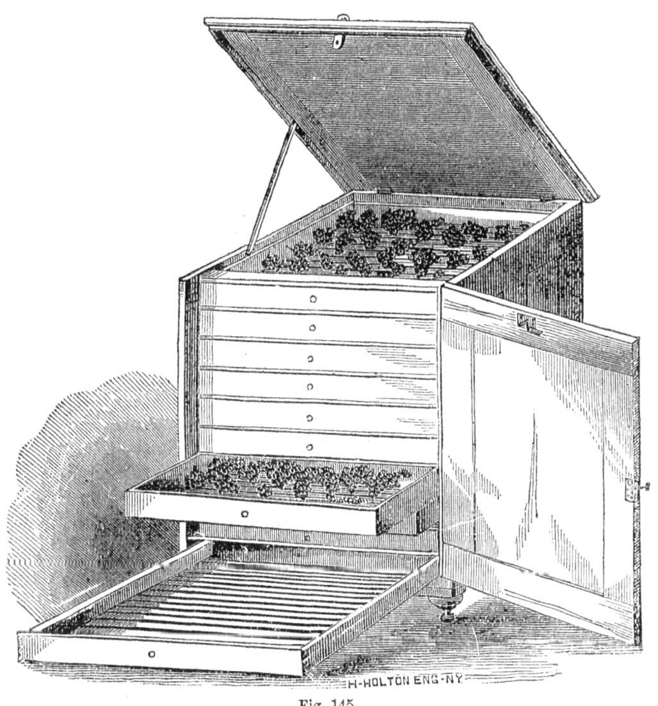

Fig. 145.

struction will be readily understood from an examination of the engraving. The drawers should be deep enough for one layer of grapes, or about four or five inches, and the bottom made of slats. The bunches must be carefully laid on the bottom, and not touch each other. When filled, the lid must be raised and propped up, and the door opened, and remain so till the weather gets cold, when the lid must be let down and the door closed, and kept so. Ventilation will not be needed except on an occa-

Fig. 146.

sional warm day, when the door and lid may be opened for a while. A little frost will do no harm; but if there should be danger of freezing, it may be prevented by throwing a blanket over the chest. In this way some kinds of grapes may be kept till spring. *Fig.* 146 shows the chest closed.

For winter keeping, only the best and evenly ripened grapes should be selected. All bruised and imperfect berries should be cut out, and the bloom preserved as far as possible, for it has something to do with the keeping of the fruit. The bunches should be gathered when they are dry, and handled with care, so as not to loosen the berries from the stalk. Whether suspended from wires or laid in drawers, the bunches should not come in immediate contact with each other, and they should not be handled, except to remove decaying berries. Ventilation should be regulated with reference to a uniformly low temperature, ranging from five to ten above the freezing point. Much moisture in the air should be provided against, either by removing the cause of it, or, where this can not be done, using some good absorbent, such as the sulphite or chloride of lime. If moisture is deposited on the fruit, it is apt to produce mildew. With these precautions, grapes may be kept well during the winter.

Shelters for Protecting and Ripening Fruit. —It sometimes happens that a temporary shelter, even for a single night, will save a vine from an early frost, thereby adding two or three weeks to the season, and insuring the full maturity of the crop. It may be some favorite vine, the fruit of which is highly prized, or it may be a new kind which we are anxious to test, and an unseasonable frost, if not provided against, will blight our hopes. In such cases, a shelter like that shown in *Fig.* 147 will serve to protect a single vine, or a whole row, as the case may be. The cover can be made of straw, or thin boards; or a light frame may be made, and

Fig. 147.

covered with brown muslin, which might hang over the sides a foot or so with advantage. The manner of bracing the posts is plainly seen in the engraving. It is in use by the French.

Fig. 148 shows an arrangement for protecting vines growing against walls. Though intended for the first two rows of a Thomery, it can be made narrower, and used for any wall. It is the application that we want to illustrate here. The projecting cap or eave, No. 1, is of itself a good protector; but if more should become desirable or necessary, then the sash, No. 2, may be used, and will protect the two front rows. It may be let down as shown at No. 4. If No. 3 is used, then we have a protection that can not fail to secure the crop in full maturity.

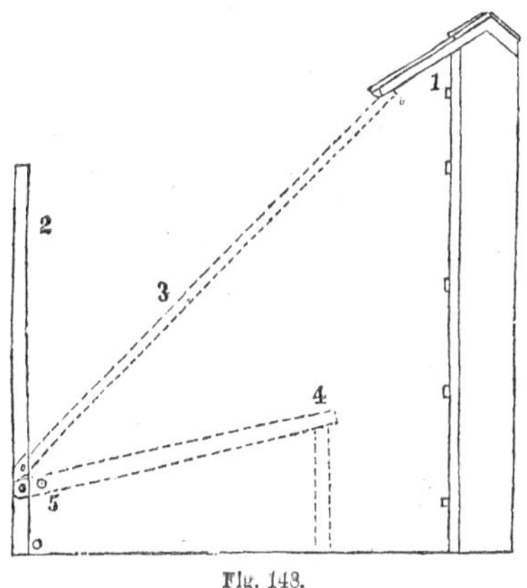

Fig. 148.

The principle may be extended so as to protect a full Thomery. Where sashes and similar conveniences are not at hand, straw mats, pieces of carpet, or muslin, may be suspended from the cap of the wall or fence. If protectors such as we have described, or something similar, are used in a small way, so as to make their advantages apparent, it will not be long before they become somewhat general in the vineyard. If it be first demonstrated on a small scale that the gain is very much more than enough to pay for the additional labor and expense, self-interest, if no other motive, will in time make shelter a necessary appurtenance of the vineyard. To encourage such trial is the object of introducing the illustrations.

Manures.—A few additional words on manures will not be out of place. We should depend chiefly upon barn-yard manure composted with muck. It should be prepared at least one year before it is used, by being laid up and repeatedly turned, till it has become thoroughly decomposed or carbonized. The leaves from the vines, or some from the woods, should be added to the heap, as may also most other things that go to the barn-yard, but all must be thoroughly decomposed. And let it be always remembered, in saving barn-yard manure, that the liquid is always of very much more value than the solid portion. Besides furnishing in itself the most precious of fertilizing materials, it performs the important office of a solvent, thus rendering available many essential materials already in the soil, but which can not be appropriated till they are made soluble. Special manures, such as ashes, bone-dust, etc., are best applied as top-dressings. The prunings should be dried and burned, and the ashes spread on the surface. We must apply nothing to the vineyard, either in kind or quantity, that will produce a gross, succulent growth. The time to apply manure is in the fall, after applowing has been done. The fall rains will dissolve a part of it, and carry it down a few inches, and the remainder will be covered when deplowing is done in the spring. There is some waste, to be sure, but it can not be helped; for we can not apply and plow in the manure as we would for a crop of corn. The feeding roots of the vine adjust themselves near the surface, and the rains carry the manure quite deep enough for their appropriation.

How often manures should be applied will depend upon circumstances. In a soil that is naturally very rich and deep, it should be applied only at long intervals, except it may be ashes; while in one that is lean it should be applied more frequently. The condition of vigor in the vine should guide us in some degree in the application of manure, but we should by all means avoid letting the vines "run down" for want of nourishment in the soil. Manuring the vineyard is one of those cases in which we must be guided chiefly by our good judgment, avoiding the two extremes of rankness or poverty of growth.

Non-Manuring.—We have already cautioned the student against overmanuring, or making the soil too rich. A word or two in regard to the opposite extreme will not be out of place. There are some virgin soils so rich in plant food as not to need the addition of manure at the time of planting, and for some few years afterward. There are others that need the addition of but a small quantity, and so on. There are those who have planted on naturally rich soils who entertain the idea that no manures will in the future be needed; that plant food will be perpetually furnished by the gradual resolution of the mineral constituents of the soil. This is a delusion that has been fruitful of evil, and nothing but evil. It has reduced portions of the country to barrenness, and will reduce others to the same condition if persisted in. With the fruits of it staring us in the face daily, it is amazing that people will not heed its lessons. Inexhaustible fertility is a chimera. Nature has bountifully supplied large portions of the earth with plant food, that man's first and most pressing wants, in taking possession of new territory, might be easily supplied; but she has given us to understand, plainly and sternly, a thousand times over, that beyond the first instance she will only work with us, and not for us. This first supply of plant food seems to us like a providential beneficence for which we are not sufficiently grateful. If we approach the subject with just views of the economics of nature, we shall not only see the impolicy of exhausting the soil of its fertility, but the magnitude of the evil we are inflicting upon our own posterity and the country at large. As every crop we raise consumes a certain amount of plant food, we can not, by any kind of logic, escape the conclusion, that cropping without feeding will ultimately produce barrenness and starvation. It will be wise, therefore, to begin to supply food before the stage of starvation, with its attendant evils, is reached. The wants of the vine, in this respect, should be anticipated. If the supply of food is withheld till the vines show their want of it by feebleness and lessened crops, an injury will have been done which can not easily be repaired.

CHAPTER XXI.

DISEASES AND INSECTS.

Diseases.—The laws of health and disease are very much the same in animal and vegetable life: plants, in common with man, will become liable to disease by an infraction of these laws. The subject is so broad that we can only treat it in a general way here. We wish to establish the analogy, however, since it will do away many illusions in the mind of the novice. Different kinds of animals have their allotted periods of life: in one kind it may be ten years or less, while in others it may be fifty or more; the elephant, for example, lives to a much greater age than the dog. It is so with plants: some fulfill their life in a single year, while others count "the years of their life" by thousands. The average life of plants is greater than that of man. The existence of both is shortened by violence in various forms, and both are liable to disease. The average health and life of man is greatest when he lives in a condition of simplicity, supplying only the natural wants of his appetites; but when he places himself under artificial conditions, he loses a part of his hardihood, becomes more susceptible to disease in its various forms, and recourse is had to various means for restoring and maintaining, as well as may be, the operation of well-known physical laws, which are necessary to health. It is the same with plants. When growing in their natural condition, they are subject to few diseases; but when placed under artificial conditions, and made tender and susceptible by injudicious hybridizing, crossing, selection, propagation, etc., they become peculiarly liable to disease, and means must be used here also to restore and maintain the operation of those physical laws which apply to the case. These brief allusions sufficiently show the general analogy between animals and plants in respect to those physical laws which govern life. If the reader appreciates it as he should, he will learn to study the diseases of the vine for himself, and not look upon them as a sort of fatality not to be overcome.

We will now confine our remarks to the vine. The vine, like man, is subject to disease; and as some men are constitutionally more liable to disease than others, so some kinds of vines are constitutionally more liable to disease than others. There are conditions which favor, or even invite, the attacks of disease in men; and it is the same with the vine. All kinds of vines, no matter what their constitution may be are liable to disease, if placed under conditions favorable to its attacks; there is not a variety in cultivation that has proved an exception, and there never will be. When, therefore, it is said that a vine is healthy, it is in the sense that we say a man is healthy when he is not subject to constitutional disease; at least, that is the sense in which we use the term. What we wish the reader to understand is simply this: that all kinds are liable to disease, some more and others less; and that all kinds, without exception, if placed under conditions unfavorable to the healthy action of the leaves or roots, will become enfeebled or diseased. He will then appreciate the importance of studying the conditions which are necessary to health or strength, and endeavor to supply and maintain them; he will understand that the health of the vine is in a great measure under his control, and that he can judge of the hardiness of kinds only by their deportment under reasonably favorable conditions of growth. What we should all of us do, therefore, is to study diligently the laws and conditions which are concerned in the preservation of health in plants, or, in other words, the conditions that are necessary to normal development and hardy growth. These we have already so fully stated and so earnestly insisted upon, that it is unnecessary to dwell upon them here.

Mildew.—This is a wide-spread and destructive disease, and difficult to manage when established. It is also known by the botanical names *Erysiphe* and *Oidium.* In portions of Europe the *Oidium Tuckeri* has at times been particularly fatal. With us it has been much less injurious. Mildew is a parasite in the form of a fungus, and attacks the leaves, fruit, and wood. It first makes its appearance on the under side of the leaf, like a fine mould. The mycelium penetrates the tissue of the leaf, and destroys it, when the leaf becomes discolored in spots, showing where the fungus is at work. In this place we can not do more than state briefly some of the causes and conditions which produce the disease, with the remedies that have proved most effectual in subduing it.

The reader will get a pretty clear idea of the subject (and a general idea is all we can give him here) if he bears in mind that the sporules of this parasite are almost constantly floating in the air, waiting for a favorable moment for attack, and that the vine, to a very considerable degree, is able to resist its attacks so long as its vital force remains unimpaired and in full vigor. Any cause whatever that *impairs or lessens vital action* favors the attack of the parasite. Hence sudden atmospheric changes from heat to cold, cold rains following hot, dry weather, cold nights following hot days, extreme drought, prolonged rains, and similar causes that *lower the action of the plant more or less suddenly*, are followed by attacks of mildew. It is generally first seen on the leaf, next on the wood, and last on the fruit, though sometimes this order of attack is changed. It soon enters the tissue of the leaf, and gradually destroys it. It also penetrates the cells of the wood, giving them an inky appearance. The disease has then become what we shall call constitutional, and admits of no cure except amputation at some point below the parts diseased; even this must not be too long delayed, for we have found the disease to run through the cells with a rapidity that would hardly be suspected. It would be better to eradicate at once any vine that has become constitutionally affected, for it seldom recovers its health. Fortunately, this stage of the disease is not as yet often seen.

Now, if the reader will bear in mind that the parasite is favored in its attack by a lowering of the vital force of the plant, he will recognize the propriety of the remedies to be used, which are twofold: first, to abate the cause, if possible; secondly, to apply some remedy that will kill the parasite. The two must be combined; for, if the cause which invited the disease remains, it will only favor the multiplication of the very enemy we are trying to destroy. In the grapery these remedies are more easily applied than in the vineyard; still, we are by no means helpless. The atmospheric conditions may be against us, but we must not look idly on, like fatalists. Some effort must be made to save the crop. It may be that the soil is hard and compact; if so, simply breaking up the surface a couple of inches will be a great benefit, but the utmost care must be used not to disturb the roots. The whole vineyard, including the drains, should be carefully examined to see where and how something may be done to restore the normal activity of the plant, by the application of the principles elsewhere explained.

At the same time we must have recourse to some remedy that will destroy the active cause of the disease. Remedies without number have been suggested, but, after long trial, only one has proved so effectual as to commend itself to general use, and that is sulphur. It should be applied directly to the parts affected, but especially to the under side of the leaves. The sulphur should be in the finest state of powder, and dry; and it should be applied with considerable force, at least to the under side of the leaves, so as to penetrate the furze which generally covers this part of the leaf. Sulphur applied in this state, being acted upon by the sun's heat, would seem to combine oxygen enough to form sulphurous acid, the vapor of which destroys the mildew. We have found considerable advantage in adding a portion of finely powdered lime, which increases the action of the sulphur. In this case, sulphite of lime is formed.

Various contrivances have been invented for applying sulphur, one of the simplest of which is the bellows of De la Vergne, which resembles a common bellows without a valve, *Fig.* 149. The sulphur is poured into the hole on the top, B, which is stopped with a cork attached to a string. The nozzle A, is about an inch in di-

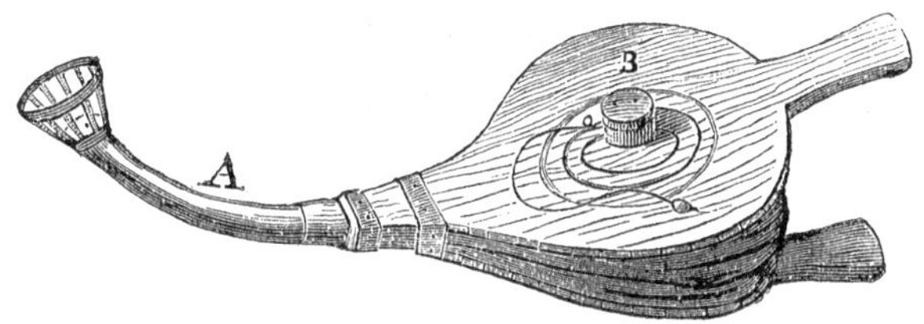

Fig. 149.

ameter, made of tin, and curved upward, and the hole at the end covered with wire gauze for dividing the sulphur, and surmounted with a

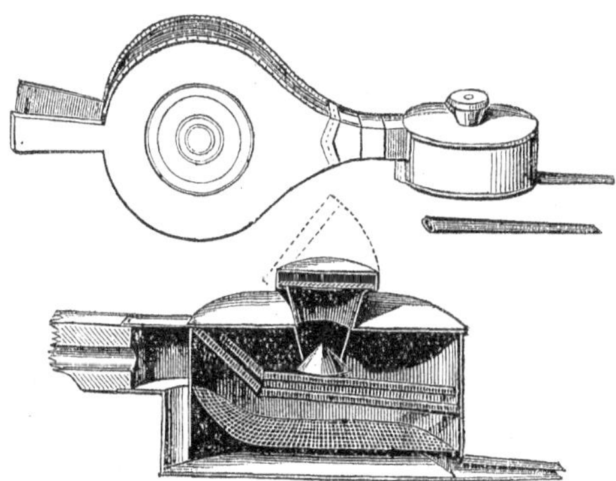

Fig. 150.

spreading or basket-like end piece to give it direction. A similar contrivance, but more complicated, is shown in *Fig.* 150. The sulphur is held in a circular tin box, which forms a part of the nozzle, the arrangement of which is shown on a larger scale. Still another form is shown in *Fig.* 151. In this the sulphur is forced through the nozzle by wind generated by a fan-wheel. The first bellows is much the simplest, and answers the purpose well, enabling one to apply the sulphur rapidly, and in a very thorough manner

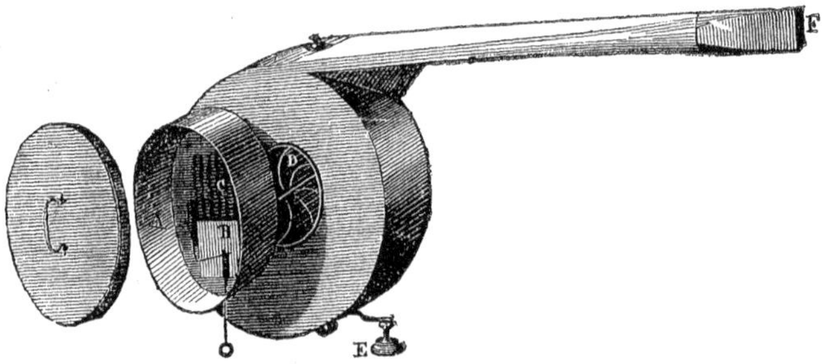

Fig. 151.

But sulphur is best applied as a *preventive* rather than a cure; for if the disease is allowed to become firmly established, it is exceedingly difficult to eradicate. The proper course, therefore, is to apply the sulphur thoroughly to all parts of the vine early in the spring when vegetation begins: many gardeners apply it in the grapery as soon as the vines are pruned in the fall. It should be applied again in June, or as often as we have reason to apprehend such a change in the weather as usually favors the attack of mildew, and before it has visibly appeared. If, in addition to this, we faithfully preserve all the conditions that are necessary to the health and well-being of the vine, mildew will be robbed of most of its terrors, and become a comparatively manageable disease. In this connection, the young vineyardist should especially see that no water is standing in or on the soil, avoid weakening his vines by overcropping, provide for a circulation of air among the foliage by so tying the canes as to prevent the leaves from becoming a tangled and impenetrable mass; in short, apply faithfully the principles that have been fully explained in the progress of this work.

Rot.—Under this name, two or three diseases are known, variously called *brown rot*, *bitter rot*, *black rot*, etc., the names in some places being interchanged. The brown rot, which is infrequent, is a brown spot on the side of the berry similar to those seen on the apple and pear, disfiguring the berry, but not injuring the quality of the fruit. The bitter rot, on the contrary, destroys the quality of the fruit, rendering it too bitter and acrid to eat. The black rot, the most common and destructive of the three, makes its appearance as a small diffused spot, which soon spreads, and involves the whole flesh. The disease spreads through the bunch, and continues its ravages till the berries begin to color, when it disappears. In appearance it resembles the potato rot, and is about equally destructive. It is of fungous origin, though its nature is not well understood. There can be no doubt, however, that the predisposing causes are very much like those that produce mildew on the leaf. Some varieties of the grape, as, for example, the Catawba, are peculiarly susceptible to its attack, and in unfavorable seasons the fruit proves an entire loss. The Diana, Isabella, Concord, and others also suffer from its attacks in bad seasons, but in a much less degree. We know of nothing better calculated to arrest the disease than the general course of treatment recommended for mildew, and sprinkling the bunches with finely powdered lime, the treatment to be used as a preventive. The berries, however, should be removed when they become diseased, carried from the vineyard, and destroyed. If the disease is of fungous origin, it is plain that leaving the berries on the bunch, or on the ground as they fall, only serves to increase and intensify it.

Sun Scald.—This makes its appearance on the leaves in spots of greater or less size, and destroys the tissue. It is of a brick-red color, and this may have given rise to the absurd brick-yard theory by which it was attempted to account for it. Its cause is not certainly known, but it is no doubt of atmospheric origin. It is supposed, with some reason, that globules of moisture are formed into lenses, and the sun, acting upon these, burns the leaves. It does not often affect the general health of the vine seriously. We know of no remedy.

These are the principal diseases of the vine, in regard to which it may be said, that they are mostly of such a nature that remedies, to be effective, must be used as *preventives* rather than cures.

INSECTS.

It would be somewhat difficult to say whether the vine suffers most from insects or disease, but we think insects might easily be managed by concerted action. In every fruit-growing district there should be an "Insect Society," which should have a grand spring and fall exhibition, with smaller weekly ones *ad interim.* At these exhibitions prizes should be offered for the "biggest bushel" of rose-bugs, the "largest quart" of curculios, and so on. These prizes should be liberal enough to enlist the services of men, women, and children, among whom there are always idlers enough to keep the "insect plague" within harmless bounds. We have tried the experiment with the best results. The insect collectors had access to all the trees and vines in the neighborhood, and they very seldom injured a plant. It is only by some kind of united action that much good can be effected. With its aid, the rose-bug has been made to disappear from some localities, and so might other kinds of insects.

The Rose-bug, (*Melolontha subspinosa*, *Fig.* 152.)—This is one of the most destructive pests that troubles the vine. It makes its appearance in great multitudes about the time the vine comes into blossom, which it soon destroys, and often injures the foliage. If the vine is jarred, the beetles drop to the ground, but soon make their way back. This dropping propensity has suggested the best method of destroying them, which is to hold a basin of water under them, and jar the vine, when they immediately drop. A couple of active men will soon go over an

Fig. 152.

acre; but the operation will have to be repeated several times. When collected in this way, they must be killed by crushing or pouring boiling hot water on them, for they have as many lives as a cat. We have kept them in a barrel of water for half a day, and had most of them come out alive. They are too stupid to know when they are dead. Birds will not eat them, for their hooked claws cause them to stick in the throat. We remember once seeing a cat-bird have one in its bill; it seemed to be deliberating whether it should run the risk of swallowing it, but we finally got tired of waiting the result, and left. It has been said that poultry are very fond of them, but any body can convince himself that this is not so. The only effectual remedy is the basin of water and a stout foot. We have tried many others, but found them all wanting.

May Beetle or Cockchafer.—There are several of this family that are hurtful to the vine, but the most numerous and destructive is the common May Beetle, (*Phyllophaga quercina* of Harris,) of a dark brown color, and about three quarters of an inch long. At night the air is full of them, and a light will entice large numbers into the house. They destroy the fruit and leaves in the beetle state, and prey upon the young and tender roots of all kinds of plants when in the larva form; they are especially destructive to the roots when the larvæ get to be three or four years old, when they are about three eighths of an inch in diameter, and quite an inch and a half long; the head is brown, the body yellowish white, and the tail a dull blue. Multitudes of the larvæ are turned up in plowing and spading. Poultry eat the larvæ as well as the beetle greedily, and they should be allowed to run at large when these operations are performed.

Late at night and about daylight in the morning are the best times for destroying the beetles. If the plant is jarred at this time, they will generally drop, and may be caught on a sheet or in a basket. At midnight and later we have stripped them from the vine, guelder rose, etc., by handfuls, the plants seeming to be black with them. In the evening they are on the wing. It is only between midnight and daylight that they can be found congregated together in this way. Birds are very fond of them, but the beetles conceal themselves during the day, and are not easily found.

We have no remedy for the larvæ, except exposing them by turning up the soil, when large numbers of them will be destroyed by poultry and birds. The moles help a little, for we have found both the larvæ and the beetle in its stomach. Fortunately, all the cockchafers prefer grass land for their nidus, so that the depredations of the larvæ are confined mostly to young vineyards made on newly broken land.

Fig. 153.

The spotted bug (*Pelidnota punctata*, *Fig.* 153) is also an enemy to the vine, destroying the fruit and the leaves. It is a large yellowish brown beetle, with three dark spots on each wing cover, and a similar spot on each side of the thorax. They appear in July and August, and, unlike the May beetle, fly by day. They are usually found on the under side of the leaf, and must be destroyed by hand, like the rest. They are not numerous, however.

About the size of this, but appearing as early as May, is the golden bug, (*Areoda lanigera*,) a very beautiful beetle of a bright lustrous yellow. It sometimes eats the leaves of the vine, and very rarely the berries. The larvæ of this and the Pelidnota are like that of the

May beetle. We have several times hatched both these beetles from larvæ found in old manure heaps, thinking we had the larva of the May beetle.

The *Vine Chafer*, (*Anomala cœlebs*,) resembling a small May beetle, we have found one of the greatest beetle pests that infests the vine. They appear in June and July, are about three eighths of an inch long, rather broad, and of a muddy brown color; we have sometimes seen them blackish brown. On the least jar they double their legs up quickly and drop to the ground. Catching them on sheets as they fall is the best way to destroy them. There is another beetle resembling this in color and form, but only about one third the length, that eats the unexpanded bud. Sometimes they are quite numerous.

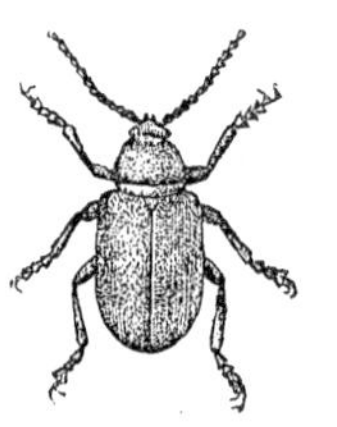
Fig. 154.

Steel-blue Beetle, (*Haltica chalybia*, *Fig.* 154, enlarged four times.)—In some seasons and places this beetle, though quite small, does a large amount of harm, appearing in great numbers, and attacking the buds just as they begin to swell. They sometimes bury their whole bodies in the bud, eating out the young bunches and leaves. They continue their depredations until the fruit has set. Where they are numerous, grapes become very scarce. They seem to be somewhat migratory in their habits. The only remedy that we know of is to knock them off and kill them.

Vine Hopper or Thrips, (*Tettigonia vitis*, *Fig.* 155, enlarged four times.)—This has become one of the most formidable insect enemies that the vineyardist has to contend with. Its general appearance is like that of a cicada or locust, but it is very diminutive in size, less than an eighth of an inch, but as "lively as a cricket." It is of a pale straw color or whitish yellow, with two little red lines on the head. They begin to appear in June on the under side of the leaf, and are then wingless. As they increase in size they shed their skins, and finally become winged. They suck the juice from the leaves, causing them to turn yellow, and unfitting them for their functions to such a degree as to impair the ripening of both the fruit and the wood. They sometimes abound in such myriads that, if the vine be disturbed, it is impossible to breathe without inhaling them. Some of the remedies proposed for their destruction are altogether impracticable in the

Fig. 155.

vineyard. Of all the remedies we have tried, we have found lime and sulphur to be the best. Two parts of sulphur and one of powdered caustic lime should be well mixed, and applied with the bellows above described. It should be thrown on all parts of the foliage, but especially the under side. Under this treatment they will cease to be formidable. Rain or high winds will make it necessary to repeat the application. The best time to apply it is in the morning when the air is still.

The *red spider* (*Acarus tellarius*) is sometimes found on the under side of the leaf, and succumbs to the sulphur remedy above. It should be applied when they first appear, for they soon spin a fine web which is not easy to penetrate. A species of black *Aphis*, *Fig.* 156, is also sometimes found on the ends of the canes, but is readily destroyed by drawing the cane through either the gloved or naked hand.

Fig. 156.

Caterpillars.—Several kinds of caterpillars are more or less injurious to the vine. The large green caterpillars of some of the *Sphinges*, like those so common on the tomato, are sometimes destructive to young vines, in a very short time consuming every leaf on the plant. Those that live on the vine have been placed in a group by Harris, and called *Philampelus*, or lovers of the vine. *Fig.* 157 is the larva of one of these, of the natural size. Killing by hand is the only remedy.

Fig. 157.

The bluish brown caterpillar of the *Eudryas grata*, which appears early in July, is a great pest in some localities. It not only consumes the entire foliage, but eats off the bunches of fruit. They are so small at first as scarcely to be seen, but grow fast. Lime and sulphur, as well as a solution of whale-oil soap, or the Gishurst compound, will destroy them; but it is difficult to make solutions reach them, and hand-picking is tedious, as they conceal themselves on the under side of the leaf. Birds are very fond of them; hence in the cities, where there are no birds, these caterpillars make sad work with the vine. The lime and sulphur remedy may drive them off, but we have not tried it.

The caterpillar of the *Procris Americana* is also a pest, but less formidable than the preceding, since it is gregarious; the whole nest keep together, feeding along side by side. It first consumes the surface of the leaf. It is yellow, with black tufts along its back.

The caterpillar of the *Selandria vitis*, a species of saw-fly, is also gregarious, feeding in rows on the under side of the leaf. It is light green, with a black head and tail. Both these kinds of caterpillars should be looked for early; being in schools, they are easily killed. They may be found in July and August. Better still, look for the eggs on the under side of the leaf, and destroy them.

The leaves of the vine will sometimes be seen rolled up. This is done by one of the *leaf-rollers*, a lively little green caterpillar, which, on being disturbed, will speedily roll itself out and fall down, suspended by a fine web. They may be crushed in the leaf.

Early in the season, when the young shoots have grown an inch or so, the young leaves will be found drawn together so as to seriously interfere with the upward growth. If the leaves be drawn carefully apart, there will be found a small, brownish-yellow caterpillar, covered with short hairs, *Figs.* 158 and 159. It destroys the young bunches of fruit as well as the leaves. The caterpillar is very tender, and a slight pressure will crush it. The young leaves may thus be pressed together sufficiently hard to kill the caterpillar without injury to them, and then drawn apart. In this way they can be disposed of pretty quickly. Unless they are killed early, the crop will be materially lessened.

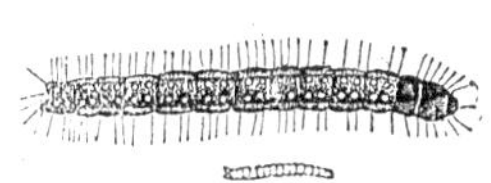

Fig. 158, Caterpillar.

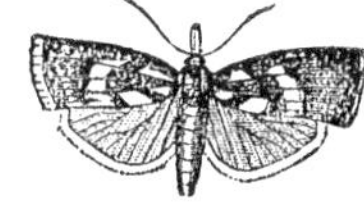

Fig. 159, Moth.

Occasionally the leaves near the end of the growing cane will be found covered with protuberances, which, on being opened, are found to contain a small yellow slug, which seems to be the larva of some gall-fly, but which we do not know, not having yet succeeded in maturing them. They do not seem to materially check the growth of the cane, but still it would be well to destroy them.

Young vines that start from a bud under or very near the surface are sometimes eaten partly or entirely off by the *cut-worm.* Sometimes the damage done in this way is quite serious. The worm may be found near the plant, and about an inch under the surface. Young vines in similar condition are also, but not so often, attacked by the wire-worm. The young vine makes a good start, but after a while stops growing, and finally sickens away and dies. The mischief is discovered only when it is too late. The course of the vine is similar to this, also, when the roots are preyed upon by the larva of the May beetle; but the May beetle preys upon the roots of young and old alike.

It would be curious to learn how much of the damage to fruit trees, of all kinds, now imputed to drought, winter killing, etc., really belongs to grubs of various kinds constantly preying upon the roots, and thus unfitting the plants to withstand changes and extremes of any kind. We are now investigating this interesting question, and have already reached the conclusion that "drought," "winter killing," etc., are by no means as great sinners as they are made to appear. A "scape-goat" has always been found a convenient animal, and horticulturists have two or three almost as big as elephants.

Those who wish to make themselves familiar

with the habits of insects should consult the works of Harris, Fitch, Trimble, etc., and the monthly publication called "The Entomologist."

Delaware.

PART SECOND.

CHAPTER XXII.

PLAN OF QUESNEL—MODES OF BEDDING VINES—PLAN OF CHARMEUX—GROUND TRAINING—TRAINING WITHOUT STAKES—TRAINING ON TREES AND TRELLIS COMBINED—RINGING THE VINE—A MILDEWED LEAF—A RACK FOR STAKES—"HEELING IN."

WE have endeavored, as far as possible, to preserve the elementary character of this volume, and have, therefore, confined the subject of training to the explanation and application of its principles, and working them out on the most useful forms, giving only a few examples of what is commonly called "fancy" training, as "studies" for the student, to aid him in a more thorough application of the principles to forms or systems in general. To this end we might have added a few more in the body of the work, but we wished to avoid distracting the reader's mind with unusual forms or references till he had fully mastered the principles of training, and hence no reference is made to this part. The examples now presented will further assist the student in applying the principles of training to a variety of cases that occur in the surroundings of the home. He should study the principle as well as the form.

Plan of Quesnel.—We have elsewhere alluded to the ingenuity of the French in working out forms to meet the wants of cases as they arise, or rather to anticipate them. *Fig.* 160 is an example. It is a literal copy from Du Breuil, and shows, among other things, how the French alternate the double and single spurs, a practice quite common among them when the necessity of the case calls for it, either for renewal or to favor the length of the arm. It affords facilities, also, for replacing an arm in the manner elsewhere described. It has been explained that there is a difficulty in keeping arms in full bearing when extended much beyond four feet in length. Where there is a necessity for making them longer, as in the example before us, the introduction of the single spur will aid materially in keeping them in full bearing. They should be started, as a rule, from base buds;

and with the attention that may always be given to the limited number of vines grown in this way, these single spurs may be kept reasonably short. When they get long, they must be renewed.

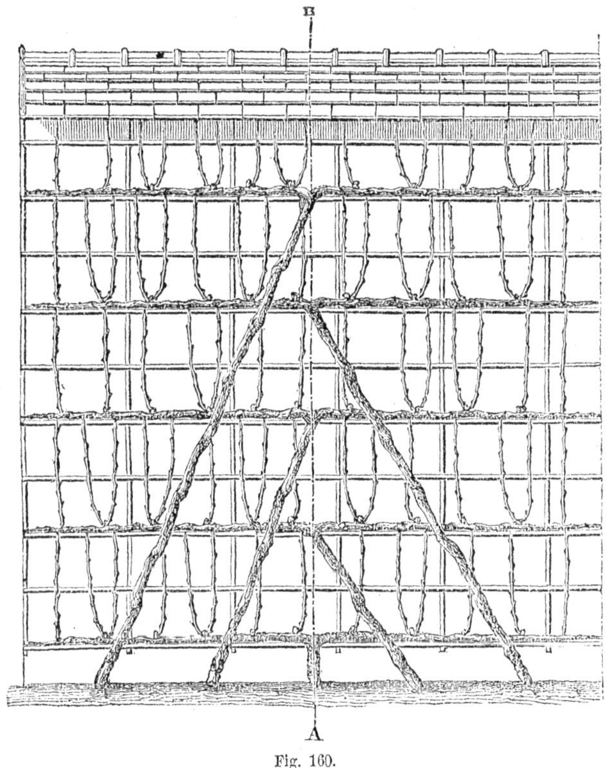

Fig. 160.

The form in *Fig.* 160 may be adapted to high walls, sides of cottages, extensions, stables, etc. In the figure the wall is about twelve feet high and twelve feet wide, and the vines are planted two feet apart. The plants should be of the best possible description, such as is shown in *Fig.* 3, p. 36. Such vines will have stout canes, which will hasten materially the formation of the upper tiers. The stocks that support the upper tiers should be carried up so as to shade equally the arms of the lower tiers, as shown in the engraving. The arms are formed in the usual manner. The vines are planted about a foot from the wall, and the trellis set the same distance from it, so as to allow of a circulation of air between the vines and the wall.

Modes of Bedding Vines.—But vines that are planted two feet apart, and only a foot from the wall, speedily interfere with each other by the intermingling of their roots; and the weak are gradually overpowered by the strong. The soil being warmest next the wall, the roots congregate and work there, so that the weak vines have but a remote chance of recovering. This difficulty is overcome, and the soil more evenly filled with roots, by planting the vines several feet from the wall, and bringing them up to it by layering or bedding. The wall will not be so soon covered, it is true, but the vines may be fruited while being brought to the wall, and in this respect there need be no special loss.

Let us illustrate the manner of doing this. *Fig.* 161 will help the reader to understand the operations to be performed. The vines may be planted from three to six feet from the wall, but

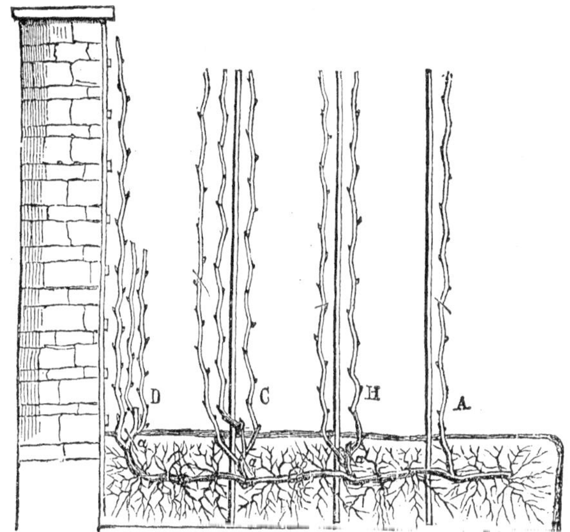

Fig. 161.

in the illustration the lesser distance will be taken. Proceed as follows: Three feet from the wall, and parallel with it, dig a trench, and in it plant the vines two feet apart. Put a stake to each, and grow a single cane the first year, as seen at A. In the fall prune this cane about eighteen inches long, and lay it down for the winter. In the spring of the second year move the stakes one foot nearer the wall, and bed or layer the canes to the stakes, bending up the ends and tying them to the stakes. On the end of the cane bent up select two buds for canes, and disbud the rest. The lower bud should be on the side facing the wall, and low down, to facilitate the next bedding. The bedded portion of the cane should be treated as directed for *layers*. From the selected buds grow two canes, as seen at H. They may carry two bunches of fruit. In the fall, cut the upper cane entirely away at the cross-mark *a*; then cut the lower cane about eighteen inches long, and cover for the winter.

In the spring of the third year move the stakes one foot nearer to the wall, and bed the canes to the stakes as before. Select three buds for canes this year, like C, having the lowest bud on the side next the wall. The bedded cane must be treated as usual. The canes may carry two bunches each. In the fall, cut the two upper canes entirely away at *a*, prune the lower cane about eighteen inches long, and cover for the winter. In the spring of the fourth year, the canes are bedded to within a foot of the wall, and three buds selected for canes on the vines that are to form the two lower tiers; on those for the upper tiers select one bud. In this way all the arms may be begun at the same time; for the vines are now so strong that those restricted to one bud will

Fig. 162

make canes reaching to the top of the wall. Each of the canes may carry two bunches of fruit. The upper canes in all the above instances should be pinched two or three leaves above the fruit, and the pinching frequently repeated. The object is to make the lower cane as stout as possible, and to confine the action in the other canes as much as possible to the fruit, this being the only purpose for which these canes are grown; if the action is very strong, they may be bent down. In the fall of this year, the vines will present the appearance shown in *Fig.* 162. The upper canes must now all be cut off at *a*, and the lower canes pruned at the points where it is desired to form the arms. To ascertain these points, the vines must be bent to their places on the wall. The pruning finished, the vines are to be laid down for the winter. From this point the training is proceeded with as explained above in *Fig.* 160.

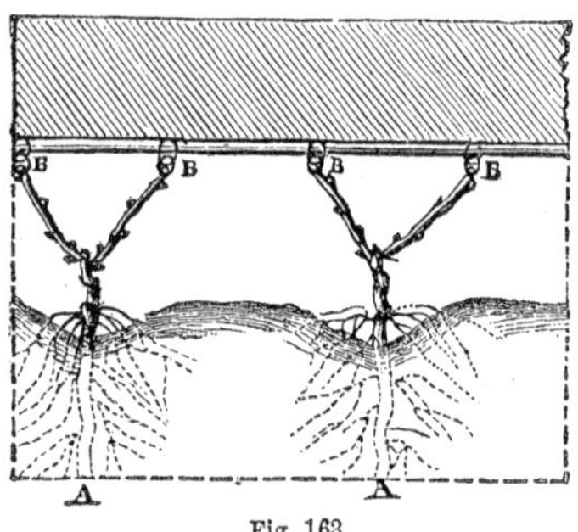

Fig. 163.

By the plan shown in *Fig.* 163, half the number of vines may be saved, which is an object where good vines are scarce; but it will occupy a year more to establish the vines in full bearing. In this case, the vines are planted four feet apart instead of two, and brought to the wall in the manner above described till the last bedding is reached, when two canes are bedded instead of one, and at an angle, as seen in the engraving. The ends are turned up, and one cane grown on each for stocks.

Still another method may be pursued, which will be found very useful where the number of stocks required is so great as to make very close planting indispensable. Let us suppose we have a building so high and narrow as to require the stocks to be one foot apart in order to furnish the necessary number of tiers of arms. In this case proceed as follows: six feet from the building plant a row of vines two feet apart; six feet in front of these, or twelve feet from the building, plant another row of vines two feet apart. The vines in these two rows must alternate each other in the line of direction to the building, so that the vines in the outer row, when bedded, will come between the vines in the first row. The first, or inner row, must be bedded to the building. The second row must be bedded to within five or six inches of the line where the first row was planted. At this point grow one good cane on each, and in the fall prune it about six feet long. In the spring, dig a very narrow trench, about six inches deep, from these canes to the building. Now procure some small round tile, pass the cane through the tile, lay the tile in the trench, and cover, turning up the end of the cane about a foot from the building. The object of running the cane through the tile is to prevent it from emitting roots, and interfering with the vines planted in the first row, which are already so close together as to need all the border adjacent to the building. Instead of running them through the tile, they may be grown above ground till two years old, when the disposition to root will be less; but the best plan is to use the tile, and put the vines in their places at once. If the number of vines required for the tiers makes it necessary, three rows of vines may be planted, allowing five or six feet of border for each row.

The manner of performing the operation once understood, the reader will readily comprehend how it may be modified and adapted to a variety of circumstances. For example, we may wish to grow vines on the side of a house, but there is no suitable place for a border within ten or twenty feet of it. In this case, the canes may be brought to the house gradu-

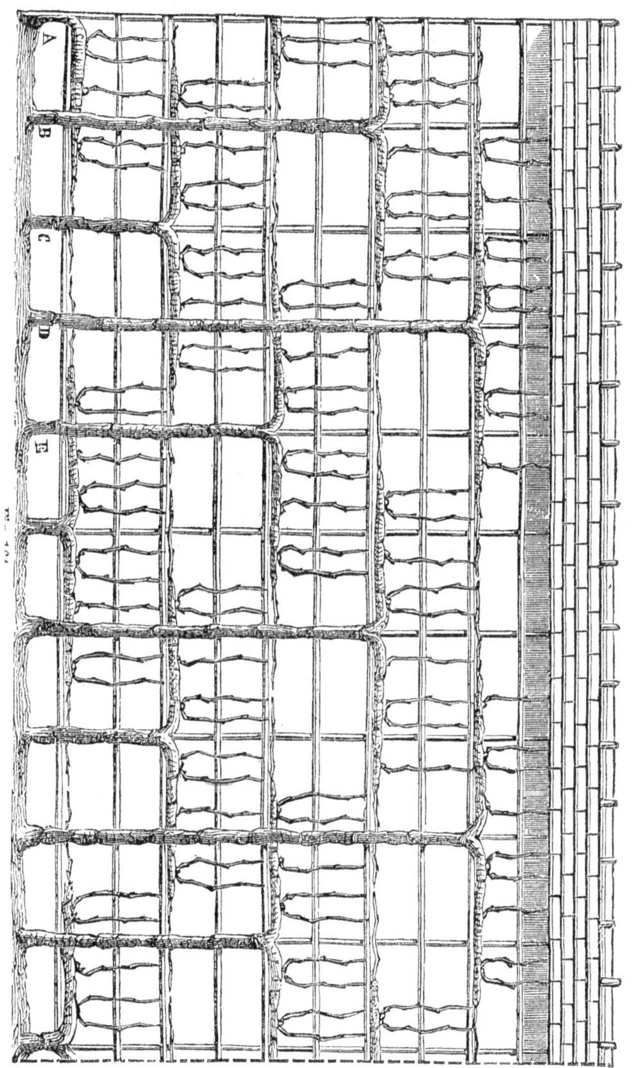
A
B
C
D
E

ally through tile, or the canes may be grown along the border till they are sufficiently long to reach the house, and then carried there through the tile, and brought up through neat earthen pedestals. There are many other cases in which the plan may be usefully applied, such, for example, as making a border on one side of a house while the vines are trained on another.

Plan of Charmeux.—Fig. 164 presents another good "study," which may be applied to a wall, a high trellis, or a house. It is another literal copy from the French, showing the alternate single and double spurs, and also an improved arrangement of the stocks, by which the arms in the lower tiers are more equally shaded. It is the plan practiced at Thomery by M. Charmeux. It was found, in the course of time, that the shading of one arm more than another produced an unfavorable effect, destroying the balance of the arms, and the present arrangement was made to counteract it. It will be seen, on examination, that the stocks of the upper tiers shade the lower arms in about the same place on each side. This is a matter of more moment than would at first sight appear. The stocks might, indeed, be carried up behind the trellis, and shading the arms thus avoided, but it would involve considerable trouble. The reader will notice here, again, that the spurs are alternately single and double; and this he will find to be very often the case in French training, where the arms much exceed four feet in length, and in some cases where it does not. By lessening or increasing the number of tiers, this plan can be readily applied to a wall, trellis, or house of any height. The mode of training the reader already understands.

Ground Training.—In *Fig.* 165 the reader will

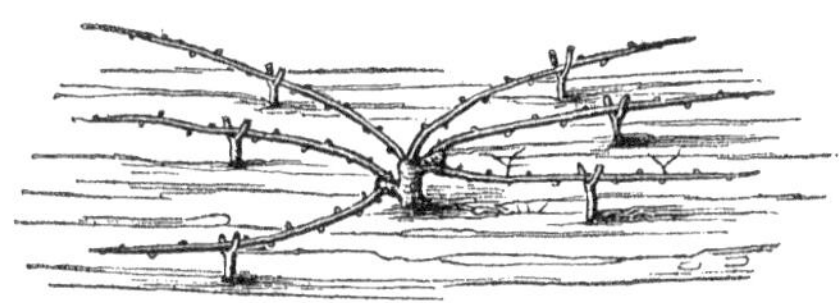

Fig. 165.

find another "study," called ground training. It consists of a system of three double spurs, with the fruit canes bent horizontally in ray form, and tied to low stakes, from twelve to eighteen inches high. It is practiced in the north of France. A good stout cane must first be grown, and this pruned so as to get three canes for spurs at the proper height. These three canes must be pruned to the two lowest buds for spurs, and the spurs bent down horizontally, so as to bring them all on the same level. To do the training neatly, at three feet from the stock, six stakes should be driven in at equal distances, so as to form a circle six feet in diameter. Connect the opposite stakes together by wires crossing each other in the middle at the stock. From each spur two canes must be grown, making a cane for each wire. The canes may carry two bunches each, and

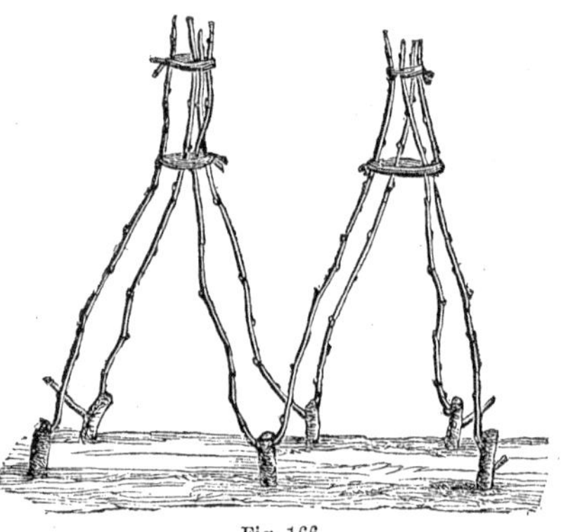

Fig. 166.

should receive their first pinching three leaves from the fruit. Athallage will need pretty constant attention. The fruit, in consequence of receiving so much radiated heat from the earth in the fall, will ripen finely. An early frost may easily be kept off by throwing a sheet over the vine.

Training without Stakes.—*Fig.* 166 is an example of growing vines without stakes. It is given for information, rather than as an example to be followed here. It was first proposed by M. Miramont. Its primary object seems to have been to secure shade for the fruit as much as any thing else. The vines, of

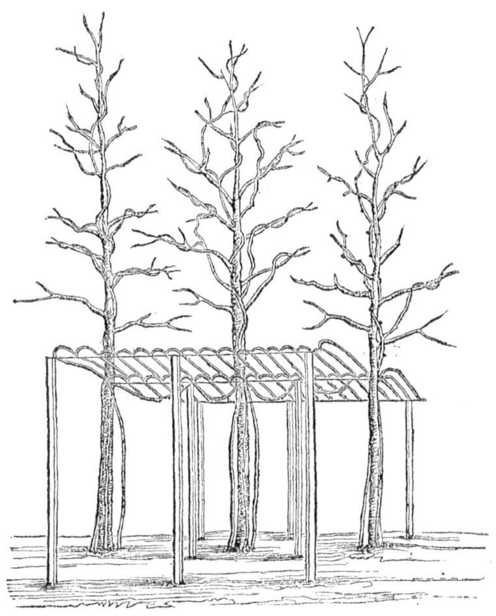

Fig. 167.

course, must be grown close together, and furnished with two single spurs.

Training on Trees and Trellis combined.—*Fig.* 167 presents another example of French training, by which trees and a trellis are so covered as to form a beautiful rustic arbor, affording a grateful shade as well as fruit. The student will find a good deal of pleasure in working this "study" out. The trees should be planted at the same time as the vines, and should be open headed, or made so by pruning. Trees already planted may be adopted, however, if they are suitably located. The soil should have a thorough preparation; the vines must be planted some five or six feet from the trees, and brought to them by bedding. There should be three vines for each tree, except the last, which should have only one. One of these three should form an arm on the trellis on the right of the tree, another an arm on the trellis on the left, and the third trained over the tree. The arms should be extended and spurred in the usual manner. The beauty of the arbor will be enhanced if a vine is planted at each trellis post, and trained on a low stock with one or two double spurs. With these explanations, the student will, no doubt, be able to work this "study" out, and apply it wherever the conditions are found.

Reversed Horizontal Arms.—We present, in *Fig.* 168, an example of the reversed horizontal arm, in order to give the student a clearer idea

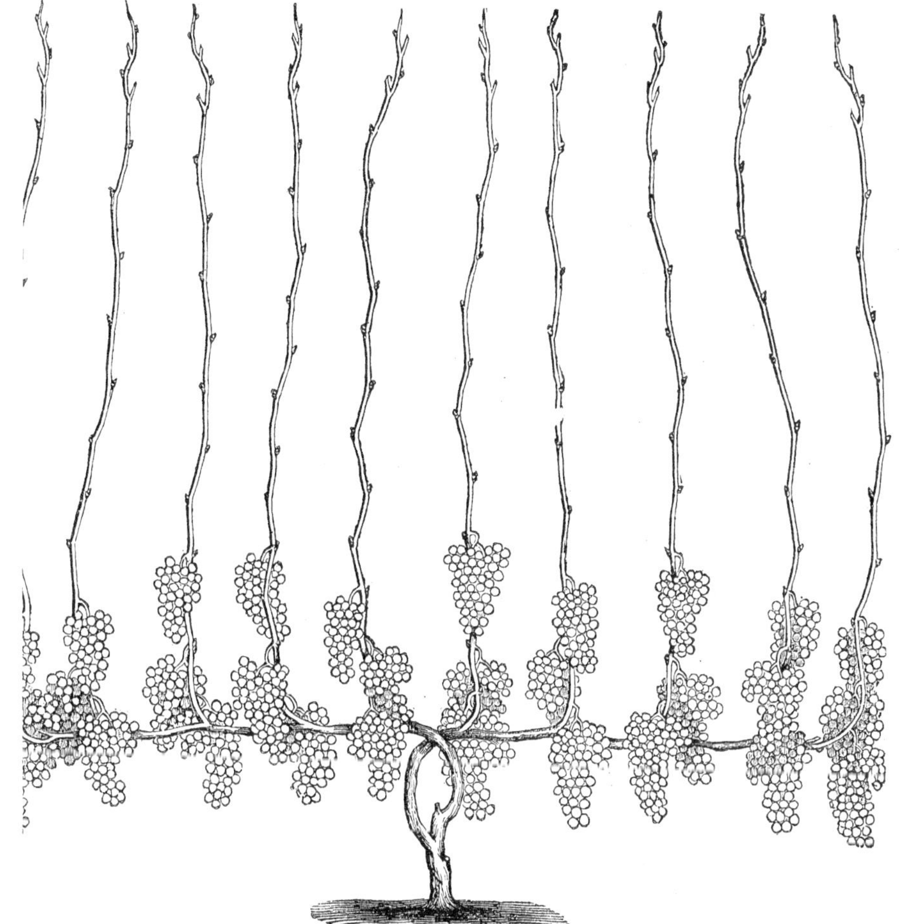

Fig. 168.

of the manner in which it is formed. It is not intended as a substitute for the gradual lengthening of the arm, but as particularly applicable to such varieties of the vine as grow rankly, and in consequence do not develop their buds strongly on the lower part of the cane. It is a very certain mode of getting strong canes for spurs near the stock. With the exception of the reversal, the arms are formed in the usual way.

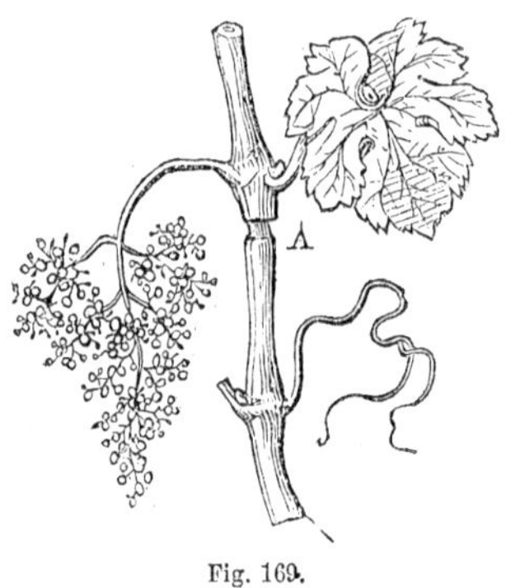

Fig. 169.

Ringing the Vine.—This is a very simple as well as a very old practice. It consists in removing a ring of bark from the fruit cane, just below the fruit, or even from old wood or an arm; but is generally confined to the fruit cane, since it renders the wood above the incision useless. It may be applied to any fruit-bearing tree. The operation is usually performed with a knife, though a peculiar kind of shears has been invented, with which it is neatly and quickly done. *Fig.* 169 is a copy of a fruit cane on which the operation has been performed. Two incisions are made half an inch or less apart, nearly an eighth of an inch deep, and extending entirely around the cane. The bark between the incisions must be taken out clean. If done early in the season, the bark will peel off; but on old wood it becomes necessary to use the knife. By this operation the return of the sap is mostly prevented, vital action is intensified above the incision, and the ripening process greatly hastened. As the result, the berries are increased in size, and ripen before their natural time; but the ripening process, in consequence of being driven too fast, has elaborated the juices of the fruit imperfectly, and the fruit is, therefore, deteriorated in quality. In other words, we have gained size and earliness at the expense of goodness, which is no gain at all. The deterioration will be in proportion to the earliness at which the operation is performed. It may be done at any time between the formation of the fruit and the period of coloring; the later the better, so far as the quality of the fruit is concerned. It is one of those operations in horticulture which the novice will do well to have recourse to only as an amusement.

A Mildewed Leaf.—The beginner, unaided, may not readily recognize the appearance of mildew. To assist him, we have copied *Fig.*

Fig. 170.

170, from Du Breuil. This is a leaf in an advanced stage of the disease, and gives a very good idea of its appearance. It should first be looked for in the angles made by the veins on the under side of the leaf.

A Rack for Stakes.—Stakes soon decay when left on the ground during the winter. *Fig.* 171 shows a simple and convenient rack for keeping them.

"*Heeling In.*"—We have elsewhere described

the operation of "heeling in." *Figs.* 172 and 173 will help the reader to a clearer idea of the

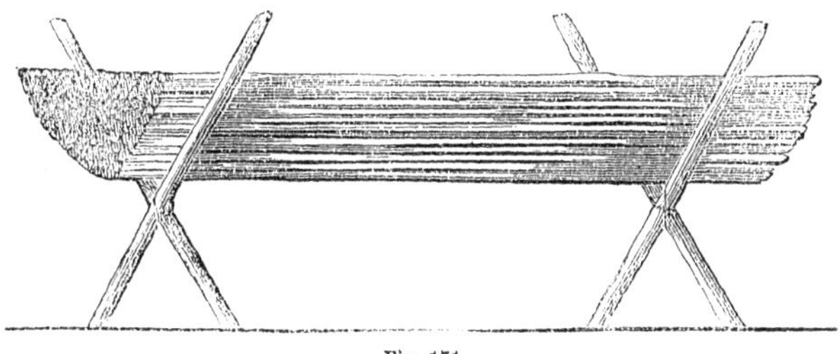
Fig. 171.

operation. *Fig.* 172 shows the trench opened and the plants laid in, ready to be covered.

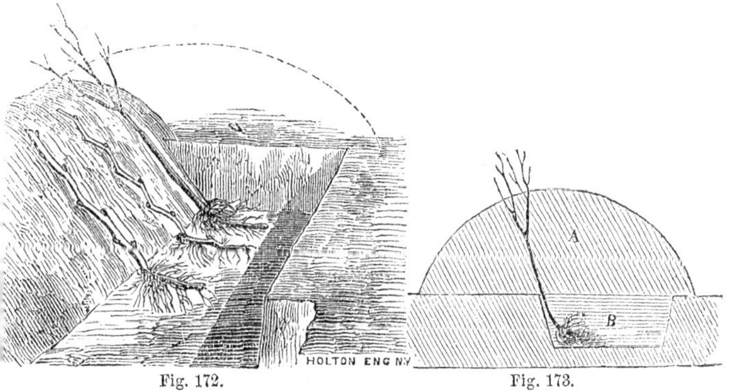

Fig. 172. Fig. 173.

Fig. 173 shows the trench filled and the plants covered.

CHAPTER XXIII.

WINE MAKING.

In this chapter we shall condense experience, reading, and the memoranda of one of the most accomplished connoisseurs among us. A bibliography will be furnished elsewhere.

Wine making is regarded by some as a mysterious art, to be acquired only by a few specially gifted for the purpose; and by others as something that follows in due course from planting any kind of grapes, and treating them in some fancied manner. Those who follow us through this chapter will see that it partakes of neither, but is a manly art, very simple in its general principles, but exceedingly attractive in its comprehensive details when pursued to its ultimate results. It needs no extensive scientific acquirements for its successful practice, and the following directions will carry their reasons with them so obviously that no one need feel any doubt as to the proper course to be pursued to reach a *good* result; the *best* results, however, will only be attained by the utmost diligence and care.

The good housewife, who makes the best of bread, exercises as much skill, and of as fine a quality, as is required to make the best of wine; and in both cases there are few who are able to appreciate fully the excellence either of the product or the maker. The illustration may be homely, but a better one could scarcely be found. A loaf of bread, perfectly balanced in farina and gluten, neither too moist nor too dry, exact in lightness, with its fermentation carried to just the proper point of sweetness, is a work of high art; nay, practically, of the highest art, for it is the foundation upon which happy and healthful living is built. It will not do to say that this is an every-day performance, for it is nothing of the kind. Moreover, no matter what the skill and experience of the housewife may be, she must have *good* flour to make the best of bread. And it is just so with wine. No matter what the skill and experience of the wine maker may be, he must have *good* grapes to make good wine, and the *best* of grapes to make the best of wine.

Wine making is so new in this country that its grand simplicity can scarcely be comprehended by any of us. While chemistry has done much in explaining the action of the different processes, it has done very little in directing how the operations should be performed. The only difficulty in the way of uniform success in wine making, either for family use or commerce, is that of persuading all to begin the subject at the beginning, and then pursue it in due order. Some will persist in efforts to make good bread out of bad flour, just as others will persist in efforts to make good wine out of bad grapes.

For the first step toward obtaining good wine, directions were given when we advised the planting of good grapes. That is the only step that leads in the right direction. Good wine can come only from the pure, unadulterated juice of good grapes that have been well ripened. The succeeding steps have also been fully described, but it may be intimated again, in view of its importance, that the bunches should be left on the vine to attain the greatest measure of maturity that is possible, even to the degree of shriveling in some cases. A slight frost will not damage them. The grapes should not be gathered when covered with dew or moisture. The bunches should be gathered without bruising them, using the scissors before mentioned, and the baskets or tubs usually made for the purpose. The assorting must be done with the utmost care, as elsewhere described. We repeat, *none but sound, thoroughly ripe berries must go into the wine press.*

The *implements* used in wine making are not numerous, and consist principally of tubs, crushers, press, casks, vats, saccharometer, thermometer, siphon, etc., all of which are made for the purpose, and are readily bought.

There is one item largely concerned in the manufacture of good wine, which, to save repetition, must be insisted upon from the beginning, and that is, the most *scrupulous cleanliness*, as respects the vessels, persons, and every operation performed. Those who reflect that a beverage is to be made, the goodness of which depends in a great measure upon its delicacy and purity, will at once recognize the absolute necessity of this. Wine of high character depends for its excellence upon fine, pure, delicate flavors, and these are marred or destroyed by want of cleanliness and the introduction of foreign substances, or by suffering any thing whatever but the juice of *good ripe grapes* to enter the must. Wine making is a careful, painstaking business, in which persistent and conscientious well doing and right doing are munificently rewarded.

The Cellar.—The cellar is of much importance where wine making is largely pursued. It must necessarily be modified more or less by the location in which it is built. There are three leading objects to be attained, and these are pretty nearly of equal importance: first, a considerable degree of evenness of temperature, which is best secured by sinking the cellar in the ground, and building the walls hollow. Second, freedom from wetness, which is secured by selecting a dry spot for the cellar, and, where this can not be fully secured in this way, laying the walls in cement, and grouting and cementing the bottom. Third, ventilation, the means for which should be placed in the upper part of the cellar, and so arranged that the temperature can be altered gradually when necessary, sudden changes being hurtful. The cellar may be built over or not with rooms, offices, etc., to suit the convenience of the owner. The lower tier of casks should rest upon cradles, and be elevated from six to twelve inches above the floor of the cellar. Under certain circumstances carbonic acid gas will accumulate in the cellar in sufficient quantity to be detrimental to health. This must be provided against by careful ventilation.

Casks.—Large casks, for very good reasons, are generally claimed to be better than small ones. They are not only more economical, but a large body of wine will ferment more perfectly than a small one. Still, we can not do without small casks, and their size must, therefore, be regulated by circumstances. They should be made of well-seasoned oak, and finished smooth inside and out to facilitate cleaning. When new, they should be soaked for a week or so in water, and then rinsed with hot water, to sweeten them; or they may be washed with lime water, and rinsed. They should never be used except when perfectly clean. If hot water will not cleanse them, they may be washed with a weak solution of sulphuric acid. First put the acid in cold water, pour this in the cask, and then add the hot water. After being well shaken, the cask should be thoroughly rinsed with cold water. This is used in France, and is highly recommended by those who have tried it.

Bottles.—Bottles should be made of glass sufficiently tough to withstand considerable pressure. The style is very much a matter of taste. They should be thoroughly clean. Shot are often used for cleaning; but they are not safe, as the lead washes off. Clean coarse sand has been found to be equally good, and free from objection.

Color of Wines.—The color of wines is in some measure an index of certain properties, but affords no indication of quality. The coloring matter resides in and near the skin, and consists of various extractive matters, which impart flavor and characteristics that are prized by some, but which are neither agreeable nor wholesome to others. White wines have a purity as well as an animation that never belongs to the red. It should be observed that high color is often used as a mask for adulteration. There is an unfounded prejudice in favor of the quality of red wines that is largely taken advantage of by makers.

Wines are often colored with elderberries, beets, Brazil wood, and other substances not so innocent; but the best color is the natural one, or that obtained from the coloring matter adjacent to and in the skin of the grape. This is obtained by cuvage, or fermentation on the skins. If the juice is pressed before fermenting in this way, the wine will be white, no matter what the color of the grape may be.

Fining or Clarifying.—Wines, particularly the dry, usually clarify themselves, the impurities gradually falling to the bottom when fermentation ceases. Isinglass and other substances are used, but albumen or the whites of eggs will answer the purpose well. The whites of three or four eggs will usually be sufficient for forty gallons; some use more, but this number is generally enough. The whites should be "beaten up," mixed with some water or wine, and poured in the cask, the wine being well stirred up. It should be used, if at all, after the second fermentation.

Several preliminary operations should here be noticed.

Stemming.—This is done by hand, or by drawing the bunches through teeth attached to a grooved board, the purpose of the grooves being to convey to the tub the juice that flows from the bruised berries. Stemming is so much a matter of circumstance that no general rule for it can be given. In some cases wines are found to be better with a small portion of the stems in the marc; in many red wines they are not at all admissible; while in most white wines they are either admitted entire, or with only the larger branches removed. In making Johannisberger the stems are all carefully removed, while in the case of some of the best French white wines they are admitted entire.

Crushing may easily be done by hand in a tub, where not more than a barrel full is wanted; but any way will do that crushes the berries without breaking or bruising the seed. Rollers like those used by grocers for crushing sugar, only channeled, will answer the purpose. In Europe it is sometimes done, even on a large scale, by trampling with the feet. It may be well and quickly done, however, by the press mentioned below, being careful, however, to so set it as not to crush the seed.

Pressing should be done with a press that has neither copper nor lead about it. Presses are made for the purpose, but a very good one is the cider and wine press now so common, which may be bought of any convenient size. Directions for use accompany each. Only one pressing should be put in the same cask when the finest and most delicate wine is wanted. The juice that runs from the marc by its own weight is called the "first running," and what is really the "first pressing" is the "second running." It is not safe to mix different kinds of must, unless they are all good; when this is the case, one may be used to impart flavor or color to another, or for some similar purpose. In pressing, the marc becomes hard, and forms what is called "cheese." This is cut down at the side from time to time, and the parings placed on the top of the "cheese" for further pressing, so as to secure all the juice possible.

Racking.—Its object is to transfer the wine from one vessel to another in such a way as to prevent the access of air, and at the same time not disturb the lees which have settled at the bottom. There are various contrivances for doing this, some of which are expensive; but if bought, directions for their use accompany them. In Europe, Hilton's is thought to be one of the best. While the wine is running at the bottom, air must be admitted gradually at the top or bung, or the disturbance will be so great as to muddy the wine. The siphon, however, is often used, and it is both simple and good. It is only a tube with arms of unequal length.

Some are made with a side pipe for starting the flow. When plain, it is first filled with wine, the short arm put into the cask to be emptied, and the long arm into the cask to be filled, which should stand lower than the first. When the siphon is filled, the finger must be held over the hole in the long arm till the siphon is inserted into the cask. Those who make wine on a large scale will, of course, purchase the apparatus made for the purpose.

Wines, briefly, are principally of two kinds, *dry* and *sweet*. In *dry* wines the sugar and acids are so nicely balanced that neither seems to predominate. In *sweet* wines the sugar is in excess, and some, like Sherry and Madeira, may be called spirituous or alcoholic wines. *Sparkling* wines partake more or less of the nature of both. Dry wines are the best, and the only ones that are suitable for daily use, to invigorate and refresh the body and mind.

With a view to make the details more readily intelligible, we propose first to describe the process of wine making in its simplest form.

After stemming (if done) and crushing, put the "marc" into a tub or any convenient vessel, and place it where a pretty equable temperature may be maintained, not falling below sixty-five degrees; a range between seventy and eighty will be very good. Cover the vessel with a cloth that will not admit insects; and for further safety, boards may be put over the cloth, with an inch or two of space between them for the admission of air, which the cloth will permit with sufficient freedom. Crash cloth is very good for this purpose.

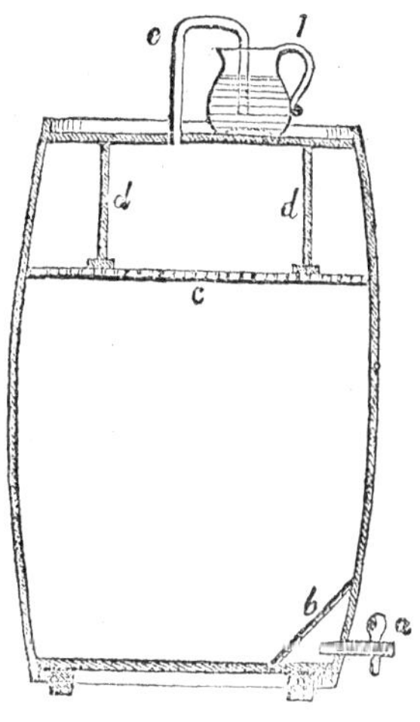

Fig. 174.

Fermentation will begin about the third day, or soon after, which may be ascertained without uncovering by placing the ear near one of the spaces between the boards. After this has continued actively for twenty-four to forty-eight hours, the free juice may be drawn off through a cock prepared for the purpose, (as seen at *a*, *Fig.* 174,) and put into a cask. The remaining "marc" must be pressed immediately, so that the juice may be put at once with the first. The cask should be of such size as to be filled without taking all the juice, some being left for filling, from time to time, the vacancy that will be continually forming in the cask in consequence of the slow fermentation, which will continue for a length of time proportioned, in some degree, to the strength of the must, and also to the temperature. When the fermentation has so far abated that a bung may be driven tight without causing pressure from the collection of carbonic acid in the cask, the wine may be said to be made, although a second fermentation will be necessary for its completion.

After the first fermentation has ceased, and the wine become clear, which will not be later than January, it should be drawn off from the lees, and put into a cask of proper size, which must be filled quite full. The second fermentation may be expected to occur about the following June, or as soon as the heat becomes sufficient for its excitement, and will continue, if the must be rich, during most, if not all, of the summer. In the following winter, after the second fermentation has ceased, the completed wine may be drawn off and bottled, when it is *new* wine, and ready, as such, for use.

This, in brief, is the history of wine making in its most simple form: a plain statement of the processes without any attempt at explanation by theory; and a general statement of what is known of the chemistry of wine making is quite as simple. The sugar of the grape, by a chemical action called *vinous fermentation*, is converted into alcohol, setting free carbonic acid, which escapes into the air in the form of gas, while the former remains dissolved in the water of the grape with the other constituents, chiefly unchanged. What fermentation itself is, is quite another question. If the vinous fermentation were perfect, every one hundred parts of the sugar would be converted into 51·11 parts of alcohol and 48·89 parts of carbonic acid. The action of the ferment depends for its force upon the rapid absorption of the oxygen of the air, without which it can not take place.

Two modes of fermenting are practiced, *above* and *below*. In the first, the cask is kept full, so that the yeasty parts flow out at the bung.

In the second, a small vacant space is left at the top, and the apparatus of Gervais is used, or a sand-bag, or something similar, laid over the hole; in which case the sediment sinks to the bottom when fermentation ceases. The apparatus of Gervais is seen in *Fig.* 174. In the engraving the cask is represented as standing on one end, this position being necessary to secure the advantages of its fixtures; but ordinarily it rests on the side in a "cradle" prepared for the purpose. The outlet of the cock is covered at *b* with a perforated diaphragm, to prevent the settlings from running off with the wine.

In wine-making countries the must from rich, well-ripened grapes goes through fermentation so surely that acetous fermentation is not feared. There are, however, large quantities of grapes grown from kinds that are not rich, and not calculated for making good wine, but which will make poor light wine in such quantity as to yield a valuable return, if it can be done without vinegar fermentation. In very bad seasons, the best kinds, from imperfect ripening, fall into the same defective condition in a greater or less degree. Overcropping and premature cropping, there as here, are constantly producing their disastrous effects, which are always shown in weakness of must. These musts will not bear the freedom of treatment that is not only safe, but advantageous to those of better quality. If some restriction is put upon the admission of atmospheric air during fermentation, its violence is abated in some degree, and the danger of the formation of vinegar instead of wine is lessened in the same proportion. Upon this the invention of Mlle. Gervais is founded. The bent tube, with its mouth under water, permits the escape of the excess of carbonic acid gas, but at the same time keeps the surface of the wine covered with it, and excludes the atmospheric air. On trial, however, the apparatus was found to have so little practical value, that it has been generally laid aside in Europe. It has been used here pretty extensively in fermenting the must of the Catawba and other grapes, but with what benefit does not appear.

A more recent question is, whether entirely free or partially closed fermentation is most advantageous for rich musts, and this is now generally settled in favor of the latter, which is usually conducted in pretty large vessels set on end, with a movable outer cover, and an additional inner cover, as seen in *Fig.* 174. Without going into detail, the rule may be briefly stated thus: rich musts are benefited by, and even require, a freer admission of air and a higher temperature than light and meager musts can endure. Thorough fermentation is indispensable for making wholesome wine; not necessarily the conversion of all the sugar into alcohol, but the conversion or deposition of all the yeast or ferment with which the must is charged. This is one of the prime conditions of that "fineness" which is so essential for health as well as enjoyment, that it may be said that no wine can be good without it.

The temperature under which fermentation takes place actively, ranges from about sixty-five to one hundred degrees, and the quantity of sugar decomposed decreases as the temperature falls below seventy; in other words, thorough fermentation requires at least seventy degrees of temperature. When it is much above eighty, there is danger that fermentation will go on too rapidly, even to the destruction of the wine, if the must is not rich in sugar, and also free from the destructive elements that belong to unripeness in the fruit.

Wine has heretofore been commonly treated of as something without life, indeed, but unlike any mere mixture, and yet not a chemical combination. Dr. Guyot, however, speaks of it as "a thing of life, which has youth and manhood, old age and decrepitude." A late French writer, M. Pasteur, attributes all the changes which the juice undergoes by fermentation to living action, and bases his discoveries upon apparently good microscopic revelations. In this country, a similar view was taken of the subject by Prof. Gardiner some fifteen years ago. It is a question of cause and effect, which can only be determined by the most careful microscopic investigations. We shall adhere to established formulas, but propose to recur to these discoveries hereafter.

We have given the reader a general idea of the processes by which good grapes are made into wine; but there are minor details of no little importance that claim our attention.

After the grapes are assorted, every operation should proceed rapidly. The stemming should be done speedily, as also the crushing, and immediately thereafter the pressing, unless we have in view fermentation of the "marc," or, as it is sometimes called, fermentation on the skins. For this operation we need a short, expressive term, and may as well adopt that used by the French, *cuvage*, so called from the vessel in which it is done; literally, tubbing. Whether immediate pressing or cuving is to be adopted will depend mainly upon the character of the grapes and the color of the wine; for it is from the coloring matter in and adjacent to the skins that the wine derives its color. When a white wine is to be made from colored grapes, the skins should not be fermented. The rule may be stated in general terms as follows: kinds that yield light musts do not require or admit of cuvage, and even in large casks must be treated with care, both as to the free admission of air and the temperature of the cellar. Those kinds only are benefited by cuvage that have rich and pure-flavored skins, and yield a must of great general richness; and these are benefited also by a pretty free admission of air. Fermentation in casks is always safe, and should always be resorted to in cases of doubt. If any of our "foxy" kinds are fermented on the skins, the odor appears in the wine stronger, if possible, than in the fruit. The Concord is bad enough in this respect, but Ives's Seedling can only be borne by those whose sense of smell has lost its best points of discrimination. Cuvage is admissible with the Delaware, probably also with the Diana, and is highly advantageous with the Iona. The skins of the Delaware have very little decided character. Those of the Diana have considerable aromatic richness, but are rarely without some degree of their characteristic offensiveness. The skins of the Iona are pure, rich in aromatic properties and tannic and tartaric acids, and give the wine a peculiar but beautiful rose color.

The need of expedition arises from the facility with which small masses of the marc that are not immersed in the juice take on acetous fermentation. When the marc is put into the tubs, it should be kept a little below the surface of the free juice by a false cover kept at the proper depth by weights, or, better, by fastenings made for the purpose, as shown at *d* in *Fig.* 174. A false bottom is also required, as therein shown, and both this and the cover should be made so open by perforations and crevices as to permit the passage of the juice, while the skins and the more solid parts are retained.

The Catawba is not fermented on the marc, and can not be successfully managed in the manner described. Its juice has very rarely any margin of alcoholic richness above the point that is safe from acetous fermentation when managed with the utmost care in the best of cellars after immediate pressing. It may be stated here that very little still Catawba wine, entirely free from adulteration by sugar at least, finds its way into the general market; a great proportion of that which professes to be pure is rather a sirup than wine.

After crushing, the marc is taken immediately to the press. A considerable portion of juice runs off before any pressure is made. This is called "first running," and is carefully tested by the saccharometer, and the degree noted before putting it into the large casks for fermentation.

When pressure is made, the juice takes another grade, which is also measured and noted, and this is called "second running." This will not measure so high as the first. When the ordinary press is used, the pomace, called "cheese," after receiving a strong application of the screw, is cut down at the sides, and the portion cut off piled upon the top preparatory to the last pressing. This juice is also tested and noted, and is of still lower grade than the last in sugar, but contains more tannic acid. This excess of tannic acid in the Catawba, although giving a degree of acerbity and bitterness to the wine, is indispensable to make it enduring.

On comparing the degree of the different "runnings," an estimate is made of the average sugar of the whole; and if this is found not to be above eighty degrees, it is not thought safe to trust to its own foundation of sugar, and cane sugar is added to the must before fermentation, and, of course, an impure Catawba wine is the result. The best Catawba wine that has been made was from must that registered at least ninety degrees on the average of all runnings.

In the vicinity of Cincinnati the Catawba generally ripens early enough to ferment thoroughly by the natural temperature of the cellars; but further north, along the lakes, artificial heat is required. To exclude the action of atmospheric air during fermentation, the apparatus of Mlle. Gervais is used. (See *Fig.* 174, p. 431.

When the first fermentation has subsided, and the wine become still, it is "racked," or drawn from the lees; and if much sediment forms during the winter, it is racked again before warm weather. After the second fermentation, if every thing has gone on favorably, the wine becomes clear, and does not need the operation called "fining."

Almost every maker of wine has some peculiarities of his own, but all dry wines are made upon the same general principles. Let us next present an example of making good wine in a small or domestic way. We have some excellent wine thus made from the Iona. As we were interested in the proceedings, we will detail them so far as to enable the reader to repeat them. The object was to test the wine-making capacity of the Iona under a variety of circumstances, and specimens were, therefore, procured from different localities, and gathered at different times, but all north of New-York.

The grapes were crushed by hand and the juice strained through a cloth, a part of it, however, having been fermented on the skins. It was then put in clean demijohns and bottles, and these placed on a shelf in the room, each specimen having been first tried by the saccharometer, (Œschle's,) and its degree noted. All were above eighty-five degrees, and some above a hundred. Some were reduced to sixty-eight by the addition of water. There being no proper facilities for maintaining an even temperature, the mercury ranged from sixty-five to ninety-five. In the moderately rich must, fermentation began in about three days, and in the others later in proportion to the richness.

Fermentation lasted more than a week in all cases, and in the richest more than four weeks. The "racking" was done by simply transferring the wine very carefully from one bottle to another. The progress was naturally watched with deep interest, and notes made daily; but we present here only the result, which was in every instance a perfect wine, varying greatly, however, in important characteristics, as these were affected by the different times of gathering the grapes and by the different localities in which they were grown, the first exercising much the greatest influence, the last gathered and ripest grapes producing far the richest must and finest wine. These experiments demonstrated not only that the Iona will make excellent wine in this way, but that the must is free from those destructive elements which produce acetous fermentation, a point of great weakness in most of our native grapes. In this way, small quantities of good wine can be made from pure, rich must in an ordinary living room, if care is taken not to let the temperature sink below sixty-five at night.

Let us suppose, here, that this new wine is wanted for immediate use, and we may introduce the results of some of M. Pasteur's most recent experiments. They can be easily repeated by any one. In experimenting for the destruction of fungi, which he supposed to cause the diseases of wine, he found that they were destroyed by heating it. His later experiments seem to show that a temperature not exceeding one hundred and fourteen degrees Fahrenheit is sufficient for the purpose. The question is, Will this injure the wine? and just here is the point we alluded to. According to M. Pasteur, it not only does not injure the wine, but hastens its ripening, producing in a few hours all the fine qualities that we have been in the habit of expecting to come from years of careful keeping in good cellars. The process is applicable to all wines, and renders them, he says, capable of long, if not indefinite, preservation. We suggest, therefore, that the experiments of M. Pasteur be repeated on wine made in bottles, to hasten its ripening; for it may be that we can have good wine to drink generally the first winter, instead of the second. It was so in the trial of the Iona above given.

To enable the reader to obtain a fuller knowledge of the principles of wine making, we propose now to give a connected summary of all the various processes.

The grapes should in all cases be thoroughly ripe. For making sweet wine, those that will bear it may be left till they shrivel. They should be gathered when dry, since moisture on them will weaken the must, and our grapes have generally no strength to spare. They may even be kept some days in a suitable room. They should be cut with scissors, received in suitable baskets or tubs, and carried at once to the cellar or house. They should next be carefully assorted, retaining for wine only those that are thoroughly ripe. The next operation will be stemming, if this is to be done. As soon as stemmed, the grapes are crushed, either in tubs or by passing through the rollers of the press. If crushed in tubs, these should have false bottoms with small holes, a faucet, and a cover, as already described. When cuvage is practiced, the marc should remain in the tubs from twenty-four to forty-eight hours, when the free juice must be drawn off by the faucet and the marc pressed. The tubs should be covered as before directed, to keep the skins below the free juice, and exclude dirt and air.

The pressing is next in order, and should be done immediately to prevent souring. The press should be in the cellar, the temperature of which should be kept from sixty-five to eighty, and fire heat used if necessary. When pressing for wine is done, water may be added to the skins, and the juice used for making vinegar; or they may be used for making brandy.

As fast as pressed, the juice is put in casks of suitable size, the larger the better, but not so large that they can not be filled. The advantage of using large casks consists in the fact, that a large body of must will produce more heat than a small one, and fermentation may, therefore, be carried on at a lower temperature than would be consistent with a small body of must. If the temperature of the cellar is too low, it must be raised by artificial heat. The beginning of fermentation may be hastened by the addition of warm must, in the same manner that we hasten or restore the heat in a hot-bed by moistening it with hot water. When fermentation ceases, the cask must be bunged up. It will be prudent not to drive the bung tight at first; for if fermentation should not have pretty nearly ceased, gas would accumulate and burst the cask. It must, therefore, be examined occasionally. There will be some leakage or waste in the casks, and the vacancy caused in this way must be filled up.

After the first fermentation has ceased, which will not be later than January, the wine must be "racked" off, or separated from the "lees," or settlings. In doing this the wine should not be exposed to the air, or it will lose a portion of its spirit and aroma by evaporation, if not injured in other respects. The flow of the wine must be stopped as soon as it ceases to run clear. The muddy portion and the lees are put in a separate cask, and generally distilled into brandy. If much sediment settles during the winter, the wine must be racked again before warm weather sets in.

About the following May or June the *second fermentation* will begin, and will continue a greater or less length of time, according to the richness of the wine. In our best wines it may be expected to continue a greater part of the summer. The casks during this time will need watching, as the fermentation may in some cases become so active as to endanger the cask by the rapid accumulation of gas, unless it is allowed to escape. In the following winter, after the second fermentation has ceased, the wine will be ready to bottle. In rich wines, however, there are always left traces of sugar and ferment, and in consequence a slow, insensible fermentation will go on, in some cases for years, during which the wine is said to be "ripening." We are only just beginning to have that kind of wine. This insensible fermentation may, under favorable circumstances, become active, and should be checked, which can usually be done by "racking." Dry wines, it may be remarked, generally fine themselves, and resort need not be had to fining.

Bottling should be done in cool weather, and not till fermentation has entirely ceased, otherwise the bottles will be liable to be broken by the accumulation of gas. The wine is usually drawn from the cask by a faucet, and passed into the bottle through a funnel. The bottles should only be filled to within a couple of inches of the mouth, so that, when corked, there shall be a small space between the cork and the wine. The corks should be of the best description, and compressed at the bottom when put in. They should then be sealed by dipping them in melted sealing-wax, and placed upright till the wax cools. The bottles should then be packed away in the cellar on their sides, so as to cover the corks, which will prevent the accumulation of mould. A sediment will collect after a time. If this consists of cream of tartar, it may remain; otherwise the wine must be transferred to other bottles, leaving the sediment behind.

Wasting.—Even in the best of casks there is more or less evaporation of the spirit and water of the wine, which leaves a vacancy at the top. A vacancy is also caused by drawing off portions of the wine. This vacancy should be filled within a day or two. When this can not be done, it is usual to sulphurize it from time to time by burning a sulphur match. If, in filling up, there should be mould on the wine, the filling should be done through a small pipe, the end being put under the surface. When full, the mould should be carefully removed.

Use of Husks.—The husks are used for various purposes, such as making vinegar, brandy, potash, etc. If used for brandy, they must be kept from the air, and worked up with as little delay as possible. The pomace or "cheese" is mixed with water and sugar, again fermented, and then distilled. But nobody will undertake to make brandy without providing suitable apparatus for the purpose. If *vinegar* is made, water must be added to the husks, which must be stirred up, and fermented till vinegar appears. If, however, the husks are "foxy," it will be better to press the husks after watering them, and ferment the juice: there will then be less of the "foxy" impurity in it. Potash is also made from the husks, but they are probably quite as valuable for manure for the vineyard.

Sediment or Lees.—These may be distilled into brandy or made into potash. The crust or salt that collects on the sides of the casks is crude cream of tartar, and as such may be sold.

Changes or Diseases.—Certain changes take place in wine, which are called diseases. What is called *souring* is the commencement of acetous fermentation, which is generally remedied by racking and sulphuring. Weak or watery wines are very apt to sour on exposure to the air. A remedy would be to add good wines of greater strength. Where the disposition to sour exists, suddenly increasing the temperature a few degrees will give it activity, or, in other words, bring on active fermentation. If a wine poor in sugar and rich in ferment gets stirred up, and the temperature at the same time increased, fermentation will be renewed, and soon pass to the acetous state unless checked. In this and similar cases, racking and fining should be resorted to; and this is also the proper course to pursue with wines that are oily, sticky, or slimy. In the case of *mouldy* wines, the mould should be removed, and the wine racked and fined. This is often caused by not keeping the casks well filled. *Cloudiness* or *muddiness* may be removed by fining.

M. Pasteur, however, a distinguished French physiologist, at the instance of the French government, has devoted several years to the study of diseases in wine, and has arrived at conclusions which must be regarded as of very great importance to the wine-making interests of all countries. These results may strike some of our readers as being quite improbable; but experiments of a somewhat similar kind conducted by others give a great degree of probability to M. Pasteur's theory in regard to wines. We can not here do more than give an outline of the theory as applied to the diseases of wine, which is as follows: That all the changes that wine undergoes find their appropriate cause in a specific vegetable fungus. Thus, "souring" or "acetification," "mould," etc., are each produced by a different vegetable parasite or fungus, which, if allowed to go on to mature growth, will spoil the wine. Before the germs of these fungi are called into active life, no harm has been done, according to his theory. His remedy is to destroy them by heating the wine. For this purpose he submitted wines to a degree of heat reaching two hundred and fifty or more degrees; but his latest experiments would seem to show that one hundred and fourteen degrees of Fahrenheit are quite sufficient to insure the destruction of the parasite. The question will naturally arise, whether this degree of heat will not injure the wine. M. Pasteur answers it by saying that, so far from injuring the wine, it hastens its ripening, and brings forth in a few hours those fine qualities that we have been in the habit of expecting only from many years of careful keeping in good cellars. The process is applicable to all kinds of wines, and renders them capable of long, if not indefinite, preservation. There is good reason to suppose, however, that these fungi will make their appearance again if air is allowed access to the wine; but then the process is very simple, and easily repeated. We commend this theory to the consideration of wine makers, with the hope that the experiment may be repeated. M. Pasteur's book is embellished with many fine microscopic illustrations, which materially assist the reader in comprehending his theory, and would seem to throw additional light on the hitherto inscrutable mystery of fermentation.

Adulterations, Gallizing, etc.—Wine is the fermented juice of the grape: nothing more and nothing less. When a foreign substance is added to it, it becomes, to that extent, something else. The fermented juice of the grape is essentially different from the fermented juice of any other fruit. The elements of the grape, during the process of fermentation, react upon each other in some mysterious way that deprives the alcohol of its chief consuming and destructive qualities, and thus produces a beverage that may be safely and beneficially used for strengthening, invigorating, and sustaining the body, while it gently exhilarates and cheers the mind. This is wine, pure and simple, and pure and simple we wish to keep it. The poetry of words may surround it with certain charms, but it can make nothing more of it. It is one of those productions of nature which man can not reproduce by any of the means at present at his command, however closely he may seem to imitate it; and it is of these imitations, which are all more or less hurtful, that we now propose to speak.

It will have become very plain to the reader that we have taken uncompromising ground against adulterations in all their various and specious forms. We did this many years ago, after having witnessed their uniformly pernicious effects, and we have neither read nor seen any thing since to shake our faith in simple purity. We do not mean to court popularity with any class of men at the sacrifice of our conscientious convictions; neither shall we forget our self-respect by applying opprobrious terms to those who may differ from us. Our position is not such a bad one that it needs bad arguments to sustain it. Notwithstanding, we shall state our convictions very plainly, but without meaning to offend any one.

There are certain kinds of adulterations, practiced especially in large cities, that are so generally recognized as being destructively poisonous that it is needless to waste time on them here: those who indulge in them are hopelessly beyond the reach of argument as well as the influence of moral law. There is another kind of adulteration, however, of a more specious kind that claims a brief notice. It is very largely practiced, both by those who do not know that it is an adulteration, and by those who do, but who claim that it is not injurious. We allude to the practice of adding sugar to the must, or Gallizing, as it has more recently been called after Gall, who enjoys the unenviable reputation of having reduced it to a system. The practice is an old one, having been in common use for the fabrication of so-called domestic wines long before the days of Gall, Chaptal, Maupin, etc.; but it was only at a comparatively recent period, and by slow degrees, that men could be educated into marring the noblest of all beverages. The "golden argument" in this case, as in too many others, alas, in the end became irresistible, and the addition of sugar to the must of the grape is now nearly as common as the addition of sugar to the juice of rhubarb or the currant.

What Mr. Gall has done is simply to tell us how much sugar or how much water to add to weak or strong must, or no must at all; nothing more, notwithstanding all the mystery that has been attempted to be thrown around the subject. In other words, he has told us how to make forty gallons of wine out of four, and even how to make forty gallons of wine out of no wine at all; but in all this he has told us nothing new. He and his *confrères* have reduced the formulas to a tabular form, and published them to the world, and to that extent have done what they could to make fraud an exact art; for to publish the formulas is only to invite to their general practice. It is a pity that the talents of these men could not have been devoted to a nobler purpose. If we are told that in bad seasons the vintage would be mostly lost if some such practice were not resorted to, we reply that this need not be so; and even if it were, it is better that a few men should suffer a temporary loss than that many should lose their manhood, and even their souls. Some reader may expect to find these formulas here, but he will be disappointed. Their publication has been productive of nothing but evil, and we do not mean to multiply it.

But it is said that some of our native grapes will not make wine without sugar.

That is very true; and it may be added that they will not make true wine with it. They are clearly not wine grapes, and that is the best that can be said of them. There need be no argument about that. It is further said that the addition of sugar is not injurious, and many arguments derived from chemistry are adduced to support this position, chief among, which is the assertion that cane sugar is nearly identical with grape sugar, and potato sugar quite so, and that the result produced by fermentation is precisely the same in all.

This is the little triangular argument that supports the arch. Weaken this key-stone, and the whole structure falls to the ground. Now, let us look at a few facts. Chemistry itself has much to learn yet, and its formulas are by no means fixed. What a few years ago were supposed to be simple bodies have been discovered to be compound. The elements of the grape are not yet clearly and fully known. Fermentation is a profound mystery, and at best we only know its most striking results; the most learned men are not yet even agreed as to how many kinds of fermentation there are, and, of course, never will be until it is first ascertained what fermentation really is. It is too soon, therefore, to say that grape sugar and potato sugar are precisely identical, or to say in what manner the peculiar elements of the grape react upon each other in the process of fermentation. But suppose present chemical analysis to reduce grape sugar and potato sugar to the same elements, can we be certain that we have all? It is a well-known chemical fact that the same elements are sometimes so combined by nature as to produce quite different results; and it is now equally well known that the same element exists in more than one form. The diamond is pure carbon; yet we can no more make real diamonds from carbon than we can make real wine from potato or cane sugar, or bread from the maple. Aside from this, however, we have the highest authority for saying that these sugars are not precisely identical; and each individual, without resort to chemistry, may convince himself that they do not produce identical results by fermentation. The pure juice of the grape yields a beverage that produces an exhilarating glow, at the same time that it refreshes, strengthens, and satisfies. The sugar of the cane and potato yields a beverage that stimulates to intoxication, at the same time that it weakens, stupefies, and depraves, leaving an unnatural thirst for more. That is precisely the difference between the effects produced by the two beverages, and upon that difference is founded our objection to the adulteration. It produces other evils by no means of a minor kind; but these are enough to condemn it. The case might even be put so broadly as to say that the one gives rise to drunkenness, while the other does not, and it would by no means be difficult to prove it. We put the subject upon the broad ground of public health and public morals, and affirm that no man has a right to conduct his business in such a manner as to imperil either. In the name of American wine making, we enter a solemn protest against it.

But let us look a little further at the subject of Gallizing, and see where it leads us. It is claimed that by this method wine can be made from green grapes. We reply, that in the same way wine may be made from the stems, the leaves, or the green wood; wine just as good, and in which the taste shall not be able to detect any difference. What matters it, then, whether the fruit ripens or not? Why not give our whole attention to the production of leaves and green wood, and make wine as abundant and cheap as water? Why not? Are we coming to this? If so, then it would be better at once to abandon the vine, and make plantations of rhubarb, currants, and the elder. But, in fact, why plant any thing? Gallizing has already produced its legitimate results in the fabrication of wine, into the composition of which no portion of the vine enters. The imitation is so well done that the majority of those who taste it say it is good wine. If nothing but the taste were concerned, the subject would not be worth a moment's argument; but it is the demoralizing effects which follow the use of these beverages which should alarm us. No man can study these effects as we have without feeling deeply concerned for the future.

While we have an innate dislike for deception in all its forms, we are at the same time jealous of the character of American wines. So long as we have grapes that will make a pure and good wine, there is no excuse for growing those that will not. There is a higher motive than mere gain underlying this question, in which every member of the community is personally interested. We ask all, whether wine makers or wine drinkers, to examine the subject in the light in which we have put it; to investigate the effects produced by pure and by adulterated wines, and then decide, each one for himself, how far he can conscientiously approve and encourage the fabrication of factitious wines. We ask chemists, who feel jealous of their reputation, to consider, not how cleverly they can produce a fraud, but how surely they can detect one. We ask that science may be made the hand-maiden of virtue, and not of vice.

Champagne, Sparkling, or Effervescing Wines.—These form a distinct class, their sparkling or effervescing quality constituting a well-marked characteristic.

Champagne is so called from the district of Champagne, in France, where many suppose it to be chiefly made. It has been said, however, and we believe with no great departure from the truth, that more so-called champagne is made in New-York alone than in the whole district of Champagne. The name is commonly, though erroneously, applied to any sparkling wine. With us, the wine should take the name of the grape from which it is made, such as Sparkling Catawba, Delaware, Iona, etc., and this has already been begun.

The making of what is called champagne

is such a complicated art, and requires so much observation and experience, added to thorough knowledge, that it is proposed to indicate only its general principles, with a view to show what *real* sparkling Champagne wine is, and how much more enjoyment there is in the true than the false, if people could only be induced to look for it where it may be found.

In the district of Champagne, still and dry as well as sweet and sparkling wines are produced. In the general use of the term champagne only sparkling wines are meant, which are divided into two classes, according to the degree of effervescence, the more moderate being called "creaming," and the more active "effervescing;" but the general term sparkling best meets the popular idea.

The body or foundation of Champagne is still wine of the richest quality that has undergone the first fermentation. In the management of the second fermentation, a part of the carbonic acid gas is retained, and, under great pressure, induced to form some degree of cohesion with the wine, so that when the bottle is opened the gas escapes with much less freedom than if it had not been firmly imprisoned in the wine. Science has given to this part of the art, theoretically, a great degree of exactness: a given amount of sugar converted into alcohol and carbonic acid will produce a certain pressure, which good bottles made for the purpose are able to withstand. About two atmospheres, or sixty pounds to the inch, are deemed the lowest admissible degree. This may be considered a pretty high pressure, but the bottles are made to endure two-fold more than that. If the pressure becomes very much higher, the bottles burst; if very much lower, the wine lacks the force of effervescence that is deemed so desirable. Our present knowledge, however, will not enable us to control or precisely estimate the strength of fermentation from given quantities of material, and hence some loss will occur under the best management. After the closest calculation has been made, and the excess of sugar reduced, there will still be much left to experiment. The second fermentation is brought on in warm rooms, and carried to the point of breaking some of the bottles. When it is jduged that fermentation has reached the proper point, two methods are resorted to for checking it: first, sprinkling cold water on bottles; the second, removing the bottles to a cool cellar. The practice, however, varies, some taking the bottles to the cellar first, and the fermentation room afterward, according to circumstances.

In the second fermentation there is one nice point to be attained besides the proper degree of fermentation, and this, to good judges of wine, is of the first importance. At the end of the first fermentation there is always, in rich wines, a considerable quantity of sugar awaiting conversion by the second fermentation. The "fineness" that is indispensable to excellence requires that this fermentation should be carefully conducted to the proper point; for, as elsewhere remarked, pure champagne is wine of the highest character with the sparkling quality added. This may be a difficult point to attain, but it is not beyond the reach of painstaking skill. It is such wine that some have learned to enjoy; but it is not in demand by the generality of customers in this country, and special provision is therefore made for them by various additions, the chief of which are alcohol and sugar. Advantage is taken of this fact, and champagnes for exportation are made to suit the tastes of various nations, the makers, of course, having due regard to their own interests. Thus it is that pure Champagne is not made for general exportation; much of the cost and care consequent upon making it is rendered unnecessary, and the excellence for which it was praised has been lost under the mask of sweets, spirits, and flavorings. Under the circumstances, still wines of tolerable quality, and without offensive odor or taste, are just as good as those possessing the richest qualities, since the effervescence, which has come to be regarded as the chief consideration, is not made to depend upon the natural sugar of the grape, but solely upon that added in the operation called "working," and the wines are hence called "worked wines." This "working," which consists in the addition of prepared liquor, (chiefly alcohol and sugar,) generally averaging from twenty to thirty per cent, enables the makers to keep their wines at nearly the same quality, irrespective of the seasons. In other words, the grape has much less to do with it than skillful confection.

The most recent apparatus for adding this liquor in exact quantity is one of the most elaborate and complicated pieces of mechanism used in champagne making. It must take a partly filled bottle, add just so much liquor, and leave

30

just so much space in the neck, and all this it does like an automaton. Besides this, there are many other kinds of apparatus used for various purposes, of which a mere description in words would be useless.

We have given but a brief glance at this part of the subject, and can not avoid saying that it has been the least satisfactory part of our labor. We have not alluded, in this connection, to the making of sparkling wines in this country: both the apparatus and the art, however, have been imported. Our object has rather been to serve American wine makers by showing the difference between a true and a spurious Champagne, with the hope of leading the way to the formation of a class who will create a demand for American Champagne in its purity. We live in the hope that a better taste will call for sparkling wine that, like the best still wines, will not only "leave the head clear and the mouth cool," but also afford the stomach that grateful refreshment from carbonic acid and pure wine that we now look for in vain except in wines of special importation. There are many who would pay liberally for such a luxury if they could learn its worth, and knew where to obtain it.

It is unnecessary to say any thing here of the processes whereby such immense quantities of drink, called Champagne, are made: we have said quite enough elsewhere. It is only another phase of Gallizing. The carbonic acid is added by machinery, very much as it is added to soda water, and it is made nearly as cheap. These fabrications bear to pure Champagne the same relation that Gallized wine bears to pure wine.

We have stated that there are two classes of champagne, the dry and the sparkling. The first is the best. Of the last, there are innumerable brands, and two or three grades, being more or less sweet or dry, and of these the driest is best. There is a sparkling brand called "Consular Seal," imported by Tomes & Melvaine, of three grades, "dry," "drier," and "driest," indicated respectively by a red, blue, and black seal. The reader can prove for himself that the driest champagnes are best by trying the "Consular Seal," which he will find to improve as it gets drier. If he compares the "driest" with the common brands, his head will tell him the difference, if his taste does not.

Israella

CONCLUSION.

Our labor of love is now done, except a few words of explanation and acknowledgment. Some five years ago, in our "Hints," we promised to write a work on Grape Culture, the design then comprehending two volumes, and we have been constantly reminded of it since; but circumstances unnecessary to explain prevented us, till within a few weeks past, from even beginning the text. The engravings, however, were put in hand; but their execution was so unsatisfactory that they were thrown aside. There is but one man that we know of who can make a really truthful engraving of the wood of the grape vine, and he has acquired the ability to do so after years of training under Dr. Grant. We refer to Mr. Henry Holton, whose work is so truthful and spirited in execution as to extort our praise. There has been nothing done in this country or Europe to compare with it. Even copies from the French, it will be seen, become new things in his hands. To Mr. Holton, then, we had recourse; but for various reasons the engravings "dragged their slow length along." They might have been hastened by copying and transferring; but that would not quite suit our sense of propriety. We therefore applied to Dr. Grant for permission to take electrotypes from some of his engravings, and got more than we asked for. The answer came that we could have whatever we wanted. It therefore becomes our pleasing duty to make an acknowledgment befitting such generous liberality, and we do it very heartily. It may not interest the public, but it concerns us much whether we make use of the property of others with or without their approbation. It is thus that we have been enabled to illustrate the present volume with the most beautiful vine portraits that have ever been given to the public, and the minute truthfulness of which the reader will find of material assistance to him.

One word more of encouragement to the beginner. There can be no doubt that grape culture, under proper conditions, is one of the most profitable departments of horticulture, and may be entered upon without misgiving by any one who has a suitable location, and will study and apply the conditions of success. We can not promise, neither can you expect, a full measure of unvarying success from year to year; for grape culture, like all other branches of industry, is occasionally liable to unfavorable seasons, and at long intervals one that is exceedingly so, like that we have just passed through. But even such a season is not without its lessons. We may learn something, not only of the reliability of varieties, but also of the value of thorough preparation of the soil and judicious training. It has given us renewed confidence in our preferences and treatment, for we have heard of no cases in which similar treatment has been adopted in which the effects of the season were not comparatively light; and it has furnished additional evidence of the greater reliability of our best grapes as compared with the poor ones. There is nothing to dishearten in adverse seasons like the past; for they occur so rarely as to be but little feared, and less with grapes than other kinds of fruits.

When we initiated the movement which resulted in the formation of the American Pomological Society, we had in view a central society which should properly *test* new fruits in reference to their excellence, healthiness, and hardiness, and indorse them accordingly. This duty, honestly performed, would have been of incalculable service to the public, and made the society a great benefactor to the country; but it has been overlooked, and the public must still continue to do its own testing unaided. That the progress of fruit culture is greatly retarded from a want of this kind can not be doubted; but there is no present help for it. The grape-grower, therefore, in common with other fruit-growers, must test for himself such new varieties as may from time to time appear. In regard to those already before the public, he must select some competent guide in whom he may have confidence, and not allow himself to be bewildered and led astray by a multitude of advisers. The intelligent amateur may try all things, if he can afford it, with profit to himself and the public; but the vineyardist, who grows largely, will find his greatest profit ultimately to consist in growing such kinds only as are known to possess excellence of a high standard, and eschewing all others; he should not, indeed, waste his time in even testing any that he has not good reason to believe possess such excellence, much less plant those that are already known to be wanting in the very characteristics which constitute a good grape. We hope the time for that has pretty well passed by. To this end, we have given you the results of a wide field of observation, as well as the benefit of many years of experience devoted lovingly to the subject, with the hope, which we trust may not be a vain one, that they may be a safe guide to you, as well as a source of pleasure and profit, in all that relates to the vine.

One word more on this point. Having selected wisely, devote yourself faithfully to the study and practice of those principles which are essential to success in grape culture. In all the pursuits of life success is measured by knowledge, and the use we make of it. Fruit growing is not an exception, however much the fact may be overlooked. Too many seem to think that they have only to put trees and vines in the ground, and look idly on while the fruit grows and ripens without thought or care from them; nay, there are not a few who begrudge even the small labor that is necessary to gather the fruit as it ripens and falls. This might, perhaps, be borne if these very men were not constantly moaning over their want of success, and disheartening the beginner with the mournful cry that "it won't pay." It would be surprising if it did. How can fruit growing be expected to pay where there is such an utter disregard of the plainest conditions which Nature has made necessary to success? Fruit growing is a business, and, like other kinds of business, has its laws, which can not be disregarded with impunity; but, unlike other kinds of business, it must be conducted as a partnership, Nature always being one of the partners. She, indeed, is "the head of the firm," having been so made in the first instance by "Him who doeth all things well," with a promise that she should remain so "through all the ages." But this firm is in no respect a "close corporation:" all who will may enter it. Nature receives each applicant with a gracious welcome, and makes but one condition. She opens her great Book of Laws, tells him to read them, and then says, with an encouraging smile, "Obey these, and you shall partake of our pleasures and profits: otherwise, not." That is the contract we make with Nature; and as she has never been known to fail in one of her promises, we may be sure, if we come short of the pleasures and profits, that we have been wanting in the performance of some duty. This is the stand-point from which we must view success in grape culture.

Further than this, as a grape grower, you are under certain obligations to the grape consumer to give him the best in its best condition; and you owe it to yourself not to regard the great mass of the people, the "million," as an inferior and degraded class, incapable of any but the lowest forms of enjoyment, and for whom any thing is good enough that you can induce them to buy. That would be a gross outrage and insult to our common humanity. If the masses, from want of opportunity, have not yet attained to the same knowledge of excellence in fruits that you possess, remember that it is only a short time since you knew as little in this respect as they do now, and esteem it a privilege to help them to the same measure and degree of enjoyment. Be assured that all labor that tends to the improvement of public taste by placing the good within its knowledge and reach will meet its appropriate reward, not alone in that which makes rich, but also in that exalted consciousness of well-doing which riches can neither purchase nor take away. Attune yourself to the "key-note" that runs through this book, "*Good grapes for all*," and do your part to hasten the day when its vibrations shall be heard and felt in every dwelling in the land.

INDEX.

THE END.

www.ingramcontent.com/pod-product-compliance
Lightning Source LLC
LaVergne TN
LVHW020923110826
845150LV00004B/746

* 9 7 8 1 4 2 5 5 5 4 0 7 1 *